Brian Martin

Nonviolence unbound

Nonviolence unbound

Brian Martin

Published 2015 by Irene Publishing
Sparsnäs, Sweden
http://www.irenepublishing.com/
irene.publishing@gmail.com

ISBN 978-91-88061-03-4

CONTENTS

1 Introduction *1*

2 What is nonviolent action? *6*

3 The effectiveness of nonviolent action *27*

4 Transportable features of nonviolent action *89*

5 Verbal defence *104*

6 Being defamed *148*

7 Euthanasia *208*

8 Vaccination *259*

9 Conclusion *335*

Index *349*

Acknowledgements

For several decades, numerous individuals have inspired me and stimulated my thinking about nonviolence. To write about nonviolence is to be part of a community of activists and scholars, and this makes continued effort worthwhile.

Over several years I presented extracts from work in progress to members of the high-output writing group at the University of Wollongong. For their helpful textual comments, I thank Paula Arvela, Zoë Barker, Anu Bissoonauth-Bedford, Trent Brown, Kathy Flynn, Xiaoping Gao, Alfie Herrero de Haro, Nicola Marks, Michael Matteson, Anne Melano, Ian Miles, Ben Morris and Tshering Yangden.

Greg Beattie, Anne Collett, Meryl Dorey, James Lasdun, Fiona Stewart, Rodney Syme and Wendy Varney provided valuable feedback on specific points in the text. For thorough scrutiny of the entire manuscript, plus numerous probing suggestions, I thank Sharon Callaghan, Sharon Nepstad, Majken Sørensen and Tom Weber.

1
Introduction

Imagine living in a country where the government suppresses opposition and censors criticism. After a particularly appalling incident, people pour out onto the streets, despite the risks, despite beatings, arrests and even killings. Day after day, the protests continue — and after a matter of days or weeks, a seeming miracle occurs. The leader of the government steps down. The people have toppled a dictator.

It sounds almost too good to be true, yet events along these lines have occurred in dozens of countries, for example the Philippines in 1986, East Germany in 1989, Indonesia in 1998, Serbia in 2000, Georgia in 2003, Lebanon in 2005 and Tunisia and Egypt in 2011. These are examples of the power of popular resistance to repressive governments. The method of action is called by various names, including nonviolent action, people power and civil resistance.

What's actually going on in these sorts of events? The methods used by challengers include rallies, marches, strikes, boycotts, sit-ins and setting up alternative schools and markets. These sorts of methods are different from conventional actions like lobbying or voting. They are also different from armed struggle. However, nonviolent action is more than methods such as rallies and strikes: it is an approach to conflict and social change.

Many people think violence is the only way to bring down a ruthless regime. This means armed engagements with police and troops and perhaps also bombings, assassinations and taking hostages. There is a long tradition of armed struggle, for example in Algeria, China, Kenya, Malaya, Uruguay and Vietnam.

Surely using weapons makes success more likely! This is the assumption many people make: nonviolent methods might work against kindly, soft-hearted opponents, but if governments really get serious, the only possible way to succeed is through counter-violence. Yet the best evidence available says this view is wrong.

Erica Chenoweth and Maria Stephan compiled a database of 323 challenges to regimes from 1900 to 2006. They added in secession and independence struggles. They included both armed and unarmed challenges to governments; nearly all the governments used violence against the challengers. Chenoweth and Stephan then analysed the data statistically and discovered that for struggles against repressive governments, armed struggles were far less likely to succeed.[1] Surprise: violence doesn't work all that well.

Furthermore, they analysed the struggles to see if it made any difference how repressive the government was. Their finding: it didn't make much difference at all. Nonviolent challenges succeeded just as well against highly repressive regimes as against others.

---

1 Erica Chenoweth and Maria J. Stephan, *Why Civil Resistance Works: The Strategic Logic of Nonviolent Conflict* (New York: Columbia University Press, 2011).

The usual idea is that toppling a dictator must be done by beating them with superior force, the way Allied military forces defeated Nazi Germany in World War II. But this is only one way to bring down a dictator. Another is to weaken internal support for the ruler, including support from the army and police. When soldiers and police decide they won't fight any more on behalf of the government, it collapses. That is exactly what happens when people power movements succeed.

Nonviolent action is widely used in social movements, for example the labour, feminist, environmental and peace movements: workers go on strike, feminists march against domestic violence, environmentalists chain themselves to trees and peace activists blockade shipments of arms. Very few feminists or environmentalists believe armed struggle can advance their causes.

The curious thing about nonviolent action is that it is often more effective than violence even though most people assume the opposite. This got me thinking. Perhaps there are other domains, quite different from the struggles against repressive regimes or for major social change, where this same thing occurs: there is a good method available but people don't believe it is superior. This thought launched me into the investigations reported in this book.

Specifically, I decided to see if the features of effective nonviolent action could be relevant to action in other domains, for example in conversations. The other domain needed to involve some sort of disagreement or struggle. After all, nonviolent action is a method of persuasion, protest and (nonviolent) coercion, intended to challenge an injustice. So to apply it to a conversation, it wouldn't be to just any old conversation, but to ones where some disagreement, hostility or struggle is involved — for example verbal abuse.

The first step in this process is to identify the features of effective nonviolent action. That's the aim in chapters 2–4, which provide a bit more information about nonviolent action and how to determine whether it is effective. However, this isn't the definitive case for nonviolent action. Others have provided the evidence base and relevant arguments. Here I take as a starting point that nonviolent action, if done well, can be highly effective, and want to discern what makes this possible. My goal is limited: I sought to identify "transportable" features, namely ones potentially relevant in other domains.

Chapter 5 deals with how to respond to another person's verbal abuse, for example to comments like "Can't you ever get anything right?" It turns out that the features of effective nonviolent action are quite compatible with the advice from manuals for responding to toxic language.

Chapter 6 looks at a variant of verbal abuse: defamatory and damaging material on the web. When someone posts an uncomplimentary photo of you, accompanied by a nasty comment, what can you do? There are no definitive answers. The features of effective nonviolent action provide helpful guidance.

Chapters 7 and 8 deal with two controversial issues, euthanasia and vaccination. In each case, I have taken the point of view of those seeking to challenge the orthodox position supported by governments. So these struggles have similarities with challenges to repressive governments, but with some important differences. In neither case is armed struggle a serious option: no one is proposing to take up arms against orthodoxy; nor, with rare exceptions, is the government so repressive that it is arresting, beating or killing campaigners. These are domains where physical violence against campaigners is highly unusual or absent. My goal is to examine the relevance of features of effective nonviolent action.

The issues of euthanasia and vaccination involve competing injustices and often ignite deep passions. The point here is not to support one side or the other, but to examine the struggles and see what can be learned in light of what is known about nonviolent action. Others might draw different conclusions. That's fine. The most important thing is the journey.

2
What is nonviolent action?

Rallies, strikes, boycotts and sit-ins are examples of nonviolent action. There are many other types and subtypes, such as mock elections, humorous political stunts, teach-ins, excommunication (a religious boycott), refusal to rent, withdrawal of bank deposits, working to rule, noncooperation by judges, expulsion from international organisations, seizure of assets, and disclosing identities of secret agents. What these actions have in common is that no physical violence is involved and the methods are not standard, everyday sorts of actions. Leading nonviolence researcher Gene Sharp catalogued 198 different methods, but there are many others, limited only by the imagination of activists.[1]

Conceptually, nonviolent action can be identified by specifying several conceptual boundaries. On the other side of each of the boundaries are other types of behaviour or activity. Inside the three boundaries lies nonviolent action. It's not quite this simple because each of the boundaries is fuzzy and sometimes moveable. Still, it's a useful way to think about what's involved.

---

1 These examples are taken from Gene Sharp, *The Politics of Nonviolent Action* (Boston: Porter Sargent, 1973). See also Gene Sharp with Joshua Paulson, Christopher A. Miller and Hardy Merriman, *Waging Nonviolent Struggle: 20th Century Practice and 21st Century Potential* (Boston: Porter Sargent, 2005).

Boundary 1: physical violence

Nonviolent action, as its name indicates, does not involve violence, normally taken to refer to physical violence. Beatings, shootings, bombings, arrests, torture and killings are forms of physical violence. Nonviolent action excludes any such methods.

The word "nonviolent" suggests, to those unfamiliar with what is involved, that no violence is involved at all. So when police beat or shoot protesters, this is sometimes perceived as a violent confrontation. Well it is, but the only violence may be by the police. "Nonviolent action" means those taking the action do not use violence, but it is possible, and common, for opponents to use violence against nonviolent activists.

There are several types of action at the boundary with violence. One is self-immolation: setting oneself on fire, usually causing death. This is violence to oneself, which is different from violence against an opponent.

Self-immolation has been used in a number of campaigns, including by members of groups that are otherwise completely nonviolent. A famous case was Thich Quang Duc, who burnt himself to death in Saigon, Vietnam in 1963 to protest against government persecution of Buddhists. In December 2010, Mohamed Bouazizi immolated himself in Tunisia as a form of protest; his action triggered a nonviolent uprising that toppled the dictator Ben Ali the next month.

Should self-immolation be considered a method of nonviolent action? Some say yes, because no violence is used against opponents. Others say no, because violence is instigated by protesters. Gene Sharp excludes self-immolation from his catalogue of 198 methods of nonviolent action.

It is worth considering the motivations of those who use this technique. The Buddhists monks in Vietnam and Mohamed Buoazizi in Tunisia were trying to highlight their enormous concern about injustice, a concern so great that they were willing to sacrifice their lives to draw attention to it — but without any intent or threat to hurt others. This suggests self-immolation sits comfortably alongside other methods of nonviolent protest.

For the purposes here, there is no need to make a decision about whether self-immolation is *really* a form of nonviolent action. The key point is that it is at the boundary.

Another type of action at the boundary is action that seems like it could cause harm to opponents but in practice does not, or does so only very occasionally. An example is throwing stones against tanks. Throwing stones is violent: it has the potential of hurting others, causing injury or perhaps even death to someone who is unprotected. But what if the opponent is well protected, inside a tank or behind solid barriers? Does throwing stones count as nonviolent action in this situation?

Suppose you say yes. Then what about throwing eggs? The damage won't be as great as from stones, but an egg could hurt someone, especially if hitting their eye. What about throwing cream puffs? Flowers? Feathers? There is a continuum of objects that can be thrown or conveyed towards opponents. At some point on the continuum, there is a transition from violence to nonviolent action, unless we want to have a different name for the methods at this boundary. What about blowing bubbles?

Another type of action at the boundary is violence against objects, such as burning a flag, smashing a shop window, or blowing up a vacant research laboratory. This is sometimes called violence against property, which assumes the objects are owned. The usual assumption is that the objects are owned by someone else, but it's also possible to damage or destroy your own property. You might own or buy some rocks and smash them as a form of protest.

Some people treat violence against objects as just as bad as violence against people, or even worse. The question here is whether using force against objects can be considered to be nonviolent action.

One special case is sabotage.[2] During the Nazi occupation of Europe, workers sometimes slowed production in factories by covertly causing damage to their operations. This wasn't armed struggle against the Nazis, but it was a way of hindering their war efforts. Some sorts of sabotage seem more violent than others. Blowing up railway lines — another type of action taken against the Nazis — seems quite violent; using a sledgehammer to damage railway lines is less dramatically violent; putting

---

2 Pierre Dubois, *Sabotage in Industry* (Harmondsworth: Penguin, 1979); Martin Sprouse with Lydia Ely (eds.), *Sabotage in the American Workplace: Anecdotes of Dissatisfaction, Mischief and Revenge* (San Francisco: Pressure Drop Press, 1992).

stones on railway lines is even less visibly violent, though the consequences might be similar.[3]

Some environmental activists, especially those in the radical group Earth First!, have used sabotage to oppose what they consider to be anti-environmental operations.[4] They have pulled up survey stakes, hammered nails into trees and poured sand into the petrol tanks of bulldozers, among other forms of sabotage. In these activities, they are extremely careful to avoid any harm to humans or to non-human animals. For example, the idea in putting nails into trees — called spiking — is to prevent them being logged. The spikes can cause serious damage to sawmill blades.

To prevent a forest from being logged, Earth First! activists spike trees and then tell loggers what they have done. The idea is that the expense from damaged sawmill equipment will deter loggers. Activists also warn sawmill operators about the danger from broken blades. However, some activists think the risk to loggers is too great and therefore oppose spiking as a tactic.

Some forms of violence against objects cause very little physical damage. Burning draft cards — a form of protest against conscription into military forces — is largely symbolic, because the damage to an object, the

---

3 On nonviolent anti-Nazi efforts, see Jacques Semelin, *Unarmed Against Hitler: Civilian Resistance in Europe 1939-1943* (Westport, CT: Praeger, 1993).

4 Dave Foreman and Bill Haywood (eds.), *Ecodefense: A Field Guide to Monkeywrenching* (Tucson, AZ: Ned Ludd Books, 1988, second edition).

draft card, is trivial. Another example is deleting files on a computer, such as files about protesters targeted for surveillance or arrest. Technically, deleting files causes physical damage, and can be called destruction of information, but most people think of this as quite different from throwing bricks through shop windows.

Violence against objects thus sometimes appears quite violent, for example blowing up a boat with no one aboard. On the other hand, it sometimes appears to involve hardly any violence at all, such as deleting computer files. Gene Sharp excludes sabotage from his methods of nonviolent action. There is no need to make a final decision here. The key point is that violence against objects is at the boundary between violence and nonviolent action.

In most cases, it is clear whether an action should be classified as violent or nonviolent action. Shooting people and blowing them up through drone strikes are clear instances of violence; fasting and boycotting a business are clear instances of nonviolent action. Actions at the boundary, such as self-immolation, may behave more like violence or more like nonviolent action, depending on the circumstances.

You might think that some actions, for example tree-spiking or self-immolation, are distasteful or wrong. However, just because you don't like them doesn't necessarily mean they should be labelled "violent." It's best to separate personal likes and dislikes from assessments of what counts as violence or nonviolent action.

Boundary 2: Usual politics

Nonviolent action is normally seen as something different from normal political action. Where there are free elections, conventional political action includes lobbying, election campaigning and voting. These, therefore, do not count as nonviolent action. They are too ordinary and too expected. When authorities expect people to do certain things, they are standard activities. Nonviolent action is action that is different from these standard activities. It is a form of struggle with a difference.

Most discussions of nonviolent action focus on the contrast with violence — as indeed I've done in the previous section. The boundary with normal political action is discussed much less and often is not mentioned at all. However, it is just as important, and probably even more difficult to pin down.

Imagine you're living in a country where free speech and free assembly are well respected. Signing a petition is nothing special. In fact, you might sign an online petition every week, forward petitions to others or even sponsor one. Maybe you attend a meeting and several others pass around petitions to sign. In such circumstances, petitions are a routine political activity.

Now imagine you're living in a country where criticism of the government is risky: if you speak out, you might be threatened, arrested or worse. Signing a petition — especially a petition with political demands — becomes a significant political statement. It is a serious challenge to the government. It is certainly not a routine political activity.

So signing a petition can be normal political activity in one place and exceptional, unusual, challenging political activity in another. This means it counts as nonviolent action in one place but not another. Quite a few of Sharp's 198 methods of nonviolent action, such as letters and rallies, have become routine in some places.

Sharp was mainly concerned with nonviolent action against severe forms of injustice. Under highly repressive governments, letters and petitions are often seen as serious threats to the authorities and those involved are subject to reprisals. In such circumstances, letters and petitions are well outside "normal political action," which basically means acquiescing to rules imposed by authorities. In these sorts of situations, the boundary between conventional politics and nonviolent action is fairly easy to identify: any form of protest becomes a type of nonviolent action.

However, this classification breaks down in societies where freedom of speech and assembly are respected. Sharp did not put asterisks next to methods such as letters and petitions.* His 198 methods are often quoted, almost never with any qualification, so most readers assume that the methods count as nonviolent action irrespective of the circumstances.

What difference does this make? It's reasonable to say that Sharp's classification of methods provides a useful way to highlight a category of action, regardless of whether they are sanctioned or routine or so ordinary as to

---

* "This method doesn't count as nonviolent action when it is a routine form of political action."

be boring. This is a practical way of addressing the boundary, but it sidesteps an important strategic issue: whether to work within the system or to take stronger action.

In places where voting and election campaigning are routine, they do not count as nonviolent action. But in some countries, elections are staged. In others, voting fraud is rampant. If you go along with a fraudulent election, this is politics as usual. In the face of corrupt voting systems, if you try to vote or to ensure that your vote is registered properly, this might be considered nonviolent action. In Serbia, Georgia and elsewhere, massive rallies have been part of action taken against electoral fraud.

The fuzziness of the distinction between nonviolent action and conventional politics also extends into the methods of noncooperation, which are types of strikes and boycotts. In some places, strikes by workers in support of better pay and conditions are commonplace, accepted as a standard negotiating tool, and hence might be considered a part of conventional political action. In other places, strikes are seen as serious threats to the system.

In Australia, the government has placed severe restrictions on trade unions in order for a strike to be legal. Only if workers have voted to strike according to legal technicalities will the union and workers be protected from serious penalties. Following all the procedures for a legal strike might seem to make this a form of conventional political action. When workers go on strike on their own — a wildcat strike, unsanctioned — this is more clearly a form of nonviolent action.

There is yet another complication. Sometimes authorities respond differently to the same method, depending on who is using it and how. In the United States prior to and after the 2003 invasion of Iraq, there were numerous rallies and marches in opposition. Most of these were unobstructed. Police accepted these protests and seldom tried to arrest anyone. In 2011, the Occupy movement emerged, with protesters against economic inequality setting up camps in downtown areas. Some of these were left alone for a while, until police moved to forcibly evict the protesters. In different parts of the world, some Occupy camps have been permitted to continue whereas others have been attacked.

Another complication comes when laws change. If it is illegal to enter an area — such as a public square, a forest or a military base — then doing so, as a form of protest, is civil disobedience. If the law is changed and it becomes legal to enter the area, then doing so is no longer civil disobedience. Many methods of nonviolent action involve breaking the law, though this is not a requirement. The point here is that when laws change, the classification of an action as civil disobedience — and hence different from conventional political action — changes. This is another example of how the boundary can shift.

Does it really matter where the boundary is between conventional political action and nonviolent action? In one sense, the answer is no, because they are both types of action and can be judged in terms of their impact on participants and wider audiences, or treated as part of a campaign strategy.

There are, though, a couple of senses in which it can make sense to distinguish between these two categories of action. If a criterion for nonviolent action is that it is something different from, and usually stronger than, conventional political action, then it can be useful to identify the boundary between them. Secondly, to apply ideas about nonviolent action to entirely different domains, it is useful to identify its essential features. One of them is being different from conventional action.

Boundary 3: language

There is another interesting case to consider: what about verbal abuse, or what might be called "emotional violence"? Activists certainly engage in this sort of behaviour. At rallies and marches, shouting may occur, sometimes coordinated as in the case of chants. Some of this "loud speech" is directly at issues, such as "US troops — out now!" Some may be directed at individuals, such as "George Bush — out now!" There can be more abusive language too, such as when protesters swear at police. It's also possible to imagine petitions, slogans, badges and other forms of symbolic protest that contain abusive language, possibly directed at individuals. Emotional violence can also be conveyed without words, such as through gestures like the widely known "one-finger salute" — though the meaning of gestures varies across cultures.

Should this sort of aggressive language count as nonviolent action? In dealing with this question, it is helpful to set aside the question of effectiveness. Shouting and swearing may be unwise, indeed counterproductive, but so can methods such as sit-ins and strikes. Effectiveness alone is not the key criterion for deciding what is nonviolent action.

If we stick with the specification that no physical violence is involved, then verbal abuse can be part of nonviolent action. Sharp lists as one of his methods "taunting officials," and gives the example of peasants in China in 1942 who followed and mocked soldiers from the Kuomintang government who had seized their supplies of grain.[5] There are plenty of other examples in which protesters target individuals, especially government and corporate leaders, including via rallies, vigils and blockades. Leaders are prime targets, for all sorts of reasons, whether it is their policy on wars, abortion or some other contentious topic. In many cases, these protests involve verbal abuse.

Although Sharp included taunting as a method of nonviolent action, he did not discuss verbal abuse systematically. His approach is strategic, and it is reasonable to argue that he would address the question of abuse by asking whether it is effective. In other words, verbal abuse might count as nonviolent action but usually be unwise.

Gandhi offers another way of approaching this issue. For him, respect for the opponent is paramount. The purpose of satyagraha — the Gandhian search for truth — is to create the conditions for mutual dialogue. To do this may require forceful action, but does not require personal abuse. The idea of Gandhi shouting an abusive slogan is

---

5 Sharp, *Politics of Nonviolent Action,* p. 146.

absurd: it was not his style. From a Gandhian perspective, satyagraha does not involve verbal abuse.

For the time being, there is no need to make a final judgement about verbal abuse. It can remain a method at the boundary of nonviolent action.

A good cause?

Suppose the Nazis used some of the methods catalogued by Sharp, such as rallies, strikes and boycotts. Would this count as nonviolent action? To couch the question more generally, does nonviolent action have to be for a good cause? There are two main answers: yes and no.

Many activists say yes, or rather they assume the answer is yes, because they don't even ask the question. Activists who are familiar with nonviolence ideas often assume that nonviolent action is by those on the side of justice. When US civil rights protesters used rallies, boycotts and sit-ins, this was nonviolent action, to be sure. Their opponents, the segregationists, opposed the protesters using various means. The actions by segregationists are seldom analysed in terms of methods used. Activists thus may look only at one side in discussing nonviolent action (and comparing it to other options, such as violence) and completely ignore actions by the opponents.

Gandhi and those in the Gandhian tradition definitely answer yes. For them, satyagraha is not just a method, but a search for truth that seeks to overcome injustice, inequality and domination. For Gandhians, the means and the ends should be compatible. Satyagraha, as a method of action, therefore cannot be used for an unworthy goal.

Sharp, in cataloguing methods of nonviolent action, gave numerous examples, nearly all of them involving challenges to war, oppression and other bad things. Nevertheless, his definition and framework allow for nonviolent methods to be used for unworthy causes. If the Nazis organised a boycott of Jewish businesses, this is nonviolent action even though it is used by a murderous regime for a racist purpose. Sharp would say it is possible for nonviolent methods to be used for bad purposes.

Another example is the "capital strike," when business owners withdraw investment as a form of protest, such as disinvestment from South Africa under the racist system of apartheid. However, withdrawing investment, or threatening to, can also be used for the selfish purposes of owners, for example to push for tax concessions, exemptions from environmental regulations or cuts to wages. A capital strike is not necessarily for a good cause.

An advantage of restricting nonviolent action to good causes is that it broadens the concept of nonviolent action beyond actions to include purposes: activists need to examine their goals and not just use methods mindlessly and instrumentally. Most importantly, nonviolent action becomes inherently worthy.

On the other hand, saying nonviolent action can be used for good or bad purposes leads to fewer logical complications. Sometimes it's not possible to know which side in a dispute is in the right; sometimes both sides have good intentions and worthy goals. Consider, for example, protests against genetically modified organisms (GMOs). The protesters think they are right, of course, but what if there are counter-protesters who believe GMOs are beneficial in feeding poor farmers? If nonviolent action can only be used for good purposes, then the two groups of protesters will have opposite ideas of who is using nonviolent action. In such circumstances, it makes sense to look only at the methods and not try to judge the goals. The same sort of thing applies in all sorts of other disputes, such as over pornography, abortion, euthanasia and pesticides. A definitive assessment of which side is correct may not be easy.

Individuals and groups

Does nonviolent action have to involve lots of people? Not necessarily. An individual can hold a vigil, hunger strike or work-to-rule. Sometimes an individual's action is immensely inspiring to others. On the other hand, some methods of nonviolent action seem to require many people. A consumer boycott by just one person won't have much impact, unless the consumer is wealthy or politically influential. Strikes usually involve groups of workers. For a single worker to go on strike is more a form of symbolic protest than noncooperation — unless the single worker is crucial to operations, such as the sole computer programmer in a business. A rally with one person attending is better thought of using another name, for example a vigil. Then there are methods such as setting up alternative government, which require many participants.

Based on these examples, it is reasonable to say that nonviolent action can be carried out by individuals and by groups, small and large. The role of numbers is to change the character and sometimes the type of the action. Larger participation usually leads to more powerful actions, but not always, and anyway that is another matter than deciding what counts as nonviolent action.

On the other side of the confrontation or struggle is the opponent. Can the opponent be an individual? Not in the normal conception of nonviolent action. The usual picture is that the opponent is a government, a corporation or a major group such as military or police forces. Sometimes the opponent is an entire system of rule, such as the previous apartheid system of white rule in South Africa. Nonviolent action, in the usual conception, is not about a struggle against an individual or even a small group, but against something larger. It is political activity, rather than interpersonal activity.

This is parallel to the division between political science and psychology. Political scientists study collective behaviour whereas psychologists study individual thought and behaviour. Nonviolent action falls in the domain of political science, but it needs to be asked, why? Why couldn't the same approach be used for examining struggles between individuals? Well, it can be, as covered in chapters 5 and 6. Indeed, the purpose of this book is to show that features of nonviolent action can be transported to other domains and used to assess methods and strategies. For the time being, though, the main thing is to note that the usual study of nonviolent action deals with groups on one or both sides.

Conclusion

One of the challenges in understanding nonviolent action is to specify exactly what it is. Some examples seem clear-cut, such as sit-ins, boycotts and large rallies. But complications abound. At the boundary with violence there are several forms of action, such as sabotage, that may or may not be counted as nonviolent action. Even fuzzier is the boundary with conventional political action: methods such as petitions and banners, when they are legal and routine, could be considered conventional political action, but are commonly listed as forms of nonviolent action. Then there is the issue of action for a bad cause. Some would say any action by racists cannot be nonviolent action, whereas others would say racists can use nonviolent action — and that activists need to carefully consider both their methods and their goals.

It is tempting to try to decide on a definition of nonviolent action and work with it, to reduce misunderstanding. However, any definition is bound to have boundaries that are contested. Furthermore, understandings of other sorts of action — violence, conventional political action, and language — are different in different places, and change over time, so it is inevitable that the meaning of nonviolent action will have to adjust accordingly.

My goal is to identify the key features of successful nonviolent action and then find their analogues in arenas where the idea of nonviolent action is not normally applied, such as conversations where there is no physical violence. For this purpose, it is not necessary to make a final decision on defining nonviolent action, because in other arenas there will be movement from the usual meanings. My aim in outlining some of the contested aspects of the meaning of nonviolent action is to raise the issues rather than make final determinations. These issues will continue to be raised as activists discuss what to do and why.

Appendix: What to call it

I started this chapter by giving various examples of nonviolent action. Using examples is helpful because they provide a mental image of people collectively challenging something without using physical violence. If you try to provide a definition, it's likely to end up boring and confusing: "Action by one or more people in pursuit of a goal without using physical violence while going beyond the conventional methods used in politics and discourse."

The expression "nonviolent action" is not very helpful for understanding the concept. It is constructed as a negative, as *not violent,* rather than in terms of what it is. Taken literally, "nonviolent action" includes walking down a street and brushing your teeth, because they are types of action and do not involve violence. Or do they? People differ greatly in their interpretation of the word "violence." Some think shouting or insults are violent: they are "emotional violence" or "verbal violence." So does nonviolent action mean being polite in a conversation?

"Nonviolent struggle" is an improvement because "struggle" implies the existence of conflict and an opponent, thereby ruling out everyday activities. However, as noted earlier, another problem with any expression containing "nonviolent" is that it suggests no violence is involved at all, whereas violence is often used *against* nonviolent activists.

The expression "nonviolence" — as contrasted with "nonviolent action" or "nonviolent struggle" — has these problems and more, because it doesn't specify action. Sitting contemplating the moon — does this qualify as nonviolence? No, but it might be interpreted this way. A complication here is that "nonviolence" is used within activist circles to refer to several things: coordinated action towards a goal, living a life in harmony with ideals of justice and simplicity, and constructing a peaceful, compassionate society. The Gandhian meanings of nonviolence as a way of life are much broader than the idea of action towards an immediate goal.

Although "nonviolent action" is not a very good expression, alternatives are not much better. One is "people power," popularised after the mass action in Manila that helped topple Philippines dictator Ferdinand Marcos in 1986. "People power" as an expression has the advantage of being positive and indicating the involvement of "people" — in contrast to leaders or rulers — exerting power, suggesting change. However, as an expression it is vague. "People power" might be interpreted as voting, cleaning up a park or pushing for a cancer clinic. It is not much more specific than "social action," namely groups of people doing things.

"Civil resistance" is another expression. It has the advantage of being unfamiliar to most people, so they can't so easily misinterpret it! "Civil" refers to members of the public — civilians — as contrasted with "military." It is different from "civil" meaning polite as contrasted with rude. The word "resistance" is unanchored: resistance to what? By implication, resistance is to those backed by greater authority or force. This fits a picture in which opponent forces attack and civilians defend, but doesn't cover scenarios in which civilian activists initiate campaigns. Despite its ambiguities, "civil resistance" is worth considering as an alternative to "nonviolent action" and "people power."

Yet another option is "unarmed resistance," referring to campaigners who do not use weapons such as guns or missiles — they do not use "armaments" in the usual sense. Referring to "unarmed resistance" or "unarmed struggle" leaves the door open to some methods of sabotage and to symbolic yet violent methods such as throwing stones at tanks. A disadvantage of "unarmed resistance" is that it does not give much idea about what activists actually do.

In the early 1900s, what is today called nonviolent action was commonly called "passive resistance."[6] This conjures up images of protesters sitting and refusing to move, allowing themselves to be carried away by police. It is a highly misleading term, because only a few forms of nonviolent action can reasonably be said to involve

---

6 Steven Duncan Huxley, *Constitutionalist Insurgency in Finland: Finnish "Passive Resistance" against Russification as a Case of Nonmilitary Struggle in the European Resistance Tradition* (Helsinki: Finnish Historical Society, 1990).

passivity. For this reason, Gandhi invited suggestions for an alternative name. The result was the word "satyagraha" which literally can be translated as "truth-force" or "soul-force." As a new label for an unfamiliar concept, "satyagraha" is a brilliant innovation. Because the word does not have prior connotations, it is less easy to misinterpret: it has to be explained. Nevertheless, it has not caught on outside India, perhaps because it sounds alien and is hard to pronounce.

For the past century, Gandhi and others using nonviolent action — or satyagraha or whatever you want to call it — have avoided the expression "passive resistance." Yet, for some reason, "passive resistance" continues to be applied by others. This may reflect a persistent association between violence and action, so that not using violence is assumed to be passive by comparison. Efforts at linguistic education seem unable to eradicate "passive resistance." For this reason, terms such as "nonviolent action" are helpful, because "action" is the opposite of passivity.

I do not have a firm view about the best words to use. Even if I did, others might not agree. Language evolves by use, and how words in this area will be used in the future remains to be seen and heard. In this book I most commonly use "nonviolent action," but for the sake of variety use various alternatives. When possible, it is often better to be specific and refer to a strike or a rally rather than generic terms such as "nonviolent action."

3
The effectiveness of nonviolent action

Nonviolent action has been used on countless occasions. Just think of strikes by workers in support of better wages and conditions, protests against corruption, and dissidents speaking out against repressive governments. With so many cases, it might seem easy to figure out whether nonviolent action is effective, and furthermore whether it is more effective than violence, conventional political action or other options. Actually, though, assessing effectiveness is not as straightforward as it might seem.

Consider the case of a building site in which a worker is seriously hurt. The other workers stay on the site but refuse to continue with a particular task until safety is improved. Management promises to fix the problem and the workers return to the job. Nonviolent action — in the form of a refusal to work — seems to have been effective.

Examples like this are common and unremarkable. Nonviolent action in these sorts of cases is effective in achieving the goals of those taking action.

However, in some cases workers take action but are unsuccessful. The workers go on strike for higher pay but the owner refuses to budge, and brings in other workers — strike-breakers — to do the work. The striking workers lose their jobs. Does this mean nonviolent action is ineffective?

The obvious answer is that strikes are sometimes effective in achieving the goals of the strikers, but sometimes not. This is just like other types of action, such as talking to the owner (negotiation), using a formal labour disputes mechanism (conventional action), or threatening to kidnap the owner's family (violence). Each such method is sometimes successful and sometimes not. So what does it mean to say that nonviolent action is or isn't effective?

To say something is effective is to say that it does the job, achieving the goal. However, this never happens in the abstract. It might be effective to eat peas with a fork — namely, people can do it with ease — but skills are required.

The more complex and uncertain the task, and the more training, technology and skills required, the more it makes sense to compare methods of doing the job and choosing the one that works best. For a child, it's easier to eat peas with a spoon or with fingers. For a knee cartilage problem, maybe it would be better to postpone surgery and use physiotherapy instead, or investigate different surgeons, or get a second opinion before proceeding. Each of the options has costs and benefits, and there is no guarantee of success, only a probability.

The same applies to major uses of nonviolent action. It is not guaranteed to succeed, and it makes sense to compare it to alternatives such as doing nothing or using violence.

There's another complication. In many struggles, nonviolent action is one of the methods used — but others are used as well. Consider for example the struggle in East

Timor against the Indonesian military invasion and occupation between 1975 and 1999. The East Timorese resistance was initially primarily through armed struggle: a war against the Indonesian forces. Some key figures in exile, most prominently José Ramos-Horta, attempted to persuade foreign governments to take action against the occupation. The United Nations General Assembly passed a motion condemning the Indonesian government's annexation of East Timor. Finally, there were nonviolent protests, for example rallies, especially in the capital city, Dili. Following a change of government in Indonesia in 1998, the East Timorese were allowed to vote on independence. After they overwhelmingly voted yes, militias sponsored by the Indonesian government went on a destructive spree that was only stopped after UN military intervention.[1]

It's not easy to separate out the different methods of struggle and assess their effectiveness. Armed struggle in the decade after 1975 seemed to fail entirely: Indonesian troops were victorious and up to a third of the East Timorese population was killed or died of starvation. By comparison, the persistent diplomatic efforts of José Ramos-Horta and others in the East Timorese government

---

1 See, for example, Steve Cox and Peter Carey, *Generations of Resistance: East Timor* (London: Cassell, 1995); James Dunn, *East Timor: A Rough Passage to Independence,* 3rd ed. (Sydney: Longueville Books, 2003); Don Greenlees and Robert Garran, *Deliverance: The Inside Story of East Timor's Fight for Freedom* (Sydney: Allen & Unwin, 2002); Constâncio Pinto and Matthew Jardine, *East Timor's Unfinished Struggle: Inside the Timorese Resistance* (Boston: South End Press, 1997).

in exile seemed on the surface to be more successful. Only one government — that of Australia — recognised the Indonesian government's formal annexation of East Timor: all others rejected this as illegal. Nevertheless, this diplomatic disapproval was not enough on its own to bring about East Timorese independence. But it is hard to disentangle the effects of the different methods used. Perhaps the armed struggle maintained the morale of the East Timorese, enabling nonviolent resistance by a new generation. Perhaps the seemingly fruitless diplomatic efforts helped sensitise foreign governments to the plight of the East Timorese, thereby making the 1999 UN intervention more likely.

All that can be said for sure is that in the East Timorese struggle for independence against the Indonesian invasion and occupation, various different methods were used, including armed struggle, nonviolent protest and diplomatic efforts. To this could be added many forms of conventional awareness-raising in countries around the world, especially by solidarity groups and sympathetic journalists and politicians, in Australia, Portugal and a few other places. Their efforts included leaflets, talks, meetings, discussions, media stories and solidarity protests.

In the East Timor case, like many others, separating out the role of nonviolent action is not easy. There is another factor that complicates the issue — but, curiously, also makes things clearer.

When a combination of methods is used in a struggle, one particular mode usually receives most of the attention. Consider a rally with 1000 participants, of whom 995 listen, sing and cheer. However, five of the participants start fighting police, throwing punches and bricks, and are arrested. In media reports, it is almost certain that this rally will be portrayed as violent, with all the attention on the five violent individuals. The other 995 will be ignored. They might have been peaceful but, because the five upstaged them, they are considered to be part of a violent rally.

In 1987 in Palestine, there was a sudden collective uprising — called the intifada — by Palestinians against Israeli rule. This included a range of methods, including rallies, boycotts of Israeli products and businesses, home-based education systems (after the Israeli government shut down schools) — and throwing stones at Israeli troops. Of all the numerous methods used, only throwing stones involved physical violence; all the others could be called methods of nonviolent action. Some scholars have called this an "unarmed struggle," because the Palestinians used no weapons such as guns or bombs.[2] Furthermore, stone-throwing seldom hurt any Israelis — it was primarily a symbolic form of resistance. (In the second intifada, starting in 2000, Palestinians used missiles and suicide bombers, much more obviously violent means.) Is it reasonable to call this a nonviolent struggle, because nearly all the methods used did not involve physical violence? Many Israelis saw the first intifada as violent: they focused on the throwing of stones. In terms of the means for violence, it was quite an unequal struggle, given that Israeli troops had automatic rifles, explosives and tanks. Deciding whether the first intifada was nonviolent

---

2 Andrew Rigby, *Living the Intifada* (London: Pluto, 1991).

is not straightforward given the unequal media coverage to different forms of action.

In the 1990s, members of Whistleblowers Australia were concerned about the way employers sent whistleblowing workers to psychiatrists as a means of discrediting the workers and providing a pretext for firing them. Over a period of several months the group collected stories from whistleblowers, produced an information sheet, wrote letters, sent out newsletters — and, on one occasion, organised a small protest outside the agency where the dubious psychiatric assessments were made. Should this campaign be thought of as primarily using conventional means of raising awareness, or does the one rally mean the campaign was built around nonviolent action?

The rally was more visible than all the other efforts of the group, and also more dramatic, hence capturing attention. It was more memorable for most of those involved.

In many nonviolent actions, there is a lot of behind-the-scenes work.[3] To organise a rally, this might mean choosing a venue, arranging speakers, preparing flyers, putting out media releases and arranging for equipment such as loudspeaker systems. For large rallies, there can be an enormous amount of such logistical work, including arranging transport, training crowd monitors and dealing with media. The speakers at the rally receive most of the

---

3 Schweik Action Wollongong, "Behind the activism," 2010, http://www.bmartin.cc/others/SAW10.pdf

attention but usually others have done far more work, most of which is invisible.

The same amount of behind-the-scenes work is required for armed struggle. Think of cooks, accountants, maintenance workers, cleaners, communications specialists and others who are never near the front lines.

Thus, there are three important factors to consider when judging whether a campaign should be characterised as armed struggle, nonviolent action, conventional political action, community organising or something else. The first is that most struggles involve a variety of methods. The second is that there is nearly always a lot of behind-the-scenes work in major actions: what people see is the tip of an iceberg of effort. The third is that campaigns are commonly interpreted in terms of the most dramatic methods used. All these factors make it more difficult to assess the effectiveness of nonviolent action, because it is not something easily separated out from everything else that is going on.

I'm going to follow the standard way of classifying campaigns, which is to look at the most common method used as a front-line engagement with opponents. This means setting aside, for the purposes of classification, most of the behind-the-scenes work, which might be called organising, and focusing on what is most visible to opponents and observers. In violent action, often called armed struggle, there is a significant amount of force and violence used. In nonviolent action, also called civil resistance or people power, there is little or no violent action and significant amounts of protest, noncooperation and intervention. In conventional political action, there is little or no violent or nonviolent action and significant amounts of lobbying, campaigning, electioneering, advertising and voting.

It is important to note that to call a campaign nonviolent refers only to the primary mode of the campaigners. The opponents — most commonly governments, including police or military troops acting on behalf of the government — may use violence, and often do. The campaigners might be beaten and arrested, so it seems to be a violent interaction. It is, but if all the violence is by the police, the campaign can legitimately be called nonviolent.

In some campaigns, activists intentionally remain nonviolent, whereas in others, it just so happens that activists do not use violence, even though they have no explicit commitment to nonviolence. Thus in practice nonviolent action can be a conscious choice made in advance or an almost inadvertent outcome arising out of the circumstances.

Examples

The question here: "Is nonviolent action effective?" Providing examples of nonviolent campaigns is one way to respond to this question. The ending of communist rule in East Germany in 1989 is one such example. There was no armed struggle. The main protest methods were rallies and emigration. East Germans previously could not leave the country without permission. However, the government of Hungary opened the border to West Germany, so East Germans could leave via Hungary — and many did. In late 1989, small rallies were held, and very soon they became much larger. East German leaders decided not to use force, as the reliability of the troops was uncertain. In a matter of months, the leaders resigned. Thus the East German communist state, maintained by a powerful military apparatus and a pervasive police presence with extensive surveillance, did not survive a peaceful uprising.[4]

These sorts of examples are commonly used by proponents of nonviolent action. They show that nonviolent action *can be* successful. These examples usually involve:

- lots of nonviolent action, usually visible and dramatic
- little or no violence (or, alternatively, prior unsuccessful armed struggle)
- a powerful, ruthless opponent, sometimes backed by other powerful groups
- overthrow or collapse of the powerful opponent.

The East German example displays each of these features. The rallies against the regime were visible and dramatic (whereas emigration, also a method of resistance, is less often mentioned). There was no armed resistance. The East German state was powerful and ruthless — and it collapsed in a matter of a few months of anti-government protest.

---

4 Karl-Dieter Opp, Peter Voss and Christiane Gern, *Origins of a Spontaneous Revolution: East Germany, 1989* (Ann Arbor, MI: University of Michigan Press, 1995).

These four features of the East Germany case are regularly found in other examples because they highlight the strengths of nonviolent action and challenge usual assumptions about it. Having lots of nonviolent action is crucial in order to identify the example as centrally about nonviolent action. It is necessary that there be little or no violence, because otherwise the case might seem to show the success of *violent* action. The existence of a powerful, ruthless opponent is useful for challenging the common assumption that the only possible way to confront violence is with superior counter-violence. Finally, success of the campaign is needed to cement the message about the value of nonviolent action.

From the point of view of international relations scholars in the realist tradition, the collapse of East German communist regime says nothing at all about the power of nonviolent action, because they focus instead on structural conditions, such as the withdrawal of Soviet guarantees for the East German regime.[5] In much international relations scholarship, people's action is either invisible or an afterthought.

In this context, it is hardly surprising that the most frequently mentioned examples of nonviolent action are chosen in part because they counter assumptions about violence versus nonviolence. Some of these examples are:

- The US civil rights movement in the 1950s and 1960s, in which blacks (with support from some

---

5 Ralph Summy and Michael E. Salla (eds.), *Why the Cold War Ended: A Range of Interpretations* (Westport, CT: Greenwood Press, 1995).

whites) used boycotts, sit-ins, strikes and other methods to challenge the entrenched system of racial discrimination called segregation
• The Indian independence movement from the 1920s to the 1940s, in which rallies, marches, civil disobedience and numerous other methods were used to challenge British rule
• The Philippines popular protests against dictator Ferdinand Marcos, who was ousted in 1986
• The Serbian people's campaign against dictatorial president Slobodan Milošević, who was forced from office in 2000
• The South African people's campaign, with international support, to get rid of the system of white racial domination called apartheid, which finally succeeded in the early 1990s

Dozens of other examples could be mentioned, but these will do for the purpose of illustrating their typical features.

• The campaigns were largely nonviolent in the period before ultimate success, though some of them contained significant armed resistance, usually separate in location (as in the Philippines) or time (as in South Africa)
• The campaigns were successful. The effectiveness of nonviolent action is hardly likely to be shown through failed campaigns.
• The campaigns challenged powerful opponents. Overthrowing ruthless dictators is especially impressive.

> • The stories told about these campaigns are usually short, leaving out much of the detail, complexity and contradictions. Short accounts are useful for getting the central message across, but may simplify and distort the events. (The same could be said about any short account of an historical event.)

It is certainly true that nonviolent campaigns can sometimes be unsuccessful, just as military campaigns or election campaigns are sometimes unsuccessful. A few of these failed campaigns are regularly mentioned.

> • In 1989, there was a nonviolent uprising in Beijing, China, centred in Tiananmen Square, called the pro-democracy movement. It seemed like it might ignite a serious challenge to the government, but instead it was brutally crushed.
> • The 1987–1993 intifada stimulated a so-called "peace process" but did not lead to autonomy for the Palestinians.
> • In Burma, a nonviolent movement led by Aung San Suu Kyi challenged the government over a period of decades.

These unsuccessful movements seem to be regularly mentioned because they seem so courageous against an overwhelmingly powerful opponent. In the case of China, there was no armed resistance to the government, so nonviolent protest seemed like the best prospect for change. In Palestine, the Palestinian Liberation Organisation had previously relied on terrorist attacks to challenge Israeli rule, but completely failed. The intifada seemed to pose a much greater threat, and generated much international sympathy and support. In Burma, the military government has been excessively brutal; the nonviolent opposition, occurring mainly in the cities, was seen as a far more promising form of resistance than the armed struggle occurring in rural areas.

In summary, there are good reasons why the same examples of nonviolent struggle are repeatedly told. Most of them are success stories, with a feel-good factor from oppressed groups winning against brutal opponents. The stories provide a challenge to the usual assumption that a ruthless government can always win against peaceful protesters. Finally, some stories become established as traditional favourites because they involve challenges that do not threaten the interests of currently dominant groups. The US civil rights movement is the prime example: because racial equality is now accepted policy (though far from a full reality), the success of the movement resonates with dominant liberal values. Media coverage contributes to the attention given to chosen stories such as the Philippines people-power movement and the US civil rights movement.

On the other hand, many major nonviolent campaigns are largely unknown, for example ones in Bolivia 1985, Ecuador 2005, Iceland 2008–9, Morocco 1999–2005 and Nepal 2010.[6] There are several possible reasons.

---

6 For other examples, see Maciej J. Bartkowski (ed.), *Recovering Nonviolent History: Civil Resistance in Liberation Struggles* (Boulder, CO: Lynne Rienner, 2013).

- They have not been adequately documented.
- They have not been popularised.
- They led to an outcome unwelcome to dominant groups.
- They conflict with standard ways of thinking about politics.
- They are too ambiguous to provide a clear message.

For example, there are dozens of cases of the nonviolent overthrow of dictatorships in Africa and Latin America.[7] Few scholars have studied these cases, and these areas of the world are not often reported by the international media (except for a few countries such as South Africa, Egypt and Cuba).[8]

Many countries in South and Central America have been subject to US imperial control, through military interventions and corporate domination. Challenges to this control are hence less likely to be lauded in the US. Furthermore, the dominant story of resistance is armed struggle, on the model of Cuba and the Marxist-inspired approach of Ché Guevara, namely guerrilla struggle. This

---

7 See, for example, Patricia Parkman, *Insurrectionary Civic Strikes in Latin America 1931–1961* (Cambridge, MA: Albert Einstein Institution, 1990); Stephen Zunes, "Unarmed insurrections against authoritarian governments in the Third World: a new kind of revolution," *Third World Quarterly*, vol. 15, no. 3, 1994, pp. 403–426.

8 Many of the world's most deadly conflicts are ignored by the western media. See Virgil Hawkins, *Stealth Conflicts: How the World's Worst Violence Is Ignored* (Aldershot, UK: Ashgate, 2008). Nonviolent struggles are usually even less visible.

means that Latin American scholars have neglected nonviolent struggles. Who, for example, has heard of the nonviolent overthrow of the dictatorial regime in El Salvador in 1944?[9]

The military coup in Chile in 1973 is widely known. It was against the democratically elected government of Salvadore Allende. The coup was seen in left circles as a prime example of US covert operations against left-wing foreign governments. However, relatively few people know about the people's challenge to the subsequent regime led by Augusto Pinochet. This was a nonviolent struggle against a ruthless ruler, and it was successful.[10] It failed to gain visibility for several reasons. US leaders would hardly want to hold it up as an example, because it would remind audiences of the US government role in installing Pinochet in the first place. In "progressive" circles, especially in Latin America where Marxism has been a standard framework, nonviolent struggle does not fit the usual model by which change occurs. Another obstacle to recognition was that the struggle occurred over several years. Unlike East Germany in 1989 or Egypt in 2011, there was no dramatic confrontation to transfix media attention.

---

9 Patricia Parkman, *Nonviolent Insurrection in El Salvador: The Fall of Maximiliano Hernández Martínez* (Tucson, AZ: University of Arizona Press, 1988).

10 Peter Ackerman and Jack DuVall, *A Force More Powerful: A Century of Nonviolent Conflict* (New York: St. Martin's Press, 2000), pp. 279–302.

Then there is Iran. The Iranian revolution of 1978–1979 was a dramatic demonstration of the power of nonviolent action. The Shah of Iran at the time ruled the country as a classic dictator, ruthlessly repressing opposition, including with the use of torture by the feared secret police Savak. The regime was highly armed. It was supported by all relevant international players, including the governments of the United States, Soviet Union, Israel and other Middle East countries. In the face of this formidable opposition, the popular movement succeeded largely through nonviolent means, including rallies and strikes — and despite significant numbers of peaceful protesters being shot dead.

Although the Iranian revolution is a prime case of the success of nonviolent action against a highly repressive government, it is seldom raised as an example, for two main reasons. The first is that the Shah was a favourite among western governments. (He had been brought to power in 1954 through a CIA-supported coup against an elected government.) The second is that the revolution, rather than leading to greater freedom, was followed by a different sort of dictatorial regime, an Islamic government headed by Ayatollah Khomeini.

The Iranian revolution thus provides two important lessons, first that a nonviolent movement can succeed against a highly repressive regime and second that successful nonviolent campaigns are not guaranteed to lead to a better society. This is a challenging set of messages to get across, which may explain why the Iranian revolution is seldom used as an example — especially since the

Iranian government in subsequent years was demonised by the US, Israeli and other governments.

Rather than introduce such a challenging case study, it's easier to stick with stories with a simple plot and happy ending, like the US civil rights movement or the end of apartheid in South Africa. And what's wrong with that?

For the purposes of illustrating the potential power of nonviolent action, the classic examples are fine. They get the message across that there is such as thing as nonviolent action and that it can be effective against powerful opponents. They show that nonviolent action can succeed against opponents holding a far greater capacity to use violence.

However, sticking only to the classic examples can limit a greater understanding. The more complex and ambiguous cases, and failed struggles, are valuable for those who want to probe more deeply into the issues.

- Studying failed nonviolent campaigns can provide insights into what is needed for success.
- Studying successful nonviolent campaigns that led to poor outcomes can provide insights into what is needed for desirable social change.
- Studying ambiguous campaigns — in which the role of nonviolent action is hard to distinguish from other methods and activities — can give insights into the dynamics of multi-method struggles.
- Studying little known campaigns may reveal insights not so obvious from the more prominent ones.

Potentially, there is much to gain by studying campaigns that, so far, have received relatively little attention. It's quite possible that some of them could become classic examples.

Examples and case studies are the most common way in which people learn about nonviolent action. It is easier to comprehend specific cases and then generalise to the principles involved. Furthermore, for most people, examples are more interesting: they involve individuals, injustice, suffering, courage and drama. They arouse passions. In comparison, discussions of the abstract principles underlying nonviolent action are not so appealing. Nevertheless, that is next on the agenda here. To illustrate the principles, I'll toss in a few examples!

To answer the question of whether nonviolent action can be effective, examples are a good initial response. Then there is a follow-up question: what makes nonviolent action effective? If there are reasons or explanations, they can provide better understanding. Part of the argument over nonviolent action is about questions of why and how. This is a big topic, so I'll only touch briefly on some of the key factors.

Participation

Participation in action for change is important for success. In general, it seems reasonable to think that the more people who participate, the more likely success will be.

Imagine someone who wants to turn a vacant area of public land into a community garden. With just one individual, the prospects might seem slim. With dozens of people, change is more likely. Imagine a crowd protesting at a meeting of local government officials or, taking direct action, turning the land into a garden. If those involved include politicians, town planners and police officers, prospects are even better.

Greater participation has several advantages. It shows that more people care about an issue, and sometimes can produce a bandwagon effect, winning over ever greater numbers until opponents feels outnumbered and give up. It provides a sense of mutual support, as those involved are encouraged by the fact that others are too. It provides greater resources to the movement. More people means more skills, more communication, more ideas — all of which are potentially valuable for further action.

Several methods of nonviolent action allow widespread participation, more than most other forms of action. Rallies, boycotts and some types of strikes are examples. A rally allows men, women, children, elderly and people with disabilities to participate. Anyone can join a boycott of a shop or a product.

In the face of severe repression, when joining a rally would risk injury, one method of safer protest is simultaneous pot-banging. At a specified time, say 6pm, everyone in an urban area opens their windows and makes a loud noise by banging pots and pans. This is a challenge to the authorities — and most people can join in.

It is usually pretty safe to join a boycott. This might involve not buying a particular product, not going to a particular shop, not depositing money in a particular bank, or not attending a government-sponsored march.

In public meetings, rallies and marches, people congregate together: these are called methods of concentration. Boycotts and pot-banging, in contrast, are methods of dispersion: people can join, but don't have to be in one place at the same time. Some research suggests that movements are stronger when they use methods of concentration *and* dispersion rather than relying on just one type.[11]

This possibility of participation by a broad cross-section of the population in rallies and boycotts can be compared to other methods of action. In armed struggle, most participants are young fit men: there are relatively fewer women, children, elderly and people with disabilities.

In elections, only a few individuals can run for office. Voting is restricted to adults. Furthermore, voting only occurs at specified occasions. A rally can be called at any time, but not an election.

There are two aspects to participation in nonviolent action. The first is that many methods *allow* more participation. The second is that many methods *encourage* more participation. The encouragement comes in part from the relative safety of methods such as boycotts and pot-banging, and in part from the excitement of joining in when lots of other people are involved.

---

11 Kurt Schock, *Unarmed Insurrections: People Power Movements in Nondemocracies* (Minneapolis, MN: University of Minnesota Press, 2005).

Methods and goals

Another important reason why nonviolent action can be effective is that it is more likely to win over others to the cause, including opponents and those who are uncommitted. The ones who are uncommitted, namely not on one side or the other, are sometimes called "third parties," in addition to the first two parties, who are the campaigners and their opponents.

Think of yourself, for the moment, as one of these third parties. There's a serious struggle going on — over climate change, animal rights, corruption, inequality, surveillance or whatever — but you haven't been involved, perhaps because you're too busy or you don't know enough about it. Maybe it's about some new technology called picotech that no one has ever explained to you properly.

If both sides in the struggle are using violence — they're shooting at each other, or planting bombs, or whatever — you might very well say you don't want to be involved and don't want to take a stand. You might reject both sides. Why would this be?

There's a perspective for understanding people's responses called "correspondent inference theory."[12] This sounds complicated, but the basic idea is simple. If you see a person using a particular type of method, you are likely to assume the goals of the person match the method.

---

12 For application of this theory to terrorism, see Max Abrahms, "Why terrorism does not work," *International Security,* vol. 31, no. 2, 2006, pp. 42–78.

If you see a person blowing up a building, you may assume their goal is destruction.

A prominent example is the 9/11 terrorist attacks on the World Trade Center and the Pentagon. Many people assumed that the purpose of al-Qaeda terrorists was to kill Americans.[13] Few bothered to learn about bin Laden's stated goals, which included opposing the western military presence in Saudi Arabia and supporting Palestinians against Israeli government impositions.

Correspondent inference theory suggests that most observers assumed the 9/11 attacks were attacks on the US way of life. The stated goals of the attackers were obscured or dismissed.

Now imagine you're a member of the police guarding a building where there's a meeting of politicians. There's a crowd of protesters outside and it's your responsibility to make sure the politicians are safe. The protesters are obviously angry. They're shouting and chanting ugly slogans. Some are shaking their fists. Next, some of the protesters start throwing bricks at you. What do you think? You may think the aim of the protesters is to hurt you and probably to hurt the politicians. The fact that the actual aim of nearly all the protesters is to reject the economic policies being imposed by the politicians — or whatever they're doing — is lost. You're not likely to read a leaflet put out by the protesters and make your judgement based on your assessment of the views expressed there. You're too busy doing your job, or dodging bricks!

---

13 Ziauddin Sardar and Merryl Wyn Davies, *Why Do People Hate America?* (Cambridge: Icon, 2002).

Correspondent inference theory has a simple lesson: the methods used can send a message that is stronger than the stated goals of the sender.[14] This means it's vital to choose appropriate methods.

Now imagine you're back on the police line, but the protesters aren't threatening at all. They're singing and dancing. Some of them are wearing clown suits. One of them comes up to you and offers a flower, and tries to strike up a conversation. What do you assume they're trying to do? Maybe they're just having a good time. It's likely you will be much more sympathetic to this group of protesters than the ones who were throwing bricks.

This points to one of the advantages of nonviolent action: compared to violence, it is much more likely to lead to shifts in loyalty by opponents and neutrals. In other words, those on the other side find it easier to change their allegiance. Some of the opponents, such as police, may decide to be neutrals; some of the neutrals may decide to join the movement.

This is especially dramatic when police or military forces are instructed to attack peaceful protesters but refuse to obey their orders. In 2000 in Serbia, the opposition movement Otpor forged connections with the police

---

14 For a similar conclusion about press coverage of protests — namely that a group's tactics influence coverage more than its goals — see Michael P. Boyle, Douglas M. McLeod and Cory L. Armstrong, "Adherence to the protest paradigm: the influence of protest goals and tactics on news coverage in U.S. and international newspapers," *International Journal of Press/Politics*, vol. 17, no. 2, 2012, pp. 127–144.

and military; although the ruler Slobodan Milošević wanted action taken against protesters, this did not happen. A similar dynamic occurred in the so-called orange revolution in the Ukraine in 2004.[15] In Tunisia and Egypt in 2011, there were mass protests against the repressive rulers; in each case, shortly after the military decided to stand aside and not act against the protesters, the dictators stood down from their positions.[16]

In most cases, police and military forces follow commands. That's what they are trained to do. But when they are instructed to attack citizens of their own country who are peacefully protesting, their loyalty can be divided: they know their orders, but some of them feel a greater loyalty to fellow citizens, especially ones who pose no physical threat to them.

Fraternising

Fraternising is when protesters try to win over troops on the other side, by talking to them, explaining their position

---

15 Anika Locke Binnendijk and Ivan Marovic, "Power and persuasion: nonviolent strategies to influence state security forces in Serbia (2000) and Ukraine (2004)," *Communist and Post-Communist Studies*, vol. 39, 2006, pp. 411–429.

16 On the importance of military defections when challenging repressive regimes, see generally Sharon Erickson Nepstad, *Nonviolent Revolutions: Civil Resistance in the Late 20th Century* (Oxford: Oxford University Press, 2011). For a much earlier treatment, see Katherine Chorley, *Armies and the Art of Revolution* (London: Faber and Faber, 1943).

and inviting them to put down their weapons and refuse to attack the protesters, or even join them.

One of the arguments against nonviolent action is that it cannot succeed against opponents willing to use violence. This argument assumes that the "willingness to use violence" cannot be affected by what the protesters do. With the right choice of tactics, police and military personnel are more likely to refuse orders and more likely to defect. In other words, willingness to use violence can be influenced by the actions of protesters.

By remaining nonviolent, protesters pose no physical threat to opponents, thereby reducing their incentive to use violence. By careful choice of tactics and messages, protesters make their cause more appealing, increasing the chance of defections. By making themselves vulnerable — by protesting and putting themselves at risk of harm — protesters show themselves as human beings, as people who are like other people, and thereby harder to attack. By explaining what they are doing, and making personal contact — namely fraternisation — protesters can win over some police and soldiers. Through all these means, nonviolent activists can undermine the willingness of opponent troops to use violence, and thereby neutralise what is seen as the ultimate sanction by the regime, physical force.

In 1968, there was an invasion of Czechoslovakia. At the time, the country was a communist dictatorship and part of the Warsaw Pact, a military alliance dominated by the Soviet Union. Within Czechoslovakia, the government was moving towards a less repressive type of communist rule, commonly called "socialism with a human face."

This was threatening to the Soviet rulers, who launched an invasion on 21 August, with half a million Warsaw Pact soldiers entering Czechoslovakia.

The Czechoslovak military forces were oriented to defending against an attack from the west — from NATO (North Atlantic Treaty Organization) — and not from their supposed allies. In the face of the Warsaw-Pact attack, Czechoslovak military leaders thought they would be able to resist for only a few days, and therefore did not resist at all: armed defence was futile.

Instead, there was a spontaneous popular resistance, entirely nonviolent.[17] There were protests and strikes. In the capital, Prague, people removed street signs and house numbers so the invaders would not be able to find their way around, in particular to track down targeted individuals. The radio station broadcast messages of resistance, counselling nonviolent tactics.

A key to the resistance was fraternisation. Czechoslovak people talked to the invading troops, trying to win them over. The troops had been told, falsely, that they were there to stop a capitalist takeover. The people told them: "No, we are socialists like you, and want to create our own socialist future."

---

17 H. Gordon Skilling, *Czechoslovakia's Interrupted Revolution* (Princeton, NJ: Princeton University Press, 1976); Joseph Wechsberg, *The Voices* (Garden City, NY: Doubleday, 1969); Philip Windsor and Adam Roberts, *Czechoslovakia 1968: Reform, Repression and Resistance* (London: Chatto and Windus, 1969).

To get a sense of this, imagine a 20-year-old soldier, with a rifle and perhaps in a tank, under orders to invade, confronted not by enemy soldiers but instead by civilians — some of whom were 20-year-olds just like them, talking to them and explaining what was going on. As a result of this effort to win over the troops, many of them became "unreliable" — from the point of view of Soviet commanders — and were removed from the country.

As a result of Soviet domination for 20 years, many younger Czechoslovaks knew Russian and could talk to the Soviet soldiers. To avoid the threat to their troops of simple conversations, Soviet commanders brought in troops from the far east who did not speak Russian.

The Czechoslovak people's resistance, in its most active phase, lasted just a week: Czechoslovak leaders, taken to Moscow for talks, made unwise concessions that undermined the popular resistance. Nevertheless, it took eight months before a puppet regime, subservient to the Soviet leadership, was installed.

This example shows the immense power of fraternisation. What made it possible? The Czechoslovaks needed a persuasive argument and needed to believe in it — which they did. They needed opportunities to talk to the invading troops, in order to win them over. They needed to know the language of the troops. A key condition for success was that the resistance was entirely nonviolent. The Czechoslovak people were no physical threat to the troops. This made the troops more willing to listen. As suggested by correspondent inference theory, the methods used by the Czechoslovaks corresponded with their message: "We are not a threat."

Here, I've used an example from Czechoslovakia 1968 to illustrate an important part of what makes nonviolent action effective: it is more likely than violence to win over opponents and third parties, in particular by undermining the loyalty of troops. This example does not prove anything on its own. It only illustrates the general argument. Furthermore, the example can be contested, with different analysts putting different weight on the factors involved in the events. It is not a straightforward case of "fraternisation was effective" but rather a complex story that can be interpreted as showing the importance of fraternisation and, more generally, of the effectiveness of nonviolent action in winning over opponents. The value of the example is in vividly illustrating an abstract point about undermining loyalty.

You might think I'm making a big deal about loyalty — and I am! In the face of a ruthless opponent, willing to hurt people to maintain power, it is absolutely essential to neutralise or win over some of the opponent's supporters, especially police, military and security forces. One way of neutralising them is to kill or disable them, or frighten them into fleeing or surrendering. Another is to take away their weapons. And then there is winning them over or encouraging them to withdraw.

Armed struggle can neutralise opponent forces through direct use of force, but when the opponent has superior numbers, technology, resources and training, direct engagement is a losing proposition. Furthermore, armed struggle has the serious disadvantage of causing greater commitment and unity among the opponent: when troops are under attack, they will support each other to resist and fight back.

Using guerrilla methods — occasional attacks on weak outposts or vulnerable points, without direct military engagement — is a way of waging what is called "asymmetric struggle." The struggle is highly unequal in terms of numbers, weapons and resources, so the guerrillas avoid meeting enemy forces on their own terms.

Nonviolent action is a different way of waging asymmetric struggle. The activists do not use any military methods and hence do not engage with the opposition on its strongest point. Instead, they target the hearts and minds of the opponent.

Violence can backfire

This sounds very well. But what if the nonviolent protesters are met with deadly force. Surely they will lose! This leads to one of the most important points: using violence against peaceful protesters can be counterproductive. When it is seen as unfair, it can backfire.

Imagine two men standing together, having a conversation, without raising their voices. You and others are nearby watching and listening, because it's an important conversation. Then one of the men suddenly hits the other in the face, knocking him to the ground. Even worse, he pulls out a gun and shoots the man in the stomach.

Most people would react with horror or anger. They see the physical attack as unfair, unless there has been some provocation. If the two men had been shouting and started pushing each other, then a punch might be seen as an escalation, but perhaps justified. However, when there has been no provocation or escalation, a physical attack is seen as wrong. This is true legally: it's a type of assault. But even without invoking the law, most people will see it as wrong.

Barrington Moore, Jr., a prominent social historian, analysed the reaction of people in different cultures to various behaviours, and concluded that every culture has a sense of injustice.[18] One of those injustices is using violence against others who are not using violence. So it can be predicted that when police or military troops use force against peaceful protesters, many participants and observers will see this as unfair. The result is that the protesters may gain increased support. Some of the protesters themselves, and their allies, may be so outraged that they become more highly committed to the cause. Those who are neutrals may decide to support the protesters or oppose the attackers. Even some of those on the side of the attackers may break ranks, withdrawing support or even joining the other side.

Richard Gregg, from the US, went to India and observed Gandhi's campaigns in the 1920s and 1930s. He called this phenomenon "moral jiu-jitsu." This is an analogy to the sport of jiu-jitsu, in which a key technique is to turn the force and momentum of the opponent against them. Gregg saw this sort of thing when Indian police attacked peaceful protesters: the more brutal and blatant

---

18 Barrington Moore, Jr., *Injustice: The Social Bases of Obedience and Revolt* (London: Macmillan, 1978).

their violence, the more popular sentiment turned in favour of the protesters.

The classic example occurred during the salt satyagraha, a nonviolent campaign in 1930. Gandhi had the inspired idea of protesting against the British salt monopoly. The British rulers controlled the production of salt and taxed it. In the context of British colonial rule at the time, which involved all sorts of exploitation and abuse, the issue of salt was not particularly important. Gandhi realised, though, that everyone was affected by the salt tax: it was an obvious injustice that everyone experienced and could readily understand.

Gandhi and his team designed a dramatic campaign. Starting inland, they marched for 24 days towards the sea town of Dandi, with the stated intention of committing civil disobedience against the salt laws. Along the way, Gandhi gave talks in local areas, gaining more support. News of the march was reported nationally, causing a build-up of excitement about this bold challenge to the British rulers.[19]

Reaching the ocean at Dandi, Gandhi and others in the march scooped up muddy seawater and proceeded to make salt from it — and were arrested. This itself was a dramatic moment. After Gandhi was arrested, leadership of the campaign fell to others. They planned another type of civil disobedience: they would try to approach the saltworks at Dharasana.

---

19 Thomas Weber, *On the Salt March: The Historiography of Gandhi's March to Dandi* (New Delhi: HarperCollins, 1997).

Imagine this scenario. Indian activists, called satyagrahis, dressed in white, calmly walked forward towards the saltworks. They were met by police — also Indian, in the pay of the British rulers — who, using batons called lathis, brutally beat the activists, who fell to the ground, injured and bloody. Others rushed to the scene to carry the protesters away to a hospital. After protesters were beaten and taken away, others calmly walked forward for a continuation of the protest.

At a superficial level, violence succeeded: the police stopped the satyagrahis from reaching the saltworks. At a wider level, it turned out to be highly counterproductive. One of the witnesses to the saltworks confrontation was Webb Miller, a journalist for United Press. He wrote moving accounts of the courage and suffering of the satyagrahis. When Miller's reports were published internationally, they triggered an outpouring of support for the Indian independence cause, especially in Britain and the US. Hundreds of thousands of copies of his stories were reproduced and distributed by supporters. (This was huge for its time. This was before the Internet, indeed before television. Print journalism was highly influential on its own.)

If we imagine the protesters and police in a contest with jiu-jitsu moves, the police attacked and the protesters seemed to suffer a grievous blow, but the police ended up being hurt far worse. Of course it wasn't the police themselves, but the British colonial rulers whose cause suffered a major blow. Meanwhile, within India, the salt satyagrapha generated a huge upsurge of commitment and solidarity for the independence cause.

Gregg assumed that the jiu-jitsu process occurred at the psychological level, and that the police doing the beatings would be thrown off balance emotionally by having to hurt non-resisting protesters.[20] Gandhian scholar Tom Weber, writing 60 years later, showed this was incorrect.[21] The police were not, apparently, upset or deterred. Some of them became angry at the satyagrahis for not resisting, and hit them even harder. The jiu-jitsu process operated at a larger level, causing shifts in loyalty and commitment among Indians across the country and among populations in Britain, the US and elsewhere.

Nonviolence scholar Gene Sharp recognised the limitations of Gregg's analysis and relabelled the process, calling it "political jiu-jitsu."[22] The word "political" here refers to wider effects on the distribution of power, and incorporates political, economic and social dimensions.

The important message is that attacks on peaceful protesters can be counterproductive for the attacker by stimulating greater support among the group supported by the protesters (what Sharp calls the "grievance group"), among third parties and even among some of those opposed to the protesters. From the immediate point of view of the protesters, it certainly seems like they are

---

20 Richard B. Gregg, *The Power of Nonviolence* (New York: Schocken Books, 1966). The book was originally published in 1934.

21 Thomas Weber, "'The marchers simply walked forward until struck down': nonviolent suffering and conversion," *Peace & Change*, vol. 18, July 1993, pp. 267–289.

22 Sharp, *Politics of Nonviolent Action*, 657–703.

losing. The satyagrahis were being brutally beaten and carried off to hospital, some with serious injuries; a few died. This is the close-up picture, and it looks like violence is victorious. The bigger picture is the struggle for loyalties, and it is here where the protesters can have success: the fact that they are suffering a brutal attack can become the trigger for an upsurge in support for their cause.

It may seem surprising that political jiu-jitsu, which can have such a powerful effect, is so little recognised. Part of the problem is visual. People can see the physical effects of violence — the blood, the injuries and the crumpled bodies. This is vivid and gives the impression that those who are hurt are the losers in the struggle. The jiu-jitsu effects of the encounter, namely the shifts in loyalty, are not so obvious. There might be more protesters later, but there is a time delay, and often the cause-and-effect sequence is not all that obvious.

It continues to be difficult for protesters to see the big picture. Many activists want to succeed in their immediate objective, for example stopping a logging operation, interrupting a meeting of global leaders or preventing transport of nuclear waste. They focus on this objective, which, to be sure, can be important, but lose sight of the potential wider impacts of their actions.

This happened in the salt satyagraha. The immediate objectives were to make salt and to get to the saltworks, but whether these were achieved was largely irrelevant, because the primary impact of the action was on the consciousness of people in India and beyond. For this, the key was the symbolic act of challenging British law and

British rule. The challenge was principled and crystal clear. It was civil disobedience, with many satyagrahis arrested and imprisoned, or brutally beaten. The immediate goals of making salt from the sea or trespassing on the saltworks were incidental.

In some campaigns, the immediate objective is more important in a practical way, rather than mainly symbolic. Nevertheless, it is usually possible to distinguish the immediate objective from the long term goal, and important not to forget the goal.

Backfire tactics

For the beatings at Dharasana to be counterproductive for the British, it was important that the satyagrahis remained nonviolent. If they had started fighting or throwing stones, it would have turned the confrontation into a fight. In such a context, the police use of force would have been seen, by many more people, as justified. There would have been little or no jiu-jitsu effect.

Sharp, in describing the phenomenon of political jiu-jitsu, says the protesters must remain nonviolent. In presenting a set of stages of nonviolent campaigns, he emphasises the importance of "nonviolent discipline," which means remaining nonviolent in the face of provocation. If all the satyagrahis had been provoked by the police brutality and fought back, their effectiveness would have been weakened. The satyagrahis needed to believe in what they were doing and how they were going about it.

Nonviolent discipline can come from strong beliefs; it can also be built through training. Soldiers train, so why not protesters? There is a long tradition of nonviolence training. Campaigners in the US civil rights movement, preparing for sit-ins at restaurants in Greensboro, North Carolina in 1960, anticipated being insulted and physically assaulted — and practised not talking or fighting back. Nonviolence training is now a standard part of many actions in the peace, environmental and other social movements.

If beating peaceful protesters can be so effective for a protest movement, and so damaging to the police and government, then why would police and governments ever do it? Wouldn't they realise they are helping the protesters?

In many cases they do, and they adopt different tactics. At Dharasana, they could have let the protesters walk to the fence surrounding the saltworks. They could have arrested the satyagrahis rather than beating them. However, these alternatives sometimes are not so good. If the police let the protesters achieve their immediate objective, the protesters might continue on. Where might it stop? Authorities often feel like they have to "hold the line," namely prevent the protesters from achieving their immediate objective, otherwise the protesters will be emboldened and push for something more.

The Dharasana beatings became one of the most well-known events in the Indian independence struggle. They featured in the 1982 film *Gandhi* as a dramatic confrontation.

Other instances of political jiu-jitsu include the shooting of protesters by Russian troops in 1905, the shooting of black protesters by police in 1960 in Sharpeville, South Africa, and the shooting of protesters by troops in 1991 in Dili, East Timor, and the arrest and shooting of protesters on the Freedom Flotilla to Gaza by Israeli commandoes in 2010. In these and other examples, the protesters suffered — many lost their lives — in the short term, but their cause was greatly advanced by the wider perception of injustice.[23]

From this list, you might gain the impression that political jiu-jitsu, to be effective, requires protesters to be killed. Luckily, this is not the case. Although some protesters may be killed in nonviolent struggle, this is usually far fewer than in armed struggle. The instances listed are well known in part because of loss of life. In Dharasana, only a few satyagrahis died. Political jiu-jitsu occurred because of the stark contrast between the disciplined nonviolence of the satyagrahis and the brutality of the police. Another instance of political jiu-jitsu was the arrest of protesters at lunch counters at Greensboro, North Carolina in 1960. No one was killed, but the injustice was clear to many across the United States and beyond: the protesters were completely nonviolent and were asking for fairness in treatment, yet were insulted and arrested.

Given the power of the political jiu-jitsu effect, why isn't it more widely known? One reason is that most activists know of plenty of cases in which peaceful protesters have been beaten and arrested, but there was no

---

23 On the Sharpeville and Dili cases, see Brian Martin, *Justice Ignited: The Dynamics of Backfire* (Lanham, MD: Rowman & Littlefield, 2007).

upsurge of support for the cause. In fact, the historical cases of political jiu-jitsu seem to be the exception rather than the rule. How can this be explained?

The answer is that the jiu-jitsu effect doesn't happen automatically. Two conditions need to be satisfied: people need to know what has happened and they need to see it as unfair. This may seem obvious enough, but imagine that in India in 1930 the police had beaten the satyagrahis but there had been no independent witnesses. The impact would have been smaller. This is not news to police, governments and others responsible for attacks on peaceful protesters. There are five main ways they can reduce outrage from their actions.

- Cover up the action.
- Devalue the targets.
- Reinterpret what happened through lying, minimising, blaming and framing.
- Use official channels to give an appearance of justice.
- Intimidate and reward people involved.

All these methods were used at Dharasana. Journalist Webb Miller observed the beatings and wrote eloquent stories about them, but it wasn't straightforward for him to submit his stories for publication: the British attempted to block their transmission, thereby covering up the events. The British considered themselves superior to Indians, an example of devaluation. The British claimed that no police violence was involved and that the satyagrahis were faking their injuries, examples of reinterpretation by lying. The arrests of Gandhi and other independence leaders were ratified by the courts, which served as official channels that gave an appearance of justice without the substance. The beatings and arrests served as forms of intimidation, discouraging others from joining.

The British thus used all five of the methods to reduce outrage from their actions — though in this case they were unsuccessful. However, in many other instances these methods are effective, preventing a jiu-jitsu effect from occurring. Protesters are familiar with this.

At a rally, police can hurt protesters, for example with pepper spray or pain compliance holds, in ways that do not show visible damage. Police sometimes rub pepper spray into protesters' eyes. This causes extreme pain but is not visible like beatings and blood. (In 2011, a police officer was filmed casually using pepper spray against Occupy movement protesters sitting peacefully in Davis, California. The video went viral, causing outrage internationally. It was a clear example of when the two conditions for the jiu-jitsu effect were satisfied: information about the spraying was communicated to audiences, who saw it as unjust.)

Officials and opponents often devalue protesters by calling them rabble, rent-a-crowd, hooligans, misguided, terrorists and other terms of abuse and dismissal. They sometimes release information to discredit particular individuals or organisations.

When police use violence against peaceful protesters, the police and their allies sometimes claim there was no police violence (reinterpretation by lying) or that no one was hurt (reinterpretation by minimising). If the awareness of police violence is undeniable, officials may claim that only a few rogue police were involved (reinterpretation by blaming). They may say that police were defending themselves from a threatening crowd (reinterpretation by framing the action from the police point of view).

Sometimes protesters make formal complaints about police violence to government officials or to courts. These official processes give the appearance of providing justice but very seldom do so.

Police sometimes threaten protesters, overtly or subtly, with reprisals if they try to expose or challenge the police violence. Reprisals are especially severe against any members of the police who break ranks and criticise behaviour by other police. On the other hand, police who make special efforts to protect their fellow police — the ones who hurt protesters — may be rewarded by continued work, good favour and promotions.

How do these five types of methods work to reduce outrage?

Cover-up prevents people finding out about what really happened. If you don't know about something, you can't be upset about it.

Devaluation means encouraging people to think of the target as low status, as less worthy, as lacking value, as evil. If someone is perceived as low status, then when something harmful is done to them, it doesn't seem so bad. When a prominent and respected doctor is murdered, people are outraged. When someone with low status, such as a paedophile or serial killer, is murdered, it doesn't seem so bad — indeed, some people will be pleased.

Reinterpretation is a process of explaining something as different from what it seems to be on the surface. It might seem like lots of protesters are being beaten, unfairly. Reinterpretation aims to change this perception. It can include official statements that actually there wasn't any police violence or that little harm was done or that police were just doing their duty. Reinterpretation is a process of contesting the explanation of what happened. It sometimes involves lies and distortions. It is most effective when it encourages people to see the events through the eyes of the perpetrators, who have justified the events from their perspective.

Official channels include grievance procedures, courts, expert panels and commissions of inquiry. They are formal processes, involving officials who are supposed to follow procedures. Most people believe, to some extent, in the fairness of official channels, for example that courts dispense justice. If there has been an obvious case of injustice, causing public outrage, one way to reduce outrage is to refer the matter to some official channel. Sometimes protesters do this themselves, for example making complaints to the government about police brutality or suing in court for false arrest. The problem is that official channels are seldom very effective when dealing with powerful perpetrators like police or governments. In any case, they dampen outrage: they are slow, dependent on experts (such as lawyers) and focus on procedural details (such as legal technicalities). The result is that outrage declines while the official processes proceed. In a world with rapid communication, speed and delay are ever more important in the dynamics of public outrage.

It can seem counter-intuitive to say that official channels serve the powerful. Many citizens, when faced with injustice, want above all some formal vindication: they want authorities to say perpetrators did the wrong thing and apologise. With official channels, this hardly ever happens. In many cases, the perpetrators are exonerated or get off with minor penalties. In other cases, a few individuals are blamed, but these are usually lower-level operatives, not policy-makers.

Usually, official channels are only used by powerful groups when the problem is very serious, for example when protesters have been killed and there is huge negative publicity. When this happens, expect an official inquiry to be set up. Notice whether it is an internal inquiry, limiting the likelihood of a finding adverse to the perpetrators. Look for narrow terms of reference, to reduce the damage of an adverse finding. Finally, look to see how many people follow the full course of the inquiry, maintaining interest throughout. The drawn-out, technical details are often so off-putting as to discourage all but a few tenacious supporters. The result is that, for most people, the issue becomes less urgent. The official channels thus have served to dampen outrage over injustice. Note that this can occur even though all those involved in the relevant agencies — lawyers, judges, agency staff and members of expert panels — are concerned and conscientious. The effect of official channels is largely a product of the processes involved, which move an issue from one of public concern to an in-house, narrow, procedural matter to be addressed by formal rules.

Intimidation can prevent the expression of outrage. People might be angry but if they are afraid of being hurt or losing their jobs, they are less likely to express their concerns. Rewards function the same way. People might be upset but if financial compensation is a possibility, they are less likely to express their concerns. Intimidation and rewards can change people's behaviour but may not change their views.

Let's return to the phenomenon of political jiu-jitsu and examine the implications of outrage-reducing methods. Many people, when they witness or hear about what seems to be a gross injustice, are concerned, upset, disgusted or outraged. Some of them may want to do something about it. The use of violence against peaceful protesters can trigger this reaction — to many people, it seems wrong. This reaction is of the great advantages of nonviolent action in the face of an opponent able to use much greater violence: the opponent cannot exercise its superior force without the risk of triggering massive outrage. The use of violence can backfire against its perpetrators.

However, those who use violence are not helpless in this sort of situation. They can act to reduce the outrage, using the methods of cover-up, devaluation, reinterpretation, official channels, intimidation and rewards. Perpetrators commonly use these methods intuitively. No one taught them how to reduce outrage. Furthermore, they do not think of themselves as wrongdoers consciously trying to get away with an evil act. Instead, most of them believe they are justified in their actions or serving a higher purpose.[24]

Sharp's political jiu-jitsu thus is not as easy or automatic as his examples seem to suggest. He cited jiu-jitsu effects in Russia in 1905, India in 1930, South Africa in 1960 and elsewhere. These are all important cases, but they are the exceptions. Sharp argued that a key precondition for political jiu-jitsu was maintaining nonviolent discipline. If protesters use violence, then violence used against them seems more justified. So remaining nonviolent is important in preventing violence by opponents or triggering outrage if they use violence. But there is more to it: protesters can use five sorts of methods to *increase* outrage, each of them countering one of the five ways perpetrators reduce outrage.

- Expose what happened.
- Validate the target.
- Interpret the event as an injustice.
- Mobilise support, and avoid or discredit official channels.
- Resist intimidation and rewards.

Several or all of these methods were used in famous backfires. In the salt satyagraha, journalist Webb Miller exposed, to international audiences, what happened, getting around attempted censorship. His stories presented the satyagrahis as heroic rather than devious, and told of the beatings in such a graphic fashion as to evoke sympa-

---

24 Roy F. Baumeister, *Evil: Inside Human Violence and Cruelty* (New York: Freeman, 1997).

thy in the readers, who could sense the injustice involved. Within India, the salt satyagraha was used as a mobilising process, with supporters across the country engaging in salt-making as civil disobedience. In doing this, they were resisting intimidation, especially the threat of arrest and imprisonment: tens of thousands were jailed. Outside India, the campaign stimulated great support for the independence struggle. Outsiders had little need to resist intimidation. Internationally, the key was that supporters added their voices to the struggle rather than relying on governments.

For violence by police or troops to backfire, protesters need to remain nonviolent. They also need to anticipate the tactics of their opponents — from cover-up to intimidation — and plan how to counter these tactics.

Other factors in effectiveness

To talk of the effectiveness of nonviolent action is to assume what the goal is. This is normally taken as the success of a campaign in achieving its stated goals. However, there's a problem here, in that different participants might have different ideas about what the goals really are. As noted earlier, some focus on the immediate engagement whereas others look more strategically at the encounter as part of a longer and bigger struggle.

For Gandhi in the salt satyagraha, making salt was a symbolic challenge to British rule, not a goal in itself. The usual thinking about the campaigns in India is that the goal was independence. However, Gandhi didn't see independence as all that important, because he had even wider goals, including the elimination of social inequality (such as subordination of women and lower castes) and the promotion of village democracy with principles such as bread labour. Gandhi had a vision that challenged the dominant political and economic systems of the state and capitalism.

Not all that many activists share Gandhi's vision, nor is there any requirement for them to do so. The point here is that nonviolent action can be seen as a road to a different sort of society, and there can be more to it than the immediate objectives of an action or even the stated goals of a movement. In this context, it is worth looking at some of the features of nonviolent action that are beneficial in ways separate from campaign goals.

Compared to armed struggle, using nonviolent action is unlikely to lead to large numbers of deaths and injuries. The reason is straightforward: when faced by peaceful protesters, opponents are less likely to use as much violence. In armed struggle, the opponent fights back, and casualties are likely; in nonviolent struggle, there is less provocation to use violence and, when opponents use violence, it can backfire on them.

There are some telling examples. The Indian independence struggle, which involved mainly nonviolent methods, led to perhaps several thousand immediate deaths. Compare this to civil war leading to the communist revolution in China, in which millions died.

Sometimes it is said that in India, the struggle was easy because the British were soft-hearted colonialists, not predisposed to being ruthless. This may sound plausible on the surface, ignoring repressive measures taken in

India. It is revealing to make a comparison with another British colony: Kenya, where there was armed resistance to British rule, called the Mau Mau rebellion. In response, the British used extremely harsh measures, including ruthless military attacks, executions, torture and setting up concentration camps.[25]

Admittedly, the situation in Kenya was different from India in some important ways. In Kenya, there was a significant population of British settlers, who had a strong commitment to maintaining colonial rule, compared to India where British settlement was minimal. On the other hand, British economic interests in India, a vastly larger country than Kenya, were far greater.

Arguably, the different responses of British rulers in India and Kenya were due to different methods used by independence campaigners. When the British used force in India, as against salt satyagrahis, it provoked greater opposition. However, the British could use extreme force in Kenya with hardly any public backlash, because it was against the Mau Mau who themselves used considerable violence.

Many other examples could be cited. The point here is that relying on nonviolent methods in a campaign is likely to lead to a lower toll in injuries and deaths. This is not relevant to effectiveness in a strict sense, but it is

---

25 David Anderson, *Histories of the Hanged: The Dirty War in Kenya and the End of Empire* (New York: Norton, 2005); Robert B. Edgerton, *Mau Mau: An African Crucible* (New York: Free Press, 1989); Caroline Elkins, *Imperial Reckoning: The Untold Story of Britain's Gulag in Kenya* (New York: Henry Holt, 2005).

surely a benefit for those who might otherwise have died. Compared to armed struggle, it is plausible that nonviolent methods are more effective because the process of change causes less suffering. This is to assume that effectiveness is measured through human impacts both in ultimate outcomes and on the road to achieving them.

There is no iron rule that says nonviolent action leads to fewer deaths and injuries than armed struggle. In a provocative article titled "Heavy casualties and nonviolent defense," nonviolence researcher Gene Keyes examined the possibility that defence by nonviolent means could lead to ever mounting human costs.[26] Imagine a population prepared to sacrifice their lives to stop a takeover by a ruthless invader. The death toll could mount, apparently without limit.

A massive human cost to nonviolent resisters is certainly possible in theory, but seems unlikely in practice, going by historical examples. One of the main reasons is that protesters can use a variety of techniques, some of which are low risk, such as boycotts and banging pots and pans. Few campaigners want to be martyrs, so the prospect that millions of people would walk to a protest line and be prepared to be shot is remote.

Using nonviolent methods to defend a society from attack has been compared with guerrilla warfare: defence by civil resistance is the nonviolent analogue to a guerrilla

---

26 Gene Keyes, "Heavy casualties and nonviolent defense," *Philosophy and Social Action*, vol. 17, nos. 3-4, July-December 1991, pp. 75–88.

struggle.[27] Guerrilla forces usually avoid a head-on clash with the enemy, which has superior firepower, instead using hit-and-run tactics. In this way, guerrillas cause maximum damage with limited risk. Nonviolent campaigners typically use a similar approach: they engage the opponent on its weakest rather than its strongest terrain.

The difference is that a military force, with its trained troops and superior weaponry, has little hesitation in attacking guerrillas, sometimes causing many civilian casualties along the way. Attacking peaceful protesters is another matter. Military training does not prepare soldiers to do this easily, and there is a risk of backfire if they do.

Hence, it is reasonable to say that achieving change through nonviolent action is likely to involve fewer deaths and injuries than armed struggle. This is an element of effectiveness if change is taken to include both the process of change and ultimate outcomes. It is important to remember that some struggles last for decades. Think of the struggle against apartheid in South Africa or the struggle for independence in Vietnam.

It is also worth remembering that some struggles are unsuccessful. Major efforts may be taken over years or decades, but the goals of the campaigners are not achieved. Examples are the guerrilla struggles in Malaya (1948–1960) and Lithuania (1944–1952). In such cases of failure, it is surely worth counting up the casualties.

---

27 Anders Boserup and Andrew Mack, *War without Weapons: Non-violence in National Defence* (London: Frances Pinter, 1974).

Nonviolent action has the advantage of a lower human cost.

Another argument for nonviolent action, compared to violence, is that it is less likely to lead to centralisation of power. This is not about effectiveness in immediately winning against opponents, but is about effectiveness in creating a more egalitarian, less oppressive society.

Armed struggle lends itself to a command system. In armies around the world, hierarchy and command are central elements. Soldiers are trained to obey those at higher ranks. The penalties for disobedience are severe: in wartime, soldiers who refuse orders may be imprisoned or even executed.

Modern militaries are becoming more sophisticated in their use of psychology, recognising that loyalty is primarily to fellow soldiers and that fighting effectiveness can come from suitable training rather than arbitrary brutality.[28] Nevertheless, command and obedience remain fundamental.

Guerrilla forces are sometimes organised in a more decentralised fashion, with autonomy for separate groups, but there is still usually a system of leadership. The reason is that the risks of disunity are severe. In the face of an enemy willing to kill, it is vital that control be maintained. Secrecy and coordination are vital for military planning. If a soldier or a group of soldiers attacks too soon, or even lets off a stray shot, it can wreck the element of surprise

---

[28] See, for example, Dave Grossman, *On Killing: The Psychological Cost of Learning to Kill in War and Society* (Boston: Little, Brown, 1995).

and make the entire force vulnerable. The system of hierarchy and command is an adaptive response to the nature of armed struggle.

Armed struggle can certainly be used against systems of domination, namely against repressive states. The risk is that in the aftermath of a victory, the new government will adopt the command and control system used in the armed struggle. In other words, the method of struggle will lend its characteristics to the way the society is ruled: military leadership in the struggle may lead to military-style leadership subsequently. This has been the outcome in some prominent cases when armed struggle has succeeded against corrupt and oppressive regimes, such as in Algeria, China, Cuba and Vietnam.

This process — sometimes called militarisation of the revolution — is not inevitable. It is a tendency. If one of the goals of the struggle is a freer society, this tendency should be avoided or resisted.

Nonviolent struggle has the opposite tendency. Few nonviolent struggles use a command-and-control system, with a few leaders determining actions and imposing discipline on the activists. Participation in nonviolent action is almost always voluntary. Some people might feel pressure to join, but it is social pressure: there is no danger of being imprisoned or shot for disobedience.

Actions taken depend on participants being willing to join. If there's a rally, people can join or not. Likewise if there's a boycott or banging of pots and pans. If some people decide to organise a different sort of action, they can. (Whether it is an effective choice is another question.)

Because participants have choice and autonomy, relationships are more by mutual agreement than by command. This lays the foundation for a post-struggle society based on citizen participation rather than centralised control.

Following this line of argument, it is plausible to hypothesise that the longer a struggle takes, the more the method of struggle is likely to influence the form of the post-struggle society. A lengthy armed struggle is more likely to lead to militarisation and a lengthy nonviolent struggle to a less repressive outcome. Several prominent cases seem to fit this pattern.

- China and Vietnam: lengthy armed struggle, centralised post-revolution government
- India and South Africa, lengthy nonviolent struggle, representative post-independence government

Short struggles, such as Iran 1978–1979, China 1989 and Egypt 2011, gave less opportunity for the mode of struggle to influence the outcome. However, these are only suggestive examples. This hypothesis about long-versus-short struggles remains to be tested.

A more general argument in favour of nonviolence is that the means are compatible with the ends. The means are what people do to achieve a goal, and the ends are the goals. Activists — at least those challenging repressive governments, inequality, oppression, exploitation and other injustices — normally want a society that is freer, more equal, less corrupt and fairer. This inevitably means a society with less violence: far fewer beatings and killings, preferably none. For the means to be compatible with the ends, beatings, killings and torture should not be used to try to achieve this sort of society.

There are a few pacifists whose the goal is a society without any form of conflict, in which people live in harmony. For them, methods like strikes, boycotts and sit-ins are coercive and not desirable. If they subscribe to the idea of making means compatible with ends, they would support only methods of persuasion and not support methods of noncooperation and intervention.

Nonviolent activists — those willing to use strikes, boycotts and other methods that potentially coerce opponents, though without physical violence — don't often talk about their ideal society, except that it will be less oppressive. If we take seriously the idea of the means being compatible with the ends, then the ideal society for nonviolent activists is one in which there continues to be conflict, perhaps quite serious conflict, that is waged without physical violence.

There is an analogy here with organised religion. In earlier times, some religions sought to impose their views on others, including by force. Heresy was treated as a crime, with the penalty being excommunication from the community, or even death. Wars were fought over religious belief, for example the Crusades.

Today, in much of the world, most religions co-exist peacefully. Belief is considered to be a choice. There are efforts to invite or encourage others to join. Within churches, heresy can still exist, and those deemed outside the boundaries of acceptable religious belief can be challenged. Those deemed to be heretics can resist through a range of methods. The point is that nearly all this struggle occurs without physical violence.

It is possible to imagine a world in which politics has been pacified in the same way as religion. There might be strong differences of opinion about free speech, economic arrangements, cultural traditions, land use, treatment of minorities and much else — but without the use of organised violence, in particular without armies and militarised police forces. This is a vision of a world with plenty of conflict, in which conflicts are pursued using argument, evidence, community organising, policies — but without systematic use of force.

This is certainly a utopian vision, but a useful one. Most people, in most of the things they do, never use physical force in public. Social life is quite possible without violence. The challenge is to find alternatives for the uses of violence in the world today. The promise of nonviolent action is to model a violence-free world in the process of moving towards it.

This concludes a brief survey of plausible reasons for the effectiveness of nonviolent action. A key factor is potential participation of many people across diverse sectors of the population. Nonviolent action is not as threatening to opponents as violence, and has a greater capacity to win over third parties and cause defections from the ranks of opponents. Nonviolent action has the advantage of usually leading to fewer casualties.

Beyond the immediate pragmatic considerations of winning a struggle, nonviolent action seems promising for achieving longer-term goals of leading to a freer society. Participation in nonviolent action is more likely to foster the sorts of human interactions that enable a peaceful, respectful society. Nonviolent action as a method of struggle has the advantage of incorporating the ends within the means.

So far I've looked at campaigns using nonviolent action that illustrate its potential effectiveness and at arguments about why it is likely to be more effective than violence. There is a third, and most important, element in the case for nonviolent action: empirical studies.

Empirical evidence

Undoubtedly the most important study is reported in *Why Civil Resistance Works* by Erica Chenoweth and Maria Stephan.[29] They provide a statistical analysis that undermines claims for armed struggle and, incidentally, the assumptions of most social movement researchers. (In the context of their study, civil resistance means the same as nonviolent action.) The foundation for their analysis is a database of 323 campaigns, between 1900 and 2006, of resistance to regimes or occupations, or in support of secession. Many of the struggles mentioned earlier, such as the Indian independence struggle and the Iranian revolution, are included. Others in the database are the 1944 October revolution in Guatemala, the 1955 Naga rebellion in India, the 1960–1975 Pathet Lao campaign in Cambodia and the 1974 carnation revolution in Portugal. The database has all sorts of information, such as loca-

---

29 Erica Chenoweth and Maria J. Stephan, *Why Civil Resistance Works: The Strategic Logic of Nonviolent Conflict* (New York: Columbia University Press, 2011).

tions, key protagonists, lengths of campaigns, maximum numbers of participants, methods used and outcomes.

For Chenoweth and Stephan's core argument, the key bits of information are the methods used (either primarily armed struggle or primarily civil resistance) and the success or failure of the campaign. Deciding whether a campaign is successful is sometimes difficult: maybe only some of the goals of the challengers were achieved; maybe the goals changed along the way. This is only one of many difficulties faced in quantifying the elements of resistance struggles. The authors describe their careful process for validating the information in the database, including checking judgements about campaigns with experts on the countries and events involved.

With such a database, it is possible to test various hypotheses. Their most significant and striking finding is that nonviolent anti-regime campaigns are far more likely to succeed than violent campaigns.

A sceptic might claim the nonviolent campaigns were against softer targets. Chenoweth and Stephan tested this: one of the elements in the database is how repressive the regime is. The answer: the strength of the regime makes very little difference to the success of the resistance. This is remarkable. It means civil resistance can win against even the most repressive regimes, and furthermore has a much greater chance of success than armed resistance.

What happened to the idea, widely used by social movement scholars, that movements succeed because political opportunities are favourable? Chenoweth and Stephan have replaced it with a quite different conclusion: the keys to success are the methods and strategies adopted by the challengers. Conditions such as the level of government repression don't make very much difference to outcomes. This means that success depends far more on what activists do than ever realised by more than a handful of scholars, political commentators or governments.

The statistics in the book are supplemented with many illustrations, including four detailed case studies: the 1977–1979 Iranian revolution, the first Palestinian intifada (1987–1993), the 1983–1986 people power movement in the Philippines, and the 1988–1990 Burmese uprising. These vivid stories give flesh to and help validate generalisations from the statistical findings.

If Chenoweth and Stephan are right, many social movement scholars should reconsider their frameworks and focus on agency, namely what activists choose to do. Why haven't more scholars done this before?[30] One answer is that it means relinquishing some of their authority to experienced activists.

What are the lessons for activists? The first and foremost is that armed struggle is not a promising option. It is less likely to succeed and, when it does, it is more likely to lead to a society lower in freedom and more likely to lapse into civil war. Mixing armed struggle and civil resistance is not such a good idea either. The best option, statistically speaking, is to forego any armed resistance and rely entirely on nonviolent methods.

---

30 Some have, for example James M. Jasper, *Getting Your Way: Strategic Dilemmas in the Real World* (Chicago: University of Chicago Press, 2006).

Chenoweth and Stephan argue that the key to the effectiveness of nonviolent action is greater participation. Most of those who join an armed struggle are young fit men, a relatively small sector of the population. Methods of civil resistance include sit-ins and public protests, which allow involvement by a greater proportion of the population. The maximum number of participants, as a proportion of the population, is highly correlated with success of the campaign — and large numbers of participants are more likely to be achieved with a nonviolent campaign.

Participation is crucial, in part, due to spin-off effects. More participants, especially when they include a wide cross-section of the population, means the resistance builds links to more people, with the likelihood of causing shifts in the loyalty of security forces, which are absolutely vital to success. This process can happen in both violent and nonviolent struggles, but high participation is more likely in nonviolent struggles because there are fewer barriers to involvement. The case studies, each of which involves a primary nonviolent struggle in which there was a parallel armed struggle, show this vividly.

Why Civil Resistance Works is an academic work published by a university press. It contains statistical data, explanation and justification of database construction, careful analysis of contrary hypotheses, and much else. Unlike some scholarly writing, it is clearly written, logically organised and provides helpful summaries. Nevertheless, it is unlikely to become bedtime reading for activists. What then are the takeaway messages? Here is my list.

- Civil resistance works. A well-organised unarmed campaign against a repressive government is much more likely to succeed than a well-organised armed campaign. The message from nonviolent activists to those who advocate armed struggle should be "show us some good evidence that your approach works better, because the best study so far shows civil resistance has better prospects."
- When civil resistance works, the outcomes are likely to be better. Use nonviolent methods if you want a nonviolent society; use armed struggle if you want a militarised successor regime.
- The key is participation. The more people involved in a campaign, and the more diverse the participants, the more likely is success. Beyond this general conclusion, I think it is a plausible extrapolation from the data for activists to say, "let's choose actions that will involve the most people from different sectors of society."
- Winning over the security apparatus is crucial. Changing the loyalty of those who maintain order should be a central goal.
- Plan, innovate and strategise. The evidence shows that the methods used by challengers are crucial to success. In other words, how a campaign proceeds depends sensitively on the actions by the players, so it is vital to be creative, respond wisely to opponent movements and be able to survive repression.

Regimes strategise too, so there is no set of steps that guarantees success: campaigns need to innovate against opponent strategies. Struggle against injustice is like a game: to win, it has to be played well. This is why diverse participation is important, because it brings in people with different skills, ideas and contacts. Running a campaign from a central headquarters, with a fixed ideology and set of standard moves, is not a promising approach. Having widespread participation and encouraging experimentation and diversity is.

The more people who understand the dynamics of nonviolent action and learn to think strategically, the more likely a campaign is to develop the staying power, strategic innovation and resilience to succeed. *Why Civil Resistance Works* is not an activist manual, but its findings should be used by anyone writing one.

Nonviolence researchers and advocates have been arguing for decades that nonviolent action can be more effective than violence in the short and long term, but have often faced scepticism. There have been two main sources of this scepticism. The first is the common belief that violence, when used without restraint, will always be victorious over opponents who do not use violence. This belief is widespread among the general public and also among scholars. It is so deeply held that mainstream scholars have never sought to test it. This belief is also standard among Marxist-Leninists. As Mao famously stated, "Power grows out of the barrel of a gun." Gandhi was dismissed as ineffectual in the face of "real power," namely unrestrained violence.

Mainstream scholars have another reason to dismiss nonviolent action. Most of them, in studying challenges to repressive regimes, have focused on conditions that enable or hinder success, using frameworks such as resource mobilisation and political opportunity structures. Scholars have not systematically compared different methods of struggle. As a result, researchers have not provided much guidance for activists.[31] After all, if the key is political opportunities, and the prospects are not very good right now, then the methods used by challengers should not make that much difference.

Conclusion

The theme in this chapter is the effectiveness of nonviolent action. According to the best available empirical evidence, nonviolent action is more effective than armed struggle in struggles against repressive governments. However, despite this superiority, nonviolent approaches are largely invisible in histories and political accounts. Furthermore, most people continue to believe, despite the evidence, that violence, if strong enough, will always be victorious over nonviolent opposition. This suggests that there is potentially much to learn from nonviolent struggles that can be applied to other domains, because analogues to nonviolence in those domains might also be largely invisible and not believed.

How can nonviolent action be effective against violent opponents? A key part of the answer is to look at participation and loyalties. When struggles are largely

---

31 See, for example, David Croteau, William Hoynes and Charlotte Ryan (eds.), *Rhyming Hope and History: Activists, Academics, and Social Movement Scholarship* (Minneapolis: University of Minnesota Press, 2005).

nonviolent, they enable more people to be involved at lower risk, and they reduce the threat to opponents, thereby shifting loyalties more easily. In a direct engagement, violence can defeat nonviolent protesters, but potentially at the expense of causing public outrage and leading to greater long-term support for the protesters. This is the phenomenon of backfire.

However, it is not easy to assess the effectiveness of nonviolent action because many campaigns include a variety of methods, including some violence as well as various conventional methods of political action. Because of these complexities, in many struggles there is little empirical, quantitative evidence for the effectiveness of nonviolent action.

Nevertheless, there are important reasons to prefer nonviolent action to violent methods. Casualties are likely to be lower: human suffering is reduced. Because of greater participation, the outcomes of successful struggles are more likely to be participatory too: in anti-regime campaigns, the risk of a new authoritarian government is reduced.

Nonviolent action does not work on its own: it requires planning, preparation, skill, communication and shrewd strategising. Military forces do an immense amount of preparation and training, yet are not guaranteed to succeed. The same applies to nonviolent struggles. However, nonviolent activists seldom have very many resources, at least compared to governments. That nonviolent movements can sometimes succeed, despite these disadvantages, shows the potential power of this mode of struggle.

4
Transportable features of nonviolent action

In chapter 2 and 3, I examined nonviolent action and what makes it effective. The next step is more challenging. It is to try to identify the features of successful nonviolent action that can be applied in quite different domains — in particular, domains where there is little or no physical violence. The idea is to find analogies to nonviolent action in arenas such as conversations and public controversies.

This may seem a strange sort of endeavour. Why bother trying to transport ideas from nonviolent action to different domains, when people studying those areas probably already know how to engage effectively in struggle? True enough — there's no guarantee that this exercise will lead to useful insights. But there is some promise. Nonviolent action can be highly effective, yet it has been largely ignored by mainstream practitioners and theorists, who instead have devoted most attention to conventional politics and armed struggle. Therefore it is plausible that in other domains, the existence of an effective mode of struggle has been similarly neglected.

In looking for transportable features of nonviolent action, I found it was not sufficient just to look at the usual discussions, because there are some features that are so standard that they are just assumed to exist, and hence not normally noticed. Here's how I proceeded. I started with the standard features of nonviolent action, adapting some of them for different arenas. I added a few features that seemed necessary to fully specify the nonviolent-action approach in a different domain. So here is the list, with preliminary comments on how features might apply to other domains.

Non-standard

By definition, nonviolent action is a non-standard approach when compared to accepted and authorised methods such as holding meetings, lobbying and voting, which are conventional methods of political action. Whether a method is non-standard depends on the circumstances. In places where civil liberties are respected, handing out a leaflet is a standard method, whereas in a dictatorship it is definitely non-standard.

Consider the domain of organisations. In large organisations, such as corporations and government departments, there are many formal processes for dealing with difficulties, such as grievance procedures. If these are ineffective, then the organisational equivalent of nonviolent action has to be something other than the usual formal processes. It has to be something that is not spelled out in manuals, guidelines and rules.

In interpersonal interactions, rules are mostly implicit, understood by individuals in a culture, and learned through observation and through feedback on unwelcome behaviour. If you have always spoken politely with someone, being rude is non-standard. It is relatively easy to introduce a non-standard behaviour into a relationship; however, if the same behaviour is used repeatedly, it quickly comes to be expected, at least from a particular individual or in a particular circumstance.

To summarise: the key is that the action is non-standard and/or non-authorised. This criterion will help to uncover hidden, less recognised methods in all sorts of domains.

Limited harm

A central feature of nonviolent action is that no physical violence is used against opponents. As noted in chapter 2, the boundary between nonviolent action and violent action is blurry and contested, with self-immolation and violence against objects being at the boundary.

For the purposes of applying nonviolence ideas to other domains, this criterion needs to be modified. In verbal interactions, for example, there is no physical violence. So what is the relevant criterion in other domains? A prime candidate is "limited harm": not hurting opponents, at least not too much or not in the wrong way.

"Harm" can be interpreted in various ways. You can harm someone emotionally through a slightly derogatory comment, or even by failing to offer support. To make some sense of the criterion of limited harm, it is worth remembering that nonviolent action can cause harm to others. A strike can damage a business and a social boycott can cause distress. Nonviolent action can involve coercion, though without physical force or physical harm to an individual.

To progress on this matter, it's worth looking at the reasons for not using physical violence, and then apply these to other domains. Looking at reasons opens up this category, as there are several possible reasons.

Some activists refuse on principle to use violence. They believe it is immoral to hurt opponents. This is an ethical objection. This could be applied to other domains: some people refuse to shout or swear in anger at another person as a matter of principle.

Another reason not to harm opponents is because more people will be attracted to the cause. Imagine a rally in which some protesters are throwing bricks at the police. Some people, who don't want to throw bricks, might be willing to join nevertheless — but others will not. When no one is throwing bricks, participation may increase. This can be translated into other domains: the criterion for limited harm is what enables or fosters greater participation.

Closely related to this is the capability to participate (see below). Some people are too weak to throw heavy bricks or to run away from police who are pursuing brick-throwers. By refusing to throw bricks, or undertake other aggressive methods that require special strength and skill, greater participation is made possible.

Yet another reason not to harm opponents is that they are less likely to be alienated; indeed, some may be willing to stand aside or even switch sides. As is often noted, violence tends to unify opponents, because they feel under attack, whereas nonviolent action reduces the sense of danger, enables dialogue and opens the door to conversion or accommodation. In other domains, the criterion of limited harm can be assessed by its influence on opponents. If they are alienated by your action or goaded into opposing you more passionately, the action is probably too strong. If they are encouraged to reconsider, change their behaviour or switch sides, the action is being effective.

Finally, there is backfire. When police beat peaceful protesters, and this is exposed to the world, it can generate outrage and backfire on the police. However, if even a few of the protesters use violence, the police violence is far less likely to generate outrage. Backfire dynamics apply in many other domains besides physical violence used against protesters. When looking at other domains, such as a conversation, the crucial test is whether an action enables backfire when the opponent overreacts. If you raise your voice and the person you're talking to raises theirs, eventually reaching the level of shouting, observers may think this is a shouting match and, if they don't know you or know what you're taking about, have no special sympathy for either of you. However, if you never raise your voice but the other person is shouting, observers are more likely to sympathise with you: the shouting can backfire in terms of wider support.

In summary, limited harm seems on the surface to be a suitable generalisation of the criterion of not using physical violence. However, "limited harm" is not precise enough as a criterion. It can be made more specific by looking at reasons for not hurting opponents: ethical principles, encouraging others to participate, enabling participation, winning over opponents and winning over observers.

In the case of nonviolent action, these different reasons all align, pretty closely, in the stricture to avoid physical violence against opponents. However, in other domains, such as conversations, the different reasons may or may not align in a common boundary. This needs to be explored on a case-by-case basis.

Participation

Many methods of nonviolent action, such as boycotts and rallies, allow nearly anyone to join in. In a nonviolent campaign in which various different methods are used, there are bound to be several ways to participate.

The key here is direct participation. People can be part of the action, not just spectators at the sidelines, like in a sporting event.

Compare this to armed struggle. Only some people are capable of front-line fighting, and ranks are usually filled with young fit men. Others can play supporting roles, such as being cooks, accountants or weapons manufacturers.

Much conventional political action is oriented to electoral politics, especially getting people elected and influencing politicians. Only the politicians and their paid staff are fully-fledged participants. Everyone else has an auxiliary role, either promoting or supporting or opposing politicians.

Why is participation important? At a psychological level, being directly involved can be empowering. It offers a sense of meaning, of commitment, of solidarity for a cause. Politicians and soldiers gain this — and so do nonviolent activists. In terms of effectiveness, greater participation enables a greater impact.

Greater participation, and greater equality in participation, promotes greater equality in the wider movement. If only a segment of the population can join an activity, this exclusiveness can be the basis for power over others.

In armies, there is limited participation and a rigid line of command. In electoral politics, only a few people become politicians. In nonviolent action, the differences in status between frontline participants and supporters, in the rear so to speak, are smaller. In many types of nonviolent action, it is far easier to become a participant.

The feature "participation possible by all" thus has two elements. One is participation in terms of being involved. The other is fostering power equality among participants. In other words, participation is possible, and new participants enter as closely as possible as equal members.

Obviously there are limits to equality. Some activists have a lot of experience, knowledge and strategic acumen, and hence deserve to be heard. The point is not that the opinions of every participant are equally well informed or astute, but that there is less formal subordination. In an army, commanders are supposed to be obeyed on the basis of their rank, not their knowledge. In a parliament, the votes of parliamentarians are counted — and no one else's views are directly taken into account.

This suggests that the feature of participation can be divided into two: involvement and equality.

Voluntary participation

This seems obvious enough: no one has to participate in nonviolent action. This separates nonviolent methods (as used so far) from military conscription and from coerced involvement in guerrilla struggles.

Although force is not used to compel people to join nonviolent actions, there can be very strong peer pressure. Some types of peer pressure seem benign, as when a person thinks, "everyone else is going to the rally — including my friends — so I don't want to miss out." Some peer pressure has other motivations: "my boss refuses to buy this product, so I'd better not either, otherwise my job might be at risk." Some peer pressure is more pointed, and has coercive elements, such as shaming and exclusion: "I'd better go to the rally, because otherwise my friends won't speak to me, or will continually taunt me."

Few advocates of nonviolent action favour compulsion. After all, forcing someone to join a nonviolent movement seems to contradict the principles of nonviolence itself. It could be argued that it is legitimate to use pressure, so long as it is nonviolent, but perhaps a more pressing question is whether compulsion is ever a good idea. It may alienate people more than it aids the movement.

Setting aside these debates, the point here is that voluntary participation is a generally accepted feature of nonviolent struggles, with no one supporting conscription backed by force. This can be transported into other domains, such as scientific controversies, by the admonition that tactics should not involve compulsion — at least not damaging forms of compulsion. It is reasonable to expect that peer pressure will play a role, but not too much more.

Fairness

When methods are seen as unfair, they are not productive. One way to assess whether people see a method as fair is the absence of backfire.

This feature is simple and powerful. It is simple to apply: if most people think an action is reasonable, legitimate, acceptable or justified, then more people will be willing to join in, and fewer will become active opponents. It is powerful because it can be applied to many domains.

Imagine a group of protesters at a rally, in a regime where protest is treated harshly. If many people oppose the regime, the protest will be seen as reasonable. If police brutally beat the protesters, this will be seen as too harsh. Then suppose a group of protesters detonate a huge bomb, killing hundreds of government officials and some bystanders. This is less likely to be seen as fair — the bombing may result in a backlash against the bombers, and against the peaceful protesters too.

The basic idea here is to use methods that are strong enough to make a difference, but not so strong that they increase support for the opponent or give the opponent a pretext for harsh measures. This idea is relevant in other domains.

Imagine you are having a conversation with your boss, with some others listening. If the conversation is balanced and polite, then it can be counterproductive to do something so apparently minor as raising your voice. Swearing or sneering might also be counterproductive. On the other hand, if you continue to calmly present your views, and your boss starts shouting, then you gain the advantage: sympathy is likely to be with you rather than your boss.

The basic idea of perceived fairness is straightforward, but its application to different domains can involve complexities. The case studies will be useful to seeing how this criterion operates in practice.

Prefiguration

Prefiguration is a fancy word meaning that the way you do something is compatible with the goal you're trying to achieve. If you want a world without war, then don't wage a war to achieve it — instead, use peaceful means. If you want to build a harmonious workplace, don't do it by yelling abuse.

Instead of using the word "prefiguration," it's possible to talk of the means reflecting the ends or the means embodying the ends. Other expressions are "living the alternative" and "living the revolution." If the alternative involves ecological sustainability, then living the alternative means having a sustainable lifestyle now.

Nonviolent action is commonly seen as prefiguring a world without organised violence. If the goal is a world without war, then nonviolent action is a compatible way of pursuing it.

A different philosophy is encapsulated by the motto "the ends justify the means." Some revolutionaries believe armed struggle, and perhaps a lot of killing and suffering, is a necessary prerequisite to overthrowing capitalism and creating a less exploitative society.

There are several justifications for prefiguration. One is moral: it is hypocritical to say one thing and do another, for example calling for peace while waging war. Another is practical: incorporating the ends in the means enables people to learn what it's like to live in their desired future. Living the alternative can provide an example to others. It can be a way of reminding oneself and others about their goals. It can be a symbol of commitment and a source of pride.

On the other hand, the principle of prefiguration, if applied too rigidly, can become a straitjacket. An environmentalist can be castigated for driving a car or taking a long-distance flight. A pro-democracy activist can be chastised for acting without full consultation. Applying the principle of prefiguration too strictly can mean not recognising the constraints of the world we live in. There are many people who desire a world that is more cooperative and in which human needs are a greater priority than profit. "Living the revolution" might be interpreted as avoiding capitalist relationships, but this is unrealistic: to survive in a market society, nearly everyone seeks paid employment or buys goods.

In studies of nonviolent action, there is often a contrast drawn between "principled nonviolence" and pragmatic nonviolence." Principled nonviolence is in the tradition of Gandhi: not hurting opponents is a moral imperative. Pragmatic nonviolence is most associated with Gene Sharp: nonviolent action is used because it is more effective than violence or conventional political action. Prefiguration is often a feature of principled nonviolence, in which the emphasis is on foreshadowing the desired future. Pragmatic nonviolence is more instrumental: nonviolent action is a means to an end — but in many cases it is possible to ensure that the means reflect the ends.

The implication is that prefiguration is desirable but seldom essential or fully achievable. In looking at struggles outside the traditional arenas for nonviolent action, it can be helpful to examine the meaning of prefiguration and see how it applies to struggles.

Skilful use

To be effective, nonviolent action needs to be carried out capably. In an ongoing campaign, this includes choosing the most appropriate action, picking a suitable time and place, preparing for action carefully, taking into account the strategic situation, carrying out the action effectively and learning lessons from what happened. At the level of strategy, it includes setting up organisational and communication infrastructure, choosing suitable goals, liaising with potential allies, taking into account moves by opponents, protecting against attack and designing campaigns. What this means, in brief, is doing everything concerning nonviolent action as effectively as possible.

Consider other sorts of actions, like election campaigning or military manoeuvres. In elections, choosing the most suitable candidate and running persuasive advertisements are important. In wars, choosing the right tactics and carrying them out well are important. This is obvious enough, but it is worth remembering that the same applies to nonviolent action. A boycott or vigil does not work automatically: to be effective, choices, preparations and execution are vital. For the sake of brevity, I refer to these dimensions with the expression "skilful use."

Being skilled in taking action is relevant in other domains. Whether in a conversation or a policy debate, a method isn't likely to work if it is the wrong method, or the right method but used at the wrong time, or simply executed poorly. When trying out new techniques, it can be worth remembering the importance of planning and skills. A new technique is not likely to be effective unless it is used well, and it usually takes practice and experience to become adept at using it.

Features of nonviolent action potentially relevant to other arenas

Feature	Description	Examples fitting description	Examples *not* fitting description
Non-standard	Actions are not routine or authorised.	Workplace occupations, alternative government	Voting, lobbying
Limited harm	Opponents are not physically harmed.	Vigils, strikes, etc.	Shootings, bombings, hostage-taking
Participation	Many people are able to be involved in an action.	Rallies, boycotts, etc.	Tree-sitting, blockading large vessels using small craft
Voluntary participation	No one is forced or bribed to join actions.	Sit-ins, boycotts, etc.	Paid attendance at rallies
Fairness	Actions seem fair to most observers.	Vigils, strikes, etc.	Reprisals, abuse, humiliation, violence
Prefiguration	Goals are incorporated in methods used to achieve them.	Planting a community garden; consensus decision-making at a protest	Using violence to advocate for peace; high-level diplomacy to promote participatory democracy
Skilful use	Activists develop skills in planning, taking action.	Preparation and practice for nonviolent action	Unprepared actions; ignoring lessons from previous actions

Conclusion

Nonviolent action can be remarkably effective in its core domain of unarmed citizen struggle against an armed opponent, typically a government. The aim here is to identify the key features of nonviolent action that can be transported to other domains, such as scientific controversies and interpersonal interactions, in which there is little or no physical violence.

The features identified in this chapter are non-standard action, limited harm, participation, voluntary participation, fairness, prefiguration and skilful use. None of these is straightforward. With a bit of explanation, they sound clear enough, but applying them to new domains is bound to involve a fair bit of interpretation and creativity. Spelling out these features is the beginning of the investigation rather than the conclusion.

Have all key features been identified? Probably not. Some key features are so taken for granted among nonviolent activists and scholars that they are overlooked or not thought to be important, but they may turn out to be important in other domains.

There is no guarantee that analogues to nonviolent action will be equally effective in other domains. That is something to be determined empirically, namely by seeing what methods are actually effective and how they relate to the features identified here.

5
Verbal defence

Suppose you are having a conversation with a friend, who says something nasty, condescending or hurtful to you. You might think that a friend should never say anything like this, but it does happen. Your friend might be responding to something *you* said, or be in a bad mood, or think it's okay to say certain things, not realising how much they hurt you.

How do you respond? And how *should* you respond? There are lots of factors here. In the heat of the moment, you might react angrily, saying something equally nasty and causing an escalation in hostility. On the other hand, you might say nothing at all, just hoping it won't become an issue, in order to maintain your harmonious relationship. This might work — unless your friend continues with similar comments, thinking there is no problem.

Conversations are the stuff of everyday life, and it may seem obsessive to analyse every passing comment. However, precisely because conversations are so basic, it can be worthwhile figuring out how to deal with problems in interpersonal verbal interaction.

My interest here is in seeing whether ideas from nonviolent action can be applied to verbal interactions, and what the implications might be. Interacting verbally does not involve physical violence, but it certainly can cause harm, sometimes called emotional violence. However, drawing a direct analogy between the methods of nonviolent action and methods of verbal engagement may not be all that fruitful. It is possible to propose verbal equivalents to methods such as rallies, strikes, boycotts and sit-ins, but their suitability is questionable.

An interpersonal analogy to a boycott is ostracism, namely refusing to acknowledge or interact with another person. Social ostracism is a recognised method of nonviolent action. However, collective ostracism of officials serving a repressive government is quite different from personal ostracism of an individual, which can be extremely hurtful and is probably too strong for most circumstances.[1] Rather than trying to make direct analogies with methods of nonviolent action, an alternative is to look at the features of effective nonviolent action and translate them into the different realm of interpersonal communication.

Several authors have published practical guides for verbal defence. These guides typically describe modes of verbal attack and how to respond to them. Most of these are based on personal experience, with classifications of modes of attack and defence developed by the author, sometimes supplemented by some linguistic theory. These practical guides are excellent sources for assessing the relevance of nonviolence theory. Indeed, some of the authors' suggested options reveal insights that can be fed back into traditional nonviolence thinking.

---

1 On the damaging effects of interpersonal ostracism, see Kipling D. Williams, *Ostracism: The Power of Silence* (New York, Guilford, 2001).

In the following sections, I consider in turn the approaches to verbal defence of Suzette Haden Elgin, Sam Horn, George Thompson and William Irvine. For each one, I describe the basic approach, give a few examples and try to extract some ideas that relate to the features of effective nonviolent action.[2]

Suzette Haden Elgin

Elgin's book *The Gentle Art of Verbal Self-defense* was first published in 1980.[3] It tells about various types of verbal attacks and how to respond to them. Many people found this immensely useful: they felt they were under attack and wanted to know what to do about it. The book sold and sold, eventually more than a million copies. Elgin went on to write a dozen more books on the same theme.

The books are filled with insights about attacks. A basic approach used by Elgin is to give an example of a verbal attack, analyse it and describe different responses. Consider this one, from a child to a parent: "If you *really* loved me, *you* wouldn't waste so much *money*." How would you respond?

Elgin starts with four principles. The first is to realise when you're under attack. Many people don't: they come away from conversations feeling bad but not knowing

---

[2] I looked only at English-language books. Verbal interactions in other languages may contain cultural and linguistic differences from those in English.

[3] Here I cite the revised and updated edition: Suzette Haden Elgin, *The Gentle Art of Verbal Self-Defense* (New York: Fall River Press, 2009).

why. The second principle is to understand what kind of attack it is. A key part of Elgin's approach is explaining the different sorts of attack. The third principle is to design a defence appropriate for the attack. The fourth principle is to follow through your response, using the same defence.

Elgin next introduces five modes of behaviour and communication, calling them the Satir modes after family therapist Virginia Satir. First is the blamer mode. Blamers feel unappreciated and compensate by trying to be dominant: "You *never* consider my feelings, and I'm *not* going to put up with that!"

Second is the placater mode. Placaters fear the anger of others and hence try to please them by submitting: "Whatever anybody else wants to do is *fine* with me."

Third is the computer mode. Those who use this mode seek to hide their feelings, like Mr Spock in *Star Trek*: "No rational person would be alarmed by this incident."

Fourth is the distracter mode. Distracters keep changing the topic, cycling through various other modes; underneath is a feeling of panic.

Fifth is the leveller mode. Levellers will say exactly what they feel, which is sometimes useful and sometimes inappropriate. Elgin gives this example of five frightened people trapped in a lift that has become stuck between floors.

Placater: "Oh, I *hope* I didn't do anything to *cause* this! I sure didn't *mean* to!"

Blamer: "*Which one* of you idiots was *fooling around* with the *but*tons??"
Computer: "There is undoubtedly some perfectly simple reason why this elevator isn't moving. Certainly there is no cause for alarm."
Distracter: "Did *one* of you hit the *Stop button*? Oh, I didn't *mean* that, of *course* none of you would do anything like that! It is, however, extremely easy to do that sort of thing by accident. *Why* do things like this *always* happen to *me?*"
Leveler: "Personally, I'm scared."[4]

When someone is attacking verbally, it's very helpful to figure out which Satir mode they are using and to decide which mode to use in defence. Elgin makes the qualification that someone using the leveller mode may not be attacking at all, but simply stating facts. Placaters, who are trying to please, may cause much more difficulty.

Elgin says that many verbal attacks contain a presupposition — an assumption, usually questionable — accompanied by a bait, something to which it is tempting to respond. Suppose Tom says to Meg, "If you *really* loved me, you wouldn't waste so much *money*." The presupposition is that Meg doesn't love Tom; the bait is that she's wasting money.

Here is Elgin's strategy for responding:

1. Figure out which Satir mode is being used.
2. Identify the presupposition.
3. Ignore the bait (this is crucial).

---

4 Ibid., 31.

4. In a neutral tone, respond by asking or saying something about the presupposition.
5. Usually use computer mode, or maybe leveller mode if it's safe.[5]

So let's look at Tom's attack: "If you *really* loved me, you wouldn't *waste* so much money." The Satir mode is blaming: Tom is blaming Meg for wasting money. The presupposition is that Meg doesn't love Tom. Meg needs to ignore the bait and say something about the presupposition, in a neutral tone, using computer mode. One possibility for Meg is "It's interesting when men say their wives don't love them." Another, a bit more pointed, is "When did you start thinking I don't really love you."

According to Elgin, these sorts of responses are likely to make Tom change the topic. His attack didn't work. To understand Elgin's approach, it's useful to look at what happens when Meg doesn't follow the strategy.

A common pattern is for Meg to take the bait, for example saying "I *don't* waste money! Do you have any idea how much it *costs* to feed a family these days?" According to Elgin, Meg has just lost the confrontation. Tom can continue the attack by saying "Your sister manages to feed *her* kids without sending the family bankrupt." Meg might then become angry: "How would you know how much she spends on food? You never do any shopping. You wouldn't have a clue. You're spending a heap on your company credit card and you have the nerve to criticise my spending!" Tom then says, reasona-

---

5 Ibid., 38–39.

bly, "How come you get so upset whenever I discuss our finances?" — and Meg ends up apologising.[6]

With this sequence, Elgin shows how Tom wins the interaction, with Meg seeming to be the problem, even though Tom was the attacker. Meg, playing into his hands by taking the bait, is humiliated. If this sort of interaction is typical, the prognosis for their relationship is not good.

Tom has been using the blamer mode and has managed to goad Meg into counterattacking, which is disastrous for Meg. Elgin concludes from this that you should never use blamer mode when responding to someone's blamer-mode attack. It causes an escalation that might end in shouting, with the loudest or most persistent person winning in the end, though both are losers if judged by the goal of productive communication.

Elgin's advice can be interpreted as saying to avoid passive or aggressive responses, but instead to be assertive. If Meg meekly accepts Tom's chiding complaint, she is too passive. On the other hand, if she responds by blaming — an aggressive response — she has fallen for a trap, especially if Tom is more skilled at these sorts of engagements. In between is an assertive response, though it has to be skilfully used. Elgin provides guidelines on responding to a variety of verbal attacks.

Another type of attack described by Elgin starts *"Why* don't you ever … ?" The rest of the sentence might be "try to make me happy?" or "consider anybody's feelings but your own?" A variant starts off *"Why* do you always … ?" and can conclude "try to make me look *stu*pid? or "eat *so*

---

6 Ibid., 50–55. I have slightly reworded some of Elgin's dialogue.

much junk food?" or any of a multitude of possibilities.[7] This attack is also in the blamer mode. Elgin says this sort of attack is obvious but nonetheless is especially dangerous because it usually comes from someone very close to you who knows your vulnerabilities, and therefore the temptation to counterattack is strong. A counterattack could lead to a shouting match.

Elgin recommends offering something that rebuts the presupposition and offers something the attacker doesn't want.

One of Elgin's sample scripts goes like this.

> Abby: "*Why* do you *al*ways have to be *dif*ferent? *Why* can't you act like *other* people's moms?"
> Mom: "Okay. From now on, like other moms, I'm giving you a ten o'clock curfew on school nights."
> Abby: "But, *Mom* —"
> Mom: "And like other moms, I'll expect you to be in by eleven on Saturday night. Does that solve your problem?"
> Abby: "That's not fair!"
> Mom: "Really? Let me introduce you, my dear, to the real world, in which *many* things are not fair. Including lots of other people's mothers."[8]

Mom in this confrontation has rebutted Abby's claim that she never acts like other moms, and does it by offering something Abby doesn't want, as Elgin recommends. However, Elgin notes that Mom has exerted her power,

---

7 Ibid., 157–158.

8 Ibid., 168.

with the message "don't try the blamer mode on me," and communication with Abby is likely to suffer.

Here's a better response:

> Abby: "*Why* do you *al*ways have to be *dif*ferent? *Why* can't you act like *other* people's moms?"
> Mom: "Well, let's see. Would I seem more like other moms to you, honey, if I always waited up for you when you go out at night? And then you could come sit on my bed when you got home, and we could have a nice cozy chat about what your date was like, and what everybody was wearing ... Y*ou* know, *girl* talk. Would you like that?"
> Abby: "Mom, that would be *horrible.*"
> Mom: "Well, then, we certainly don't have to do it."[9]

This will only work if having a "nice cozy chat" is not their standard practice. Assuming it's not, then Abby has to accept or reject it, and Mom wins without being heavy-handed. Elgin notes that the language has to be appropriate. If Abby thinks referring to a "nice cozy chat" is making fun of her, then maybe "a discussion of your evening" will work.

Then there's the blamer mode response: a disaster.

> Abby: "*Why* do you *al*ways have to be *dif*ferent? *Why* can't you act like *other* people's moms?"
> Mom: "Because *you* don't act like other *daughters, that's* why! And until you do, I don't intend to put myself out for you."[10]

---

9 Ibid., 169.

10 Ibid., 170.

In the Abby-Mom interaction, Elgin recommends a response that avoids taking the bait and avoids counterattack. Instead, the trick is for Mom to offer something that rebuts the presupposition inherent in "*Why* do you *al*ways ... ?" and that Abby won't want. This can be a challenge, especially in the heat of the moment. Learning Elgin's gentle art takes practice, especially when patterns of interaction are entrenched. Furthermore, her recommendations are not always intuitive. This is to be expected. After all, if there was a quick and easy way to deal with verbal abuse, it's likely everyone would know about it.

This description of Elgin's approach has been brief and limited: there are many other features of "the gentle art of verbal self-defence" worth exploring. Her books are filled with insightful observations and references to relevant writings.[11] For example, in her book *How to Disagree without Being Disagreeable,* in which she presents her basic approach, she adds a new angle: hostile language is bad, but often is used and accepted as necessary and inevitable. She says that actually it can be eliminated. This has several advantages: (1) safety and security for speakers; (2) better health; (3) greater success in communication; and (4) a legacy for the future. She

---

11 Among those I've enjoyed are Suzette Haden Elgin, *Genderspeak: Men, Women, and the Gentle Art of Verbal Self-Defense* (New York: Wiley, 1993); Suzette Haden Elgin, *Gentle Art of Verbal Self-Defense at Work* (New York: Prentice Hall, 2000).

says hostile language is like pollution, except that no permanent evidence is left behind.[12]

Metaphors are commonly used to understand verbal interactions. The usual metaphor for disagreement is that it is a type of combat, but this is not conducive to agreeable interactions. Elgin says men are more likely to use the metaphor of a game — two individuals or teams competing to win — whereas women are more likely to use the metaphor of a classroom, with the teacher trying to induce children to learn. Elgin recommends a different metaphor for disagreements: carpentry, with carpenters working together to produce a quality outcome.

On a side point, Elgin states, "Few things provoke more hostility in a group — even a group of only two — than the presence of someone who never makes a mistake."[13] Therefore, rather than trying to win every time, it's better to appear cooperative, pleasant and modest by making a few strategic mistakes.

As for gender differences, Elgin says there are not many, despite prevailing stereotypes. She says men are less happy to give in when conflict is in public. However, the differences are more due to power than gender.

To recap, here are the key elements of the gentle art of self-defence. It's important to remain detached rather than make emotionally-driven responses. It's important to listen carefully to the other person, and not interrupt, using

---

12 Suzette Haden Elgin, *How to Disagree without Being Disagreeable: Getting Your Point Across with the Gentle Art of Verbal Self-Defense* (New York: Wiley, 1997), 13–25.

13 Ibid., 161.

Miller's law: assume the other person's statement is true, and try to figure out what it's true of. In response to attacks, avoid blaming, placating and distracting. Instead, use the computer mode or, if it is safe, levelling. Use appropriate presuppositions: instead of stating the other person's bad behaviour, assume it while moving towards a solution. In dealing with verbal attacks, ignore the bait and respond to the presupposition, perhaps by agreeing with it or providing a boring meandering response. Finally, reduce tension by using "I" messages — "When you do X, I feel Y because Z" — that match the other person's sensory mode, and make trivial mistakes that can be fixed with no harm, thereby providing opportunities for the other person to display dominance.

The gentle art and features of effective nonviolent action

This brief account is enough for a preliminary assessment using seven features of effective nonviolent action: participation, limited harm, voluntary participation, fairness, prefiguration, non-standard action and skilful use.

Participation
The more people who can engage in a method of nonviolent action, the more powerful it can be. An obvious example is mass rallies. What about verbal self-defence? In most cases, Elgin's methods are intended for use in a one-on-one interaction, though they can be used in a group setting too. The obvious way to expand participation is for more people to adopt the methods and use

them in their own personal circumstances. A community in which half the people used gentle-art methods would be different from one in which only a single individual used them. Furthermore, practitioners can help each other improve.

In situations where people interact verbally in groups, it would be possible to coordinate use of the techniques against verbal abuse. If two people are using Elgin's methods, each may recognise what the other is doing and reinforce the other's efforts. Indeed, a group of practitioners might join together to respond to someone prone to verbal abuse, such as a boss who bullies subordinates. Elgin focuses on one-on-one encounters; an obvious extension of her approach is to develop coordinated group responses to verbal abuse. The gentle art thus lends itself to widespread individual use, with collective use being an extension.

Limited harm
The methods in the gentle art are designed to limit harm. Elgin warns against responding in kind, for example using the blamer mode in response to blamer-mode statements, which leads to an escalation of abuse. Verbal self-defence methods are designed to reduce hostility and encourage self-reflection, and thus minimise harm to the other party. Elgin has good reason to call her approach a "gentle art."

Voluntary participation
The implication here is that no one should be required to use Elgin's techniques. This is not likely to be a problem unless her approach became so popular that it was taught

in schools and practised in all sorts of settings, so that anyone who responded using a different set of protocols was put under pressure to adopt specific gentle-art techniques. This of course would be a perversion of the approach, given that it is about defending against verbal assault. It's possible to imagine using gentle-art techniques to resist pressure to use them: "It's interesting when people try to prescribe how others should speak." This is only a hypothetical situation, because Elgin's approach is very far from becoming standard practice.

Fairness
A nonviolent defence against attack should seem fair to observers in order to win wider support; it might even win support from opponents. As applied to person-to-person interactions, this can be interpreted as implying that verbal defence should be seen as entirely defensive. If it seems, instead, like an attack — even in disguise — then it may lose credibility.

Elgin is aware of the risks of being too aggressive. In the scenario of Tom saying, "If you *really* loved me, *you* wouldn't waste so much *money*," Meg might reply "It's interesting that so many men — once they reach *your* age — begin to feel that their wives don't love them."[14] Here Meg uses the computer mode, but slips in a dig about Tom's age. This is an escalation of the encounter, which is likely to end badly.

Fairness in verbal defence is thus achieved by avoiding any form of counter-attack, while still defending.

---

14 Elgin, *Gentle Art of Verbal Self-Defense,* 56.

This means that the words used need to avoid hidden meanings and the tone of voice needs to be neutral and non-accusing. This can be difficult to achieve. It can be very specific to the two people who are interacting. Tom and Meg will have a history of shared experiences, annoyances, sensitive points and much else, so that even a single word, gesture or voice inflection can trigger a cascade of memories. In such circumstances, learning to be non-judgemental, neutral and in other ways non-aggressive can be very difficult. Furthermore, Tom might react badly even if Meg uses the best sort of technique — maybe Tom is so volatile that it doesn't matter what Meg says or does.

One of the primary differences between encounters between protesters and police — a typical scenario in nonviolent campaigning — and verbal encounters is the presence of witnesses. In a nonviolent action encounter, there are often many witnesses. This includes members of the public as well as protesters and police who are not directly involved in an encounter. If a protester throws a brick at police, or spits at them or even just calls them nasty names, this will be witnessed by others, and hence can be counterproductive. Similarly, if the protesters are all polite but the police are brutal, this will be witnessed by others. If one officer goes berserk in beating a protester, even other police might be appalled.

However, when just two individuals are interacting, often there is no external audience. Therefore, only these two individuals will be making assessments of fairness. If the person making a verbal attack treats any response at all, even one of Elgin's computer responses, as aggressive, then there is little hope of using the person's sense of fairness as a measure of suitable responses. In such circumstances — when a person seems to have an unrealistic sense of what counts as a reasonable comment — then it may be helpful to have witnesses, for example to invite friends or counsellors to be present. People who make abusive comments to a target often are more careful in their language when someone else can hear them.

Another option is to record the interaction. If this is done covertly, and discovered, it very likely will cause a breach of trust. Making a recording might be worthwhile when there is little prospect of an ongoing relationship based on mutual respect. For example, an employee might record a boss's tirade in order to document and expose the boss's abuse. The recording enables others to become witnesses.

Assessments of fairness depend very sensitively on expectations, circumstances and personal styles. Some people enjoy boisterous interactions and expect to be confronted when they go too far, and are not offended by strong language. Others are excessively polite and may take offence at the mildest comment. Often tone of voice, eye contact or body language communicate much more than words, and even a raised eyebrow can cause offence. All this is to say that in private conversations assessments of fairness are often complicated and challenging. More remains to be done in studying this issue.

Prefiguration
The idea of prefiguration is to behave in a way that is compatible with the goal being sought: if you want peace,

then behave in peaceful ways. In verbal interactions, prefiguration can mean not being abusive, and the gentle art of verbal defence certainly satisfies this criterion.

However, it is possible to ask for more. Desirable verbal interactions might be characterised by respect for others, sensitivity to needs, the encouragement of positive behaviours, building of intellectual and emotional capacities, and much else. There are quite a few models for positive human interaction that can be applied to verbal interactions. Defending against abuse is only a start. A conversationalist with a vision of a better world can aim more highly.

Consider just one option for a positive verbal interaction: attention to the needs of the other person. Needs might include recognition and autonomy; needs should be distinguished from wants, which are not necessary. The complication here is that one person's needs in an interaction can differ from another's, depending on the relationship. Needs in a close friendship will be different from needs in a commercial interaction, and will vary from individual to individual as well as varying between cultures and times in a person's life. So a prerequisite in paying attention to the needs of the other person is to spend some time finding out what those needs are. In a friendship, this is more possible than in a brief interaction in a supermarket.

In nonviolence theory, prefiguration is related to Gandhi's constructive programme, which involves building a just, equal and nurturing society, as contrasted with the usual orientation of nonviolent action, which is confronting injustice. As applied to verbal interactions, a constructive programme would involve a just, equal and nurturing verbal environment. The gentle art of verbal self-defence is compatible with this, but there needs to be much more, though what this might involve remains to be developed.

Non-standard
Nonviolent action is different from and often stronger than forms of conventional political action such as lobbying, voting and election campaigning. The gentle art of verbal defence, likewise, is different than the usual verbal responses. Indeed, Elgin frequently comments that, by using her techniques, attackers are flummoxed: their attack is stymied and they often don't know what to do, and sometimes say nothing further.

In a blamer mode attack, for example when Tom says "If you *really* loved me, you wouldn't waste so much *money*," Meg's usual response is to defend by saying she doesn't waste money, or to counterattack by blaming Tom for wasting money or doing something else. By questioning the hook, and saying, for example, "When did you start thinking I don't really love you?," Meg can disrupt the usual pattern of interaction. In the context of the most common sequences of attack and response, gentle-art methods are definitely non-standard.

It's possible to imagine children being trained in the gentle art from an early age and becoming adept at defusing verbal attacks. In this scenario, the methods would become conventional and no longer have the same shock value. This is analogous to some methods of nonviolent action. In a dictatorship, sending emails criticising the government is a serious matter, potentially leading to arrest and imprisonment. However, in places where free speech is protected, sending emails criticising the government is likely to be so common as to be ignored. It is no longer non-regular, and thus not classified as nonviolent action.

Using a method that is non-regular is not a goal in itself. The key question is whether the method is effective. In this sense, it would be an achievement if so many people used gentle-art techniques that they become routine.

Skilful use
Methods of nonviolent action do not work automatically. For example, a boycott can be a powerful method, but it will fail unless it is carefully organised. Furthermore, it needs to be the right method for the occasion. Choosing and implementing methods well is crucial to the success of nonviolent campaigns.

The same applies to Elgin's methods of verbal self-defence. She emphasises the need to understand what sort of attack is being made, to choose the right sort of response and to continue with the response, in a sustained fashion. Although she does not discuss the practising of responses in any detail, it is obvious that skill is required to use her techniques effectively. Many people develop habitual responses to verbal aggression, for example falling for the bait every time. Changing these habitual responses requires more than reading about a technique in a book. One option would be to practise the new technique with a friend over and over, until it becomes automatic to use it even in a heightened emotional state.

Nonviolence campaigners know the importance of maintaining nonviolent discipline, which means resisting the urge to respond to violence with violence. If protesters are physically attacked by police, and remain nonviolent, the attack can rebound against the police, in what Gene Sharp called political jiu-jitsu.[15] In the same way, by resisting the urge to respond to verbal attack with a counter-attack, it is possible to make the attack backfire on the attacker. Protesters sometimes spend days or even months in preparation and training so they can use their techniques effectively. Verbal defenders may need to do the same.

In summary, Elgin's gentle art of verbal self-defence has nearly all the characteristics of nonviolent action, when these characteristics are translated into the realm of verbal interaction.

Sam Horn

Sam Horn's book *Tongue Fu!* is a wonderful manual on effective verbal communication. It contains 30 short chapters, each with a key point, a rationale for the point, numerous relevant quotations, and a practical-example page with "words to lose" (namely, things you shouldn't say) and "words to use." The main parts of the book deal with (1) responding rather than reacting, (2) choosing

---

15 Gene Sharp, *The Politics of Nonviolent Action* (Boson: Porter Sargent, 1973), 657–703.

appropriate words, (3) moving towards cooperation, and (4) developing life skills such as choosing your battles, saying no, being confident and controlling your emotions.[16]

Horn developed her approach after being asked to present a workshop on dealing with difficult behaviours, especially for workers who encounter customers who are rude or co-workers who are uncooperative. The participants found this workshop highly useful, and this response led Horn to give hundreds of other workshops and to write *Tongue Fu!*

Chapter 1, titled "Fast-forward through frustration," recommends imagining yourself as the other person, trying to understand what they're going through. Rather than reacting, the idea is to understand first, and then respond. Often, a person who makes an aggressive or insulting comment is in a bad mental space, with their own problems. By thinking what they must be feeling, you can develop empathy and formulate a response that addresses their needs.

Chapter 2 offers a way to respond to comments that are especially irritating, pressing your emotional buttons. Horn suggests using humour, and preparing in advance with replies to the most frequent or annoying comments.

> A woman who was still heavy several months after the delivery of her second child reported that she often ran into people who made such tactless

---

16 Sam Horn, *Tongue Fu!* (New York: St. Martin's Griffin, 1996).

comments as "I thought you already had your baby" or "Are you going to have another one?" Instead of being tongue-tied by their tactless observations, she pats her tummy while waggling her eyebrows à la Groucho Marx and retorts, "These are leftovers," and then switches the topic.[17]

Another technique Horn recommends is simply ignoring an accusation and deftly switching the topic.[18] The key ideas presented in this chapter are to prepare answers to questions you dread and to make interactions humorous.

Horn's chapters cover such a wide range of situations and skills that summarising them is not easy. Chapter titles give an indication of some of the approaches: "Acknowledge, don't argue"; "Become a coach, not a critic"; "Listen up!"; and "Take charge of your emotions!" Some of her advice is about becoming more persuasive; some is about being tactful, such as how to say no to requests while maintaining relationships or how to gracefully exit from a conversation in which the other person talks interminably. These are not specifically about responding to verbal abuse, but are more generally about being effective in verbal interactions.

Despite the diversity of situations that Horn addresses, her advice overall can be categorised as assertion, operating somewhere between passively accepting abuse and responding aggressively. Furthermore, the aim in much of her advice is to foster a cooperative relationship.

---

17 Ibid., 15.
18 Ibid., 16.

So it is possible to say that her approach is compatible with Elgin's.

Horn describes her approach this way:

> The purpose of kung fu (a Chinese martial art emphasizing internal development) is to defuse, disarm, or deflect someone's *physical* attack. The purpose of Tongue Fu! (a mental art emphasizing internal development) is to defuse, disarm, or deflect someone's *psychological* attack. It is a spoken form of self-defense — the constructive alternative to giving a tongue-lashing or to being tongue tied.[19]

In this description, Horn positions her approach as between aggression (giving a tongue-lashing) and passivity (being tongue-tied), so it is reasonably described as a strategy of assertion. Her reference to psychological attack suggests that attacks and responses might not just be verbal. Some psychological attacks involve not speaking — this is a key element in the method of ostracism — or using gestures or behaviours that cause emotional pain.

George Thompson

George J. Thompson obtained a PhD in English literature, and then became a police officer. He was also a karate expert. As an officer dealing with belligerent and abusive individuals, he discovered that confrontation didn't work and that certain verbal techniques did — and that these same techniques also worked in other parts of life. He

---

19 Ibid., xii.

wrote a book, co-authored with Jerry Jenkins, titled *Verbal Judo,* which presents his approach.[20]

Verbal Judo is filled with anecdotes that are highly effective in getting across Thompson's main points. He likes simple, easy-to-use methods. The context is US culture, with special emphasis on what to do when you are an authority figure, such as a police officer, up against recalcitrant people. Thompson has taught his self-developed system to police across the country.

Thompson found that few of his academic colleagues could "apply what they taught."[21] The academic world is good on theory but falls short in applications, at least so far as verbal defence is concerned. Thompson found that police were eagerly seeking practical material. His academic articles generated no response, but after publishing an article in the *FBI Bulletin* in 1982, he received 600 letters.[22] He knew there was a great demand for what he had to say.

From his experiences, Thompson extracted a set of principles. The first one is always to present your professional face, in his case the persona of a police officer, and never try to save your personal face. In other words, always respond professionally, no matter how badly you are hurting underneath. His second principle is to treat others as you would like to be treated, an application of

---

20 George J. Thompson and Jerry B. Jenkins, *Verbal Judo: The Gentle Art of Persuasion* (New York: HarperCollins, 1993, 2004).

21 Ibid., 19.

22 Ibid., 59.

the do-unto-others rule found in several religions and philosophies. These two principles are the most important for police.

Thompson lists a large number of additional principles. For example, number 3 is to distinguish between reasonable resistance and severe resistance. If the verbal resistance is reasonable, Thompson says to ignore it and not be annoyed by it. If the person does what you ask, then don't worry about what they say. Principle 4 is to treat each verbal interaction as unique: as potentially different from dozens of apparently similar previous interactions.

What Thompson calls principles might be better described as rules of thumb. They are practical reminders of how to proceed. Here are some examples of how he sees verbal judo operating.

Thompson says it is vital to recognise verbal attacks. (Elgin and Horn say the same thing.) Rather than fighting back, he says to "laugh it off." Counterattacking only gives the original attack credibility.[23] Rather than resisting the opponent, it's better to move with them.[24]

Thompson gradually learned, through trial and error, a five-step approach to obtain voluntary compliance. The first step is to ask the other person to do what you want. This is a moral appeal. If this isn't enough, the second step is to explain why you've asked them. This is an appeal to reason. The third step is to describe a set of options for the other person, telling what is likely to happen to them, giving plenty of detail. This is an appeal to self-interest. If

---

23 Ibid., 37.
24 Ibid., 43

the other person cooperates, the fourth step is to confirm that they are doing so, giving feedback to encourage continued responsive behaviour. The fifth step is to act.[25]

Elsewhere, Thompson lists the five "basic tools to generate voluntary compliance." These are somewhat different from the five-step approach, which is a sequence of methods. In contrast, the five tools can be used in any order. Thompson created an acronym for the tools: LEAPS, for listen, empathise, ask, paraphrase and summarise. *Listen* means to attend carefully to what the other person is saying or, often more importantly, to appear to listen, for example when you've heard it all before. *Empathise* means to imagine you are the other person and try to understand what they are thinking and feeling. Thompson distinguishes between empathy and sympathy. Sympathy means approving of the other person; empathy means understanding their point of view. *Ask* means questioning the other person to obtain responses. Specifically, questions are about who, what, when, where, how and why. *Paraphrase* means putting the other person's complaint or concern in your own words and checking with them that you've understood it. *Summarise* means putting everything discussed into a compact, straightforward form. Thompson says the summary must be brief, concise and convincing.

Thompson provides several toolkits of techniques. As well as the five-step approach and LEAPS, he provides PAVPO (perspective, audience, voice, purpose and organisation) and PACE (problem, audience, constraints

---

25 Ibid., 96–101.

and ethical presence). Added to over 20 principles, this is quite an array of tools. Using Thompson's approach requires practice rather than mindlessly following a set of guidelines. Probably the best way to learn his approach is to try out a few techniques in an encounter, record what happened and revisit his book to better understand this interaction and to plan for the next encounter. Like much learning, the ideas sound great in the abstract but require the test of practice to acquire personal meaning and to develop capabilities.

Like the approaches of Elgin and Horn, Thompson's approach sits between passivity and aggression. It connects with all the features of effective nonviolent action, translated into the realm of interpersonal relations. The distinctive contribution of Thompson is in addressing situations in which you are the person with formal authority. He writes as a police officer seeking compliance; others in analogous situations include parents, teachers, religious leaders, judges and military commanders. In such relationships, in which one party has more formal authority, there is a greater risk of using aggressive methods, including physical force and emotional abuse. This is a special risk when those with power do not control their own emotions and actions. Just think of cases in which bosses bully subordinates or teachers humiliate students. Thompson argues for developing skills that help pull back from hurting others.

Applied to the classic confrontation in studies of nonviolent action, police versus protesters, Thompson's approach speaks to the role of police. In some rallies, protesters yell abuse at police, sometimes engaging verbally with individual officers. Police who are experienced in using Thompson's approach will be better able to engage with such protesters, avoiding violence and increasing the chance of getting protesters to do what they want.

From the point of view of protesters who are committed to nonviolent action, it has long been a challenge to figure out what to do about other protesters who yell abuse, push and shove or even assault police. Aggressive protesters like this can discredit the entire movement, lead to bad media coverage and provide legitimacy to the police, including when the police use force to control the crowd. Those committed to nonviolent action should consider another option: encourage police to learn Thompson's approach. When police are better prepared for abuse, and can use verbal techniques to turn it against the protesters, everyone is better off.

William Irvine

A different approach to dealing with verbal attacks is provided by William Irvine in his book *A Slap in the Face*.[26] Irvine is a philosopher and decided to tackle one particular facet of verbal interaction: insults. His book displays the careful thinking characteristic of a philosopher combined with engaging examples and accessible writing.

---

26 William B. Irvine, *A Slap in the Face: Why Insults Hurt — and Why They Shouldn't* (New York: Oxford University Press, 2013).

Irvine systematically classifies different types of insults. For example, he looks at direct attacks ("you're a stupid fool"), insults by omission (when others are praised but you are not), backhanded compliments ("you're pretty good for an amateur") and many others. Insults can be hurtful, sometimes exceedingly so. However, one type of insult is positive: teasing. According to Irvine, playful teasing ("how did you get to be so ugly?") is a way of bonding, among those people you know pretty well already: "Teasing implies a level of acceptance and even intimacy."[27]

Many people feel obliged to respond to insults. A common rationale, often unconscious, is that an unanswered insult leaves them opens to further insults, by the same person or others. People with low self-esteem who are unsure of their identity, and who depend on assessments by others, are vulnerable to insults. On the other hand, there are some people with high self-esteem who have a fragile self-image: narcissists. They are also vulnerable to insults. Narcissists need to counterattack to defend their sense of self. This leads to another dynamic: some people insult others to prevent being insulted first. Often this is triggered by envy, a common emotion, yet seldom recognised.[28] Imagine this scenario. Someone sees your car, your clothes, your good looks or your friend-

---

27 Ibid., 81.

28 On the importance of envy in understanding society, see Joseph H. Berke, *The Tyranny of Malice: Exploring the Dark Side of Character and Culture* (New York: Summit Books, 1988).

ships, is envious, and attacks by making a belittling comment.

Irvine, to develop a way of responding to insults, was inspired by the Stoics, a group in ancient Greece who followed a particular philosophy of life. The Stoics did things because they were worth doing, not because of the possibility of honours or admiration. The Stoics advocated what Irvine calls "insult pacifism," which means not insulting others and not responding to insults.

Irvine tried out, in his personal life, the approach of not responding and found it worked well. So does saying "thank you," in a neutral tone, without sarcasm. This baffles the insulter. If the insulter tries to explain the insult, just say, "I know. Thanks." Irvine found that this response sometimes led the person to retract the insult.

Not responding or saying "thanks" is hard enough. Even harder is the emotional side of the Stoic approach to life, which is to appear calm in the face of insults, and be calm inside. If insults don't hurt you emotionally, much of their power is gone.

There is another aspect: responding to praise. Many people get a buzz out of compliments, and a few spend a lot of effort in the hope of receiving compliments. They derive much of their self-image from what others say. However, Irvine believes that Stoics would have responded to praise minimally, for example by just saying "thanks" and perhaps adding a self-deprecatory remark such as "You are very kind." Furthermore, Stoics would seek to be calm inside, not being emotionally affected by praise.

The basic idea here is to do things because they are worth doing, not because of a fear of insults or the possibility of praise. This was an unusual capacity in ancient Greece and seems to remain unusual today. In essence, according to Irvine, the Stoic approach means opting out of the status race. He says genuine praise of others is rare because people playing the social hierarchy game know it is a losing strategy, helping others rise in estimation and hurting one's own status.

So how does the Stoic approach to verbal interaction relate to nonviolent action? It is certainly non-aggressive. However, it might not satisfy the condition of being "action," namely of being stronger than conventional methods of responding. The Stoic approach seems, at least on the surface, to be a passive method, a form of non-response. But in this it is unusual, because the conventional methods of responding to verbal abuse all involve some sort of engagement, either defensive manoeuvres or positive steps such as demonstrating compassion.

To understand better how the Stoic approach relates to nonviolent action, it is useful to distinguish between promoting social change and defending the status quo. Many of the signature campaigns cited as successes of nonviolent action involve challenges to injustice, such as the Indian independence struggle, the US civil rights movement and the numerous people power movements against repressive governments. In these campaigns, the activists use methods to confront and change the existing system. Being passive is seldom part of the repertoire in such situations.

Another type of campaign is defence of the status quo against assault. A classic example is popular resistance to military coups, such as in Germany in 1920, Algeria in 1961 and the Soviet Union in 1991. In such defensive actions, refusal to obey commands can play an important role. In Germany in 1920, bank officials refused to sign cheques made out by the coup leaders; in Algeria, many troops stayed in their barracks, not joining the coup; in the Soviet Union, commandoes refused orders by coup officials to attack the Russian White House.[29] Methods of resistance by not cooperating are well known but are often forgotten in the emphasis on bringing about change.

Applied to verbal interactions, noncooperation can be interpreted as refusing to engage with the normal scripts or patterns of dialogue. All of the methods of verbal defence involve refusal to follow the path of escalation, in which abuse leads to counterattack. The Stoic approach of non-response or polite acceptance is a special case of noncooperation. It can be thought of as a form of ostracism: a refusal to continue with a type of interaction.

The Stoic approach can become more powerful if adopted by more people. If an insulter is met repeatedly with indifference or politeness, the impulse to insult is likely to subside: there is no reinforcement of the behaviour. Some verbal attackers gain energy by the subsequent escalation: a response vindicates the original complaint. Non-response drains energy.

---

29 See Adam Roberts, "Civil resistance to military coups," *Journal of Peace Research*, vol. 12, no. 1, 1975, pp. 19–36.

Behaving like a Stoic requires considerable self-confidence and inner peace. Not responding to insults is a technique; the harder part is developing the ability to be calm emotionally in the face of insults. It certainly can be worthwhile seeking to develop this capacity. Even if you prefer to use techniques such as those suggested by Elgin, Horn or Thompson, it is helpful to be calm and focused. A possible goal would be to become a skilled and compassionate verbal defender on the outside and a Stoic on the inside.

Conclusion

Verbal interactions can involve attempts at domination and humiliation, and often cause emotional pain. Sometimes this is intentional, sometimes inadvertent and often due to habitual behaviours. Because verbal interactions are so important in people's lives, it is worth exploring how to do better. In particular, it is worth seeing whether features of effective nonviolent action are relevant to the verbal domain.

Nonviolent action, with methods such as rallies, strikes, boycotts and sit-ins, goes beyond conventional methods of social action such as lobbying and voting, but avoids any physical violence against opponents. Nonviolent action can be seen as part of a strategy of assertion, being neither passive nor aggressive. Nonviolent action is a challenge to repression and oppression that, if done well, demonstrates commitment and mobilises support without serious damage to opponents, thus opening the door to switches of allegiance.

Taking the key features of effective nonviolent action and applying them to verbal interactions gives a simple prescription for verbal defence: do something different from the usual response, without being aggressive. When someone makes a nasty comment or hostile put-down, a response inspired by nonviolent action would be respectful to the other person, while acting to challenge or sidestep the attack.

To see how this might apply in practice, I have looked at several approaches to verbal self-defence, written by different authors. Interestingly, these different approaches were developed independently, for the most part, in some cases built out of practical experience. The most systematic approach is that developed by Suzette Haden Elgin in her books on the gentle art of verbal self-defence.

The advice by these writers is varied, but there are some core similarities. They all recommend against responding aggressively. In this, they adhere to a key principle of nonviolent action, which is not to use violence in response to violence. In a verbal interaction, this means not responding to provocative or demeaning comments with similarly provocative or demeaning comments. Elgin, for example, says to avoid the bait and respond to the presupposition, usually using computer mode, which minimises the risk of escalation, instead taking the interaction in a different direction. Irvine, in response to an insult, recommends saying nothing or saying "Thanks," which defuses the attack. These authors recognise that responding in kind simply feeds the negativity, giving the verbal attacker a justification for having attacked.

Instead of returning fire — to use a military metaphor — a common theme is to respond in a way that expends the psychological energy of the attacker without any return. It is for this reason that martial arts metaphors are used: Horn's *Tongue Fu* and Thompson's *Verbal Judo*. The energy and momentum of the attacker are used against them, or are dissipated without impact. This is reminiscent of Sharp's concept of political jiu-jitsu, in which activists, by remaining nonviolent, gain support from the violence of their opponent.

Another way to think about these recommendations is as means to change the topic of conversation. Both passive and aggressive responses remain in the same arena, following the attacker's agenda, either defending against accusations or slights, or counterattacking.

One of the features of successful nonviolent action is widespread participation. Many people, and people from different social locations, are able to join the movement, and do. Applying this idea to verbal interactions implies that more people need to learn the techniques of verbal defence. If, at a meeting, several participants use verbal defence techniques, they can support each other and provide a model to those present.

An important part of making nonviolent actions effective is appropriate preparation, which can include training in responding to provocation, in particular avoiding aggressive responses for example when police use force against protesters. Remaining nonviolent is essential for triggering the jiu-jitsu effect in which violence by police generates a backlash. In verbal interactions, preparation is also essential. Caught by an unexpected comment, a verbal defender needs to inhibit the impulse to resist or counterattack, and instead use one of the numerous techniques that defuse, sidestep or transform the attack. Practice is vital. Practising among friends or work colleagues can prepare people for particular scenarios, and also develop skills that can be used in one-on-one situations. The books about verbal defence are filled with excellent techniques, but just reading about them is seldom sufficient. It's possible to imagine schools teaching verbal defence techniques.

Then there are activists, who want to be as effective as possible. In encounters with police, some protesters shout abuse. It's not physically violent, and so does not violate the usual boundary put around nonviolent action, but often it is ineffective or counterproductive. Activists could use the advice manuals on verbal defence to develop ways of expressing themselves that advance the cause. On the other side of the protest lines, police can learn how to defend against protester provocations. That is what Thompson recommends in *Verbal Judo*.

There is one final connection between nonviolent action and verbal defence: some of the most penetrating insights arise from practical experience. The practice of nonviolent action has been the driver behind most theoretical treatments, and similarly experience in verbal confrontations provides much of the insight in manuals on the topic. The common theme is learning by doing, which involves trying things out, seeing what happens and making suitable adaptations.

Appendix: other approaches to verbal defence

In this chapter, I looked at advice manuals on verbal defence, looking for parallels with the features of effective nonviolent action. There are some different approaches to this issue that I didn't pursue but which may be just as fruitful, in different ways.

Ellen Gorsevski in her book *Peaceful Persuasion* sets out to explore links between two fields: rhetoric and nonviolence, rhetoric being persuasive discourse or communication, through words, symbols or action.[30] Gorsevski covers a range of topics, ranging from speech communication pedagogy to the rhetoric of a Macedonian leader. Much of *Peaceful Persuasion* is about national and international politics, in which rhetoric plays a key role. Gorsevski makes the point that scholars of rhetoric have looked mostly at violence and almost never at nonviolent action.

Nonviolent action can itself be conceptualised as a form of communication. Wendy Varney and I identified five main dimensions of nonviolence as communication:

- conversion, persuasion, symbolic action, which are forms of dialogue with opponents
- noncooperation and intervention, which apply pressure as a way of equalising power and preparing for dialogue with opponents

---

30 Ellen W. Gorsevski, *Peaceful Persuasion: The Geopolitics of Nonviolent Rhetoric* (Albany, NY: State University of New York Press, 2004).

- mobilisation of third parties, who then can influence opponents
- collective empowerment via dialogue within activist groups
- individual empowerment, which can be connected to a person's inner dialogue.

This is a framework for highlighting the communicative aspects of familiar forms of nonviolent action, namely protest, noncooperation and intervention.[31] It does not have any obvious applications to defending against verbal attack. However, it might be useful in designing resistance against an organised campaign of verbal abuse.

There is a growing body of writing about bullying at work, some of which refers to mobbing, which is collective bullying. Many of the treatments of bullying deal mainly with documenting and explaining the nature and impacts of bullying and with formal processes for dealing with it, with little information on the practicalities of resistance. Indeed, to emphasise resistance might be seen to put the responsibility for solving the problem on the target of abuse. Nonetheless, there are some helpful hints in some treatments of bullying, which overlap with those provided in manuals on verbal defence.[32]

---

31 Brian Martin and Wendy Varney, "Nonviolence and communication," *Journal of Peace Research,* vol. 40, no. 2, 2003, pp. 213–232. See also Brian Martin and Wendy Varney, *Nonviolence Speaks: Communicating against Repression* (Cresskill, NJ: Hampton Press, 2003).

32 Treatments that I especially like include Andrea Adams with contributions from Neil Crawford, *Bullying at Work: How to*

Sharon Ellison advocates an approach she calls "non-defensive communication."[33] This involves using carefully formulated questions, statements and predictions that reduce the likelihood of opposition and open up channels of communication. At the core of this approach is avoiding defensiveness. Being honest and revealing vulnerabilities can, in suitable situations, be extremely powerful in changing interpersonal dynamics. Ellison's approach has many overlaps with the books on verbal defence.

Marshall Rosenberg's book *Nonviolent Communication* is an approach to interpersonal communication to achieve true connection, getting past various barriers.[34] It includes:

Confront and Overcome It (London: Virago, 1992); Carol Elbing and Alvar Elbing, *Militant Managers: How to Spot ... How to Work with ... How to Manage ... Your Highly Aggressive Boss* (Burr Ridge, IL: Irwin Professional Publishing, 1994); Susan Marais and Magriet Herman, *Corporate Hyenas at Work: How to Spot and Outwit Them by Being Hyenawise* (Pretoria, South Africa: Kagiso, 1997); Judith Wyatt and Chauncey Hare, *Work Abuse: How to Recognize and Survive It* (Rochester, VT: Schenkman Books, 1997).

33 Sharon Strand Ellison, *Taking the War Out of Our Words: The Art of Powerful Non-Defensive Communication* (Deadwood, OR: Wyatt-MacKenzie, 2008).

34 Marshall B. Rosenberg, *Nonviolent Communication: A Language of Compassion* (Del Mar, CA: PuddleDancer Press, 1999).

- expressing how you are — observations, feelings and needs — without criticising or blaming others
- requesting without demanding
- listening, empathetically, to the other person, without hearing criticism or blame
- listening, empathetically, without hearing demands.

Rosenberg does not give much attention to defending against verbal attack. His orientation is more about fostering good communication, which is typical of a large body of writing and practice on interpersonal communication. I mention Rosenberg's book here because he uses the word "nonviolent" to refer to his approach. However, he does not cite any writings about nonviolent action, nor does he mention any of the concepts from the field. Activists may gain the incorrect impression that *Nonviolent Communication* has some special connection with nonviolent action.

Activists can find much valuable material in manuals for preparing for nonviolent protest, in what is often called "nonviolent action training." These manuals include suggestions for planning actions, preparing participants to refrain from using violence (for example, how to react to police violence), publicity, techniques for group dynamics (especially consensus decision-making), strategic analysis, and much more.[35] Some of this material is relevant to dealing with verbal attacks.

---

35 Important contributions include *Handbook for Nonviolent Campaigns* (War Resisters' International, 2014, 2nd edition); Per Herngren, *Path of Resistance: The Practice of Civil Disobedience* (Philadelphia: New Society Publishers, 1993); Srdja Popovic,

144 Nonviolence unbound

Thomas Gordon's *Leader Effectiveness Training* is a classic book that includes communication methods for workplace leaders.[36] Then there is the huge body of writing on conflict resolution, which includes quite a bit of practical advice on interpersonal communication.[37] However, these guides do not give as much attention to responding to verbal attack as the ones covered in this chapter.

Conflict resolution can be approached by starting with Gandhian principles and applying them to interpersonal conflict.[38] Thomas Weber does this in a few pages of

---

Slobodan Djinovic, Andrej Milivojevic, Hardy Merriman, and Ivan Marovic, *CANVAS Core Curriculum: A Guide to Effective Nonviolent Struggle* (Belgrade: Centre for Applied Nonviolent Action and Strategies, 2007).

36 Thomas Gordon, *Leader Effectiveness Training* (London: Futura, 1979).

37 A classic in the genre is Roger Fisher and William Ury, *Getting to Yes: Negotiating Agreement Without Giving In* (London: Hutchinson, 1982).

38 Important treatments of the Gandhian approach to conflict include Joan V. Bondurant, *Conquest of Violence: the Gandhian Philosophy of Conflict* (Princeton: Princeton University Press, 1958); Robert J. Burrowes, *The Strategy of Nonviolent Defense: A Gandhian Approach* (Albany: State University of New York Press, 1996); Richard B. Gregg, *The Power of Nonviolence,* 2nd ed. (New York: Schocken Books, 1966); Krishnalal Shridharani, *War Without Violence: A Study of Gandhi's Method and its Accomplishments* (London: Victor Gollancz, 1939).

his book *Conflict Resolution and Gandhian Ethics.*[39] The basic approach is to internalise the principles of satyagraha, which includes working through one's own internal conflicts and obtaining a degree of clarity to enable seeing whether there is some truth in the opponent's position and, if so, admitting it. A Gandhian will attempt to find a resolution satisfactory to both parties. Weber suggests using techniques such as "I messages" (for example, "When you accuse me of not caring, I feel upset because I do care") and role-reversal, in which each person puts themselves in the situation of the other. In making these suggestions, Weber draws on conflict-resolution techniques that were developed outside the Gandhian tradition.

Mark Juergensmeyer in his book *Fighting with Gandhi* illustrates Gandhian approches to conflict using various examples, including one involving a dispute with a neighbour and another a family feud.[40] Juergensmeyer says the Gandhian process is to examine each side's principles, create an alternative resolution and start doing the alternative. He also says that not all fights should be taken up; they should be pursued when fundamental principles are at stake.

Juergensmeyer seems to assume that opponents are open to persuasion; non-rational people are not mentioned. The approach of rational persuasion has much to offer, but

---

39 Thomas Weber, *Conflict Resolution and Gandhian Ethics* (New Delhi: Gandhi Peace Foundation, 1991), 60–65.

40 Mark Juergensmeyer, *Fighting with Gandhi* (San Francisco: Harper & Row, 1984).

may miss some techniques found in manuals on verbal defence that address underlying assumptions and motivations. Elgin, for example, recommends responding to the presupposition in a comment, not to the bait. This sort of technique might be hard to discover starting with a general Gandhian approach to conflict.

Writings on bullying, nonviolent action training and conflict resolution cover some of the same ground as the books on verbal defence addressed in this chapter. It is especially useful to compare the conflict resolution manuals with the verbal defence manuals. A parallel can be drawn with two approaches to nonviolence, commonly called principled and pragmatic. Adherents to principled nonviolence refuse to use violence because they consider it to be ethically wrong, even when used for a good cause. Principled nonviolence is in the tradition of Gandhi and is sometimes called Gandhian nonviolence. Pragmatic nonviolence is the use of nonviolent action because it is more effective than violence. It is most commonly identified with nonviolence scholar Gene Sharp.

Sharp is known for identifying, classifying and documenting historical examples of 198 different methods of nonviolent action, in the three broad categories of protest and persuasion, noncooperation, and nonviolent intervention. Sharp's approach is sometimes seen as a "methods" approach, in contrast to the Gandhian approach, which is a more comprehensive programme of seeking a solution to a conflict, as illustrated by Juergensmeyer's examples. Critics of the methods approach see it as too mechanical and insufficiently goal directed, though ironically Sharp places more attention to strategic planning than just about anyone in the field.

In practice, choosing methods without an overall plan and goal is unlikely to be effective, while having a goal but lacking skills in a variety of methods is also likely to fail. The differences between pragmatic and principled approaches to nonviolence are not as great as sometimes suggested.

The same applies to verbal defence and conflict resolution. Verbal defence techniques can be likened to methods of nonviolent action, while conflict resolution approaches can be likened to principled nonviolent action. Writers on verbal defence provide many techniques, but invariably see them as part of an integrated package designed to achieve changes in relationships. Writers on conflict resolution discuss techniques as part of a wider goal. These two bodies of writing thus can be seen as complementary, just as pragmatic and principled nonviolence are complementary.

Some people start from general principles and apply them to specific situations. However, it is probably more common for people to address particular problems — whether verbal abuse or a repressive government — and perhaps gradually integrate their understanding into a broader set of principles. In this chapter, I focused on manuals for verbal defence because it is easier to assess them in relation to features of effective nonviolent action. Others may find it useful to undertake the same sort of analysis starting with writings and experiences of conflict resolution.

6
Being defamed

She emailed me with a problem. There was a picture of her on the web and she wanted it removed. It was the year 2000 and the web was less than a decade old. It was not an easy problem to solve.

Her name was Qafika Gauliflo-Edmondsen. She had been in a relationship with a fellow named John, but then she had left — she had even left the country — because he was so controlling. John was hurt, and also vindictive. He set up a web page with a revealing photo of Qafika and the word "whore" in large bold print. Qafika was mortified. When anyone put her name into a search engine, this picture would pop up as the first link. What should she do?

Defamation and whistleblowing

In 1996, when I became president of Whistleblowers Australia, one of the first things I did was write a leaflet about defamation.[1] When whistleblowers speak out about corruption, dangers to the public and other matters of concern, they often suffer reprisals such as ostracism, petty harassment, reprimands, referral to psychiatrists, demotions and dismissal. Some of them are threatened with being sued for defamation.

---

1 Brian Martin, "Defamation law and free speech," 1996, http://www.bmartin.cc/dissent/documents/defamation.html

Whenever you say anything derogatory or damaging about a person, you have defamed them. If you tell a friend that Bill is an officious bastard, you've defamed Bill. Even if you just say he's overweight, that can be defamatory. If you say it verbally, it's called slander. If it's in print or broadcast, for example in an email or radio programme, it's called libel. If you defame someone you can be sued and it can be very expensive.

This might seem absurd because most people are saying derogatory things about others on a daily basis. Gossip, including nasty comments, is routine in most workplaces. Yet rarely does anyone sue. It's simply too expensive and too much trouble for everyday purposes.

Suppose, though, that a television station runs a story suggesting you're running a shonky business, even though you're innocent. The station refuses to retract the story, so you might be tempted to sue for defamation.

One of the main problems with defamation law is that it is used so rarely. To threaten someone with a legal action for defamation can be a form of intimidation. That's why I wrote the leaflet: lots of whistleblowers were being threatened with defamation actions as a means of intimidation. Indeed, many were afraid to speak out in the first place because of the risk of being sued.

Suppose you are actually sued for defaming someone. You can defend on various grounds depending on the jurisdiction, namely the laws of the country or region. The most common defence is that what you've said is true. If Bill actually is overweight you can defend your comment, but you might need a photo in case he has lost weight by the time of the court case. When you said he is an officious bastard, you might have more trouble proving this is true. You would need to provide evidence and obtain witnesses because Bill will be claiming you're wrong.

Another defence is qualified privilege. For example, imagine you're a teacher and you write a report on one of your students, Sally, saying she's a poor performer — and Sally's parents arrange for Sally to sue you for defamation. You can defend on the grounds that your report was part of the performance of your duties; this is called qualified privilege. However, if you comment at a party that Sally is a lousy student, your speech is no longer protected.

Then there is what is called absolute privilege, including speeches given by politicians in parliament and proceedings of court cases. If you have some hot material about corruption, one way to avoid the risk of being sued is to find a politician willing to make a speech about it. News outlets can safely report what the politician said — but only when it was said under parliamentary privilege.

Just recounting these different defences gives a whiff of the complexities of defamation law. The field is a lawyer's paradise. A case involving someone making a single defamatory statement, or publishing a picture that lowers someone's reputation, can lead to months of legal claims and counter-claims, costing many thousands of dollars, long before the matter reaches court. Most cases are settled, by some agreement between the people involved, without going to court. Those few in which there are court hearings can cost tens of thousands of dollars.

My leaflet on defamation law, titled "Defamation law and free speech," was oriented to people who are threatened with legal actions for defamation. A government employee speaks out about corruption and is threatened with being sued. In the leaflet, I describe ways to reduce the risk. For example, instead of writing "Jones is corrupt," it's safer to write "Jones received $50,000 from the real estate developer and then approved the developer's application." Sticking to facts is far safer than passing judgements. It's also more effective to let readers draw their own judgements from the facts.

I checked the text in the leaflet with quite a number of people, including a barrister who specialised in defamation law. I wanted the leaflet to be accurate as well as accessible to members of the public — especially whistleblowers. When a whistleblower contacted me, I usually would send a packet of articles to them, including the defamation leaflet if it seemed relevant.

It was 1996 and I had just set up my website, gradually adding material about suppression of dissent. The defamation leaflet was there too, and it gained a considerable readership. People would contact me saying they had searched the web for information about defamation and my leaflet was the most useful thing they found. Most of the other materials available were more legalistic. This was before Wikipedia and the huge amount of material subsequently available. My leaflet was listed highly by search engines for several years. Of the thousands of items on my website, it received more hits than anything else. This led quite a few people to contact me about defamation matters.

Most of those who contacted me were seeking to speak out, or already had. Some of them were planning to circulate a document or set up a website and were worried that they might be sued. Some had been threatened with being sued for something they had said. Some had received a letter of demand from a lawyer, requesting an apology and a payment to their client. Some had received a writ requiring them to appear in court, charged with defamation. It was for these sorts of problems that I had written the leaflet: defamation law was being used for the purposes of censorship.

However, I also received another sort of enquiry, from people who felt they had been defamed. Some wrote saying that their former spouse was telling lies to everyone in their family and hurting their relationships. Others wrote saying media coverage had damaged their reputations. Yet others wrote asking my advice about choosing a lawyer to help them sue for defamation. Qafika, whose story I mentioned in the introduction to this chapter, was one of this group of people.

Years later, I wrote a short article telling about options, titled "What to do when you've been defamed."[2] Here, I want to be a bit more specific and look at options for Qafika. Then I will assess these options in light of the features of effective nonviolent action.

Being defamed: some examples

Here are some brief accounts of people who have been defamed — or believe they have been — and want to do

---

[2] Brian Martin, "What to do when you've been defamed," *The Whistle* (Newsletter of Whistleblowers Australia), no. 45, February 2006, pp. 11–12.

something about it. These are taken from emails to me, with names and details changed to disguise the identity of all concerned. If some of these seem familiar, it is probably because the same sorts of issues arise in many different places.

Fred is the father of a child who attends Frenches Primary School. Marie is the mother of two other children at the school. Marie has been telling other parents that Fred assaulted her and that he was convicted. According to Fred, witnesses said Marie pushed him and then went to the police claiming Fred had assaulted her. Fred also said police had never even charged him. Due to Marie's comments, parents and the principle have put pressure on Fred to withdraw from school activities, in order to "keep the peace." Fred wants to sue Marie for defamation.

Helen is married to Bob. Bob's former wife, Joan, seems to be pursuing a vendetta against both of them, telling police and various government agencies that Helen and Bob are unfit parents. As a result, the police and some of the agencies have carried out investigations but found nothing of concern. However, Joan's continuing claims sometimes affect Helen, Bob and the children, for example when they are applying for a loan or for approval of home renovations. Helen discovered that Joan has a history of making false claims that hurt others. Helen wants to know whether she should expose Joan's behaviour.

Wing is involved in a custody dispute with his former partner Alicia. In the family court, Alicia claimed that Wing assaulted their young daughter. An investigation by welfare authorities and police found no evidence to support Alicia's claim. Wing wants to know whether he can sue for defamation.

Zim is involved with an organisation named Farmers Against Sexual Discrimination (FASD). A fellow named Alph has posted numerous videos on YouTube making outrageous claims about FASD and seeking to shut it down. Zim has contacted lawyers, who say all they can do is write Alph and threaten to take him to court — and it will cost $15,000 just for the letters. FASD can't afford this. Zim wants to know what FASD can do.

Cenfrida, a mother of several children in a large Asian city, visited the business of her neighbour Elena and asked for a small item costing only a few cents. They had a misunderstanding over payment for the item. Elena began shouting at Cenfrida, calling her an ugly monkey from the jungle and other uncomplimentary names. Cenfrida wants to know the first step for suing.

Elsa, during a year in another country, had a relationship with Barry. He put pressure on Elsa to obtain explicit photos of her, and she eventually acquiesced. They have now broken up. Elsa asked Barry to delete all the photos of her, but heard from another woman who had seen explicit photos of Elsa and several other women on Barry's computer. Elsa is worried about her reputation, especially because she wants to obtain a job in the other country, and wants to know whether there is anything she can do.

Daniela manages a small business named Lyleservice. Adrian, a technician working for Lyleservice, failed to do his job and insulted a customer, and was fired. Adrian then set up a website, Lyleservicesucks.com, containing nasty comments about Lyleservice. Furthermore, Adrian has been posting hostile comments about Lyleservice on various other sites. Daniela wants to know how the company can handle this problem.

Raelene broke up with Alphonse over a year ago. Alphonse, in collaboration with Brett, produced a video about Raelene. Both Alphonse and Brett have spent time in prison for fraud and stalking. In the video, Alphonse and Brett make numerous derogatory claims about Raelene. They include an excerpt from a video, making Raelene appear to be an angry woman. The video is available on YouTube and several other places on the web. Raelene wants to know what she can do.

Walter runs a business linked to his full name. A year ago, police investigated him for selling heroin, and he appeared in court, but eventually the charges were dropped. Walter says the claims against him were instigated by a business competitor. A local newspaper published a story titled "Local man on drug-pushing charges" that now appears as the first link on Google when searching for Walter's business. Walter wants to know whether it is worth suing the newspaper for defamation.

Adelle runs a small business. Someone on eBay, from another country, claimed Adelle is dishonest and recommended others not to buy from her. She complained to eBay and was told to get a court order. A lawyer quoted her $1500 to write an initial letter, which is too much for Adelle, and she's not sure whether this will fix the problem considering her critic is in another country. She wants to know what to do.

Pat lives in a small community where she is a member of a church and contributes to activities in several ways, for example ushering and preaching. She started a relationship with a man. The pastor of the church disapproved of the man, and told a group at the church that Pat's relationship was immoral and that she had stolen church property. Pat said everyone was talking about this, causing her to become depressed and attempt suicide. She wants to sue the pastor.

Qafika's options

Qafika was distraught because anyone who looked her up on the web would end up looking at the revealing photo and the word "whore." She was looking for jobs and she knew employers often checked online for information about applicants. She wanted the page taken down, whatever it took. She wanted to know how to sue John, if he refused to remove the image.

The trouble was that John was pretty good with tricks online. He knew how to create anonymous webpages. Suing him would take ages and might not actually help. Qafika told me she wanted to sue, but I knew from experience that there were often other options. It's worthwhile to step back from the issue a bit and examine a wide range of options. This way, it's possible to get a better perspective on the benefits and risks of different possibilities.

Option 1: do nothing
Sometimes negative comments are best ignored. Making a big fuss causes people to pay more attention to them. If there's an embarrassing story on a news bulletin, lots of people will see it, but most of them will forget it pretty soon — it will fade into insignificance. Years later, hardly anyone will remember. How often do you meet someone and think, "I saw this story about you on television four years ago." Even if you do happen to remember the story, your face-to-face impressions with a person are likely to be more influential. If you are known to all your friends and family as honest and trustworthy, and live a modest lifestyle, they will probably dismiss a story about you swindling an elderly couple out of a million dollars as ridiculous. The media can lose credibility by broadcasting stories that are later discredited or, even worse, shown to be fabricated.

Because people's memories are short and because false and malicious information is not likely to be credible to people who know you, in many cases the option of doing nothing is a good one. However, many people are so outraged by false claims about themselves that they want to do something. This urge needs to be resisted, at least initially, until the anger dies down and a calm assessment of options can be made.

For Qafika, doing nothing wasn't such a good idea. The webpage with her photo wasn't a broadcast, shown today and gone tomorrow, but rather an ongoing sore, viewable by anyone searching the web using her name. So what other options did she have?

Option 2: sue for defamation
Qafika wanted to sue, or at least threaten to sue. Quite a few people, when they are defamed, think of the legal system as the solution to their problems. Unfortunately, it hardly ever is.

As described already, the legal system has several disadvantages: it is slow, expensive, oriented to technicalities, and reliant on experts, especially lawyers. If someone has been spreading rumours about you around the neighbourhood, suing them for defamation escalates the matter dramatically. Suddenly many thousands of dollars are at stake, and it becomes more than a neighbourhood matter: outsiders are involved. You have to collect all sorts of information and your neighbour, the one you've sued, starts collecting information to defend. The result, ironically, is that more attention is paid to the rumours than before. Before you sued, no one may have treated the rumours all that seriously. Now *you* have taken them very seriously indeed, and they have become the centre of attention.

The unfortunate result may be that more people know about and talk about the defamatory claims than before.

Rather than ignore the rumours or move on to other topics, the rumours are scrutinised endlessly. Furthermore, because the legal system is so slow, this may continue for months or even years.

If you lose the case, you're worse off than before, financially and in terms of your reputation. On the other hand, imagine that you win: your neighbour makes an apology and pays you a handsome sum of money. But what about your reputation? Have you really cleaned it up? Perhaps some neighbours will think the rumours are true and that the reason you sued was that you knew they were true and wanted people to shut up. It's sounds contradictory and it is: suing for defamation can be bad for your reputation.[3]

This may not matter if all you care about is making your neighbour pay for spreading rumours and collecting a bundle of money as well. However, if you really care about your reputation, you need to think twice before launching a court action. If nothing else, others may think you are a bully, and avoid you. Maybe that's what you want, but maybe actually you'd really just like people to think you're a decent person.

---

3 Brian Martin and Truda Gray, "How to make defamation threats and actions backfire," *Australian Journalism Review*, vol. 27, no. 1, July 2005, pp. 157–166; Truda Gray and Brian Martin, "Defamation and the art of backfire," *Deakin Law Review*, vol. 11, no. 2, 2006, pp. 115–136. See also Sue Curry Jansen and Brian Martin, "The Streisand effect and censorship backfire," *International Journal of Communication*, vol. 9, 2015, pp. 656–671.

Qafika thought that if she threatened to sue, John would remove the photo from the web. She would thus get what she wanted by using a *threat,* without the trauma of an actual court case. She didn't think ahead to what might happen if he refused. After all, he was in another country, so launching a legal action would be awkward and expensive.

Furthermore, what if he was in such a vindictive mood that he didn't care about potential costs? He might decide to post the photo on several websites. Even worse, he might get some of his friends to upload the photo anonymously. Then he could, in all sincerity, agree to remove the photo from his own website and agree to ask others to remove it from other sites — knowing that his friends would refuse. Qafika would then be in a worse situation: the photo would be all over the web. If she threatened defamation actions against John's friends, that would be costly. Even worse, if the photo was posted anonymously, she might have to use other means to get it taken down.

Is it realistic to think that John has so many friends willing to support him in a nasty act against a former girlfriend? Maybe he doesn't have any friends willing to do his dirty work. However, John knows how to do things on the web. He creates a fake identity and uploads the photo using it. He is cautious and does all this at a cybercafe far from his home where he pays in cash, so his actions can't be traced. He covers his tracks in another way: at the cybercafe, he first downloads the photo of Qafika and then uploads it on another site. Anyone who traces his actions will not have any evidence that John was involved. Anyone — John, a friend of John's or a complete stranger — could download the photo and upload it elsewhere. John can say he didn't authorise or encourage this action and be completely sincere. After all, maybe he didn't do it.

Threatening to sue thus has quite a few disadvantages. If the threat on its own isn't enough, then either Qafika has to give up and admit powerlessness or to proceed with a legal action that is likely to be expensive and slow. If John isn't worried about legal action — he might think Qafika's threat is a bluff, or he might not care — then Qafika could be in a worse situation. To thwart the intent of the legal action, John might arrange for the photo to be uploaded in several locations.

It's possible to imagine an even nastier response. John might upload other photos that are unpleasant — pictures of mutilation or grotesque objects — and include Qafika's name as a metatag — a bit of hidden information used by search engines — so anyone putting her name into a search engine will come up with these disturbing images. He has to arrange for links to these other pictures, so search engines will find them.

On the surface, legal action sounds powerful. In practice, when tackling defamation on the web, it can be useless or worse. It can be worse if it provokes John into putting more defamatory images on the web, in a way designed to be resistant to legal action.

For the moment, let's assume John is not extraordinarily nasty and vindictive, but instead just very upset and wanting to get back at Qafika. Let's consider some other options for Qafika.

Option 3: counter-attack
Suppose Qafika decided to get back at John. She had some compromising pictures of him with other women. She could post them on the Internet with some juicy comments, maybe "What John won't tell you." Suppose she wishes to hurt John even more. She has suspicions about his preference for young men, and convinces herself that he's really a paedophile. She doesn't have any photos, but she's so convinced that she creates some using a digital technique. She posts them, and sends anonymous emails to various friends of John, giving the web address.

Is it fanciful to imagine Qafika doing something like this? Others do similar things. Police often believe that certain suspects are guilty, but there's not enough evidence to enable a conviction, so they will lie in court about what happened — a practice called "verballing" — or "fit up" the suspect by creating false evidence. For example, police might plant some drugs in a house, or in someone's pocket, and then "discover" it. Some of these sorts of dealings are payback for someone the police don't like, or are reprisals against those who speak out about police corruption, but in many cases the police are quite sincere in their belief that the suspect is guilty. All the police are doing is ensuring justice is done.

Selective perception plays a part too. If you believe second-hand smoke is harmless, you are more likely to notice information that supports your view and to ignore or discount contrary information. Sometimes police form an opinion that a particular suspect is the guilty one, and thereafter look at all the evidence with that assumption: evidence that supports their opinion is readily noticed, neutral evidence is interpreted to support guilt, and contrary evidence is ignored. Furthermore, police will go looking for evidence of guilt and not follow up leads that might implicate others.[4]

Qafika is so angry at John that she is prepared to believe the worst. She reinterprets all his behaviour in a negative light. As she mulls over their time together, remembering various episodes and interactions, her suspicion that he is a paedophile — or a thief or a compulsive liar — gradually becomes a certainty. So when she manipulates photos to create incriminating images, she thinks she is entirely justified, because in her mind he is guilty.

Let's take a cool look at Qafika's plan. It very well could be damaging to John: he will be embarrassed, probably furious, and perhaps worse. But will counter-attack get what Qafika wants, namely removal of the picture of her that John posted? For this to happen, John would need to respond with an offer: "If you remove the photos of me, I'll remove my photo of you." This is possible. But there's a problem: most of the damage has already been done. John's friends have seen the photos and some of them are repelled. That can't be reversed.

---

[4] On confirmation bias and other biases that affect police and indeed anyone, see for example Margaret Heffernan, *Willful Blindness: Why We Ignore the Obvious at Our Peril* (New York: Walker & Company, 2011); Daniel Kahneman, *Thinking, Fast and Slow* (New York: Farrar, Straus and Giroux, 2011); Carol Tavris and Elliot Aronson, *Mistakes Were Made (but Not by* Me*): Why We Justify Foolish Beliefs, Bad Decisions, and Hurtful Acts* (Orlando, FL: Harcourt, 2007).

For Qafika to use her photos more effectively, she should only threaten to post them, essentially blackmailing John into removing the photo of her. But this will work only if Qafika actually has compromising photos. John isn't likely to be intimidated by the threat to post fake photos, unless perhaps he has been sexually involved with boys.

What he might do instead is escalate his attack on Qafika, posting more photos. If she has posted fake photos, he might be able to show that they can't be true, or find some expert to show this. Then he can discredit Qafika further. And there's something else he could do: sue for defamation. If the photos can be shown to be fake, there's the extra dimension of malice on Qafika's part.

All in all, counter-attack is very unlikely to be effective in helping Qafika's reputation. She might feel satisfied at getting back at John, but that's a different goal. There's a risk that counter-attack will escalate the hostility, hurting Qafika as much as John.

Option 4: inform
Rather than direct counter-attack, Qafika could have applied indirect pressure on John, by informing various people in his life about his behaviour. Potentially, there are lots of possibilities, especially if John has several circles of relationships. To start, there are members of John's family, including his parents, his siblings and his children. Assuming he is on good terms with them and respects their views, contacting them could be effective.

Suppose Qafika sends an email to John's sister Sarah explaining that they had been together, had broken up and

John had posted an embarrassing photo of her. If Sarah is sympathetic, she might say to John, "Don't be a fool. Take down that photo." And John, caring about what Sarah thinks, takes it down. Simple!

However, this scenario depends a lot on Sarah's reaction and her relationship with John. Sarah might not do anything. Perhaps she's on John's side. Perhaps she knows about John's string of relationships and never discusses them with him. Perhaps she fears John's reaction, knowing how volatile and vindictive he can be. Perhaps she simply doesn't care because she has too much else happening in her life to worry about Qafika's feelings.

Appealing to Sarah thus is potentially effective but far from guaranteed to work. The same applies to others in John's life. If John is a charmer, he may be able to convince his relatives that Qafika did terrible things to him and that posting her photo is just a tiny contribution towards evening the score. Another possibility is that John is estranged from his relatives, so their opinions don't matter to him.

Qafika could inform John's boss and workmates. John's boss Sam is a crucial figure, because John's job may depend on Sam's favourable opinion. Sam might be appalled at John's behaviour — especially if Sam is a woman. On the other hand, Sam might think that John's private life is his own business, or rather his own affair. If John is doing his job satisfactorily, what concern is it of Sam's what John does outside the workplace?

In a worst-case scenario, some of John's co-workers — including other men who have been hurt by broken relationships — sympathise with him, give him encouragement, offer him suggestions on other ways to get back at Qafika, and even join in the online harassment. Sometimes a mob mentality can develop, and Qafika might become a scapegoat for group resentments, with the men thinking it great sport to discover further ways to humiliate her.

Telling John's boss and co-workers thus is a potentially risky response. If Qafika can convince some of them to see the matter from her point of view, then they may react by putting pressure on John to be sensible and take down the photo. But if John is such a good fellow that his co-workers want to please him, all Qafika has achieved is to alert more people to the photo, thereby hurting her reputation.

Option 5: complain
Qafika would like to complain to somebody — some agency or regulatory body — to fix the problem. So she thought about complaining to the Internet Service Provider (ISP) that hosts the picture of her that John posted. Surely the ISP, being a responsible organisation, would remove this picture that she finds so offensive. So she sends an email to the ISP. What is likely to happen?

This depends a lot on the ISP. Many ISPs are just barely making money, and the staff are too overloaded to spend much time on what they consider small matters. Furthermore, they would prefer not to become embroiled in personal disputes. They don't have the time, expertise or interest to try to figure out who's right and who's wrong. Furthermore, they would rather not set a precedent for removing material, because if one request is granted, where will it stop?

The most likely result of Qafika's complaint is no response. However, suppose that Qafika is lucky and finds someone who takes her complaint seriously and removes the photo. All John has to do is find another ISP, preferably one unconcerned about complaints.

Now it's time to pay closer attention to the photo. If it were pornographic, for example a revealing shot of sexual intercourse, then it would be easy to argue for its removal. However, the photo is simply "revealing": it shows Qafika smiling in a very low-cut top. Some would say it shows her as very attractive. That's why John took the photo, after all, during better times with Qafika. What makes the posting offensive and defamatory is the addition of the word "whore."

Suppose John's ISP tells him to remove the photo, or at least the word. He can then play with options, like "sleeps around" or "my former lover" or "ready for work." There are some possibilities that skirt around defamation, and that might placate a concerned ISP.

John might also decide to post the photo on several different websites, run by different ISPs. Qafika then has the task of tracking down the ISPs and making complaints to each of them. In this scenario, the problem gets worse.

So Qafika thinks of another solution: she'll contact Google and other search engines and ask them to remove the photo from their search results. What she wants is that when people put her name into Google, they won't find the photo. This sounds like an ideal solution — except it's very unlikely Google will agree. Google will rightly say it only provides links and doesn't control the content of the material.

By the same logic, someone might complain to a library that there is a catalogue entry to a book containing lewd images or defamatory remarks. Some librarians might agree to remove the book or put it in a special collection requiring permission to see it, but are unlikely to want to remove an entry from the catalogue. Anyway, is it the library's responsibility to judge whether something in a book is defamatory? That should be the publisher's business.

The same applies to Google Books. If you think something in a book is defamatory, Google is hardly likely to agree to your request to remove the relevant page. Google is not an organisation that adjudicates claims about defamation — that's supposed to be a matter for the courts. Qafika's complaint to Google is unlikely to succeed. Furthermore, John has options to get around any restrictions placed on him.

Option 6: explain

Instead of trying to force John to remove the photo, Qafika has another option: present her own view. She could set up a website and briefly tell what happened with John, thereby framing the story according to her perspective. A website is just one possibility; others are sending emails, handing out leaflets and talking with people individually or in groups.

The advantage of explaining events is that Qafika has the opportunity of presenting information in her own terms. If she wants, she can tell about her involvement with John, positioning herself as the victim of a vengeful loser. Or she could just give the briefest details, telling about her life and her approach to it in general.

The explanation has two facets: what is told and how it is told. Giving the facts and their significance is just one part of a story. Equally or more important is the style used. If Qafika makes cruel remarks about John and expresses her hatred for him, she may give an impression that she is saying nasty things about John because she is hurt and angry, which is not necessarily convincing. On the other hand, if Qafika indicates that she is concerned about John, understands his feelings but doesn't support his actions, she will come across as tender and perhaps magnanimous. The more generous Qafika seems to be, the greater the contrast with John's hurtful posting of her photo.

Of course, Qafika's telling of her side of the story will affect different people in different ways. Furthermore, she is likely to change what she says and how she says it depending on who is listening and how they respond as she goes along. She has the greatest opportunity for adapting her story when she talks with individuals one-on-one, whether face-to-face or by telephone or Skype. Emails can be tailored to individual recipients, but there is little interaction. Putting up a website gives the least opportunity for individual variation. On the other hand, it can be more carefully crafted. Qafika can use a combination of these methods, for example by designing her website text and format mainly for people who don't already know her and speaking to individuals who do.

Explaining the situation, as well as allowing Qafika to frame the events from her point of view, has another great advantage: it is an opportunity to build connections with people she cares about. For some, it is not so much what Qafika says that is important but rather the very fact that she cares about what they think.

There is, however, a significant down side to explaining her problems with John: she may make this matter bigger than it would be otherwise. Some of her friends or colleagues may never have thought of putting her name into a search engine. After hearing from her, they may not be able to resist having a look at the source of her concern, and thus the photo gets more attention than it would have otherwise. So there is a fine line to tread between saying nothing (option 1) and explaining what happened. One way to make a choice is to wait for others to raise the matter. If a friend says something about John or the photo, she can provide her explanation; likewise, if she hears indirectly that someone has seen the photo, she can send an email.

What are friends for if not to offer advice? As Qafika tells a few trusted friends about her difficulties, she can listen to their ideas about what to do next, in particular about who else to talk to and how to raise the issues with them.

Option 7: escape
Rather than try to get the photo taken down, and rather than risk drawing attention to it by explaining the situation, Qafika can use methods of evasion, seeking to avoid being linked to the photo.

One possibility is to populate the web with positive references to her. She can put up her own website, presenting her educational qualifications and job experience, her activities or indeed anything she would feel she is willing to share with the world. By encouraging a few friends to make links to the site, it would not be long before it is the top link given when putting her name into search engines like Google.

If she wanted, on her site she could provide her own account of her interactions with John, along the lines of the option of explaining. Then casual browsers would read her version of the story first, before encountering the actual photo. She could thus frame the matter in her own terms, which greatly influences people's responses.

Another possibility is to seek to move the objectionable photo from the initial page provided by search engines, and thus put it out of sight for all but the most persistent of enquirers. To do this, she needs her name in various sites, all in positive or at least neutral contexts. How to proceed at this point depends greatly on Qafika's interests and skills. If she's a member of a sporting team, her name might appear in news reports about games. She might decide to make comments, on Amazon.com, about books in an area that interests her. She could join Facebook groups and make comments or post photos — including photos of herself. More deviously, she could set up multiple websites about herself, in different contexts, each of them linking to the others.

All this would require quite a bit of time and energy, which might seem excessive in comparison to the goal, namely moving the photo off the first page of search engine results for her name. It is possible to pay agencies to help in creating a favourable web profile.

Another way to think of this approach is one of doing "good things" that receive online recognition. Being involved in charities, churches, clubs or other groups can be valuable in itself; developing the capacity to write book reviews or make other informed online contributions is also worthwhile in itself. So the task of swamping the photo with positive references could be a motivation to undertake positive activities that are socially worthwhile and, very likely, personally satisfying. There is another immediate spin-off for Qafika: her interactions with others are very likely to create a favourable impression.

However, creating a favourable web profile takes time, and in the short term she is worried that employers will find the photo. Is there any other escape? One possibility — which I mentioned to Qafika — is to change her name.[5] If she became Jessica Smith or Sarah Parker or some other name common on the web, employers looking for online information about her would soon give up. Even if John discovered her new name and changed the tag on the photo, it would be extremely difficult to link this to her, because the photo would be too far down on search engine results.

Changing your name to avoid being linked to a photo: it sounds drastic, and it is. It is a lot of hassle, and doesn't provide complete protection, because for some jobs it is necessary to provide previous names. Neverthe-

---

5 Qafika is not her real name to start with. For the discussion in this chapter, I replaced her distinctive full name with a pseudonym with no web presence, in the hope that it isn't anyone's name.

less, a new identity sometimes offers the best way to avoid certain forms of harassment.

Qafika dismissed the idea of changing her name: her name was part of her identity. Still, it was useful to consider this possibility. Examining a range of options can help in clarifying one's values and priorities.

Analysing options

Qafika has quite a few options. How is she to make a decision? In an actual situation such as Qafika's, few people consider a range of options and systematically analyse their strengths and weaknesses. Instead, they usually latch onto what seems most obvious or most effective. This is the reason people contact me asking me to recommend a lawyer so they can sue for defamation: they have assumed a legal action is the best way, or perhaps the only way, to address an attack on their reputation.

Here, there is no rush to make a decision. Qafika's case is in the past, so we can scrutinise it at leisure, which means we can look at a range of options that she might consider. To analyse these options, I will use seven features of effective nonviolent action, as discussed in chapter 1: participation, limited harm, voluntary participation, fairness, prefiguration, non-standard action and skilful technique. For each one, I will look at different options to see how they relate to the features. This process will highlight some of the dimensions of the issue that might otherwise be neglected.

Participation

When there is greater participation in actions for a cause, there is a greater chance of success. Large numbers show a greater level of support and can demoralise the opposition and trigger defections from their ranks. When participation is from different sectors of the population — for example different ethnic groups, genders, ages and social classes — this demonstrates a breadth of support and is more likely to encourage yet more participation. When people from different sectors join a campaign, this contributes diverse knowledge and skills and thus greater capacity to counter the opposition's tactics.

For the one-on-one dispute between John and Qafika, it may seem strange to talk about participation, but in every defamation case, third parties are involved. This is because hurting a person's reputation necessarily involves others. If John told Qafika she was a terrible person, called her a whore and emailed her the photo, this would be unpleasant and might be considered harassment, but it wouldn't be defamatory, because John would be communicating only to Qafika. If others didn't know, their views about Qafika would be unchanged: her reputation would be intact.

So who are the third parties? Most obviously, anyone who sees the photo that John posted on the web. In addition there are those who Qafika or John tell about the matter. For example, if Qafika goes to a lawyer to see about suing John, she needs to tell the lawyer about the photo.

For the purposes of nonviolent action, though, participation refers to joining in the action, for example joining a rally, boycott or sit-in. It means taking sides, demonstrating support for a cause. So which options for responding to the photo involve the most supportive participation?

Of the options canvassed, informing people about the issue involves the most people in a way likely to make them sympathetic and perhaps be willing to do something on Qafika's behalf. Methods for informing people include talking to individuals and setting up a website with relevant information and then giving people the web address. In contrast, suing, counter-attacking and making complaints bring few allies into the picture, unless lawyers are counted. For Qafika to ignore the photo or change her name will do nothing to get others involved.

As noted earlier, informing others risks making some people aware of the photo who otherwise would not have known about it. However, there can still be benefits, especially if Qafika is able to obtain feedback from those she informs. Some of them might have insights about personal disputes, the law, Internet dynamics or public relations and have valuable suggestions about the best way forward. For Qafika to increase the number of people involved can expand her options. Furthermore, some of the individuals might offer to assist directly, for example by helping her set up a website or making links to it.

She can follow this approach even more by telling her story even to those she had most worried about: potential employers. After interviewing for a job, she can — if the circumstances seem right — tell them about her dilemma. If she has just been hired, her new employer should be sympathetic to reducing the visibility of the photo. If she wasn't hired, she can find out whether the employer knew about the photo, and get their suggestions on dealing with it in future.

When your reputation has come under attack, telling others and getting them involved thus has several advantages. The main shortcoming is that more people become aware of the defamatory claims.

Limited harm
When protesters take to the street and behave in a dignified, peaceful way, it is risky for police to use violence against them: it seems unfair and can generate more public support for the protesters. However, if even a few of the protesters become violent themselves — throwing bricks through windows or hitting the police — then the interaction seems quite different to outsiders: it can seem like a confrontation in which both sides are violent, even when the police violence is much greater. Not harming the police thus can be highly important in winning greater support.

Some protesters oppose using violence for another reason. As a matter of principle, they do not want to hurt the police or anyone else. They respect their opponents as human beings.

This principle, as applied to responding to defamatory comments, can be interpreted to mean not attacking the reputation of the person making the comments. In other words, in responding, try to avoid hurting the other person.

In practice, this might mean being generous rather than nasty. Qafika could say, for example, "I think John was very hurt by our break-up. I feel for him." Or she could say, "I care for John, but I don't like what he's done," thus distinguishing between John and his actions.

To some, being concerned about not hurting John may seem to be a ridiculous expectation. After all, he's gone out of his way to hurt Qafika, and surely she is completely justified in hurting him back — and it's even more justified if she is just telling the truth.

The principle of limited harm, however, is not about whether something is justified. It is about respecting the other party and attempting to open possibilities for dialogue and reaching a satisfactory resolution of a conflict. There are plenty of situations in which doing something is justified but unethical or unwise or both. If a foreign government builds a nuclear weapon, it might be justified to build one of your own and prepare to use it, but this could be considered unethical because innocent people will be killed in a nuclear strike and unwise because obtaining nuclear weapons feeds a military race.

Similarly, if someone has said false and harmful things about you, you might be justified in saying things that hurt them. However, even setting aside the ethics of making hurtful comments (which might be more harmful than you imagine), this is likely to escalate the nastiness in the interaction.

If Qafika remains generous in her comments, she retains the moral high ground. She makes it easier for John to calm down and remove the photo. If John continues his attacks, Qafika will seem to others to be the injured party, and thereby gain sympathy. On the other hand, if she seems insincere in her expressed concerns for John, she might be seen as a manipulator.

The principle of limited harm rules out the strategies of suing, counter-attacking and informing his boss. It is compatible with the strategy of informing others and defending. But the principle's implications go further, by providing guidance for what to say when talking to others or putting up a website. The implication is to avoid putting too much blame on John. When Qafika presents her side of the story, her aim should be to reduce the damage to herself and do this while limiting any damage to John. Even further, she can reduce the damage to herself *by* limiting damage to John, because the more she seems generous in her response, the more highly people are likely to think of her, and the more they are likely to focus on the problem to be solved rather than think about who to blame.

The principle of limited harm thus has important applications in defamation issues. Because it is so important, I need to say a bit more. Some people will think, going easy on John — or whoever said those nasty things — is just being sappy. They might say to Qafika, "He's a right royal bastard and deserves no mercy. So do whatever you like. It'll be nothing compared to what he's done to you."

In less blunt terms, the principle of limited harm might seem too soft, too accommodating, too weak to make a difference. Many people think, "I need to get back at them. They deserve everything they get."

This seems all very reasonable — when you've heard or seen just one side of the story. But it might be based on a mistake or misinterpretation.

It's possible that John didn't actually mean to hurt Qafika so greatly. He might have been feeling down in the dumps after Qafika left and, combined the photo with the label "whore" as an expression of his anger — an anger that oscillates with sadness and regret. He wanted to see the photo on the web, so he posted it on an obscure part of his website, with her name as the name of the image file, never thinking that search engines might push it to the top of their hits. After viewing it on his screen, his anger faded and he went back to feeling sad and remorseful — and forgot to remove it. In this scenario, John wasn't intending to hurt Qafika at all. His peculiar method of self-therapy just ended up with damaging consequences.

There's another scenario. John has a precocious daughter who saw how sad he was, and blamed Qafika. She was at his computer and composed the photo-word montage and uploaded it. John didn't even know about it.

Suppose John next receives a heavy-handed legal threat. He didn't even realise the photo was on the web, and now he's being accused of an illegal act that could cost him a huge amount. He might retreat, or he might be fired up with anger at this sort of approach, making him more committed to keeping the photo on the web. He would have been much more responsive to a gentle email saying "I'm so sorry, John. I miss you but I couldn't make it work for us. I feel really hurt about the photo you put on your website. Can you remove it so we can maintain cordial connections?"

The trouble is that Qafika doesn't know what really happened. She left and she's not privy to John's private thoughts or to what his daughter might be doing. Maybe he's a vicious, vindictive, impulsive fellow, but maybe not. The principle of limited harm protects Qafika from overreacting, or doing a greater harm to John than was done to her, or of hurting John when actually he didn't even realise what had happened.

Roy Baumeister, a psychologist, wrote a book titled *Evil: Inside Human Violence and Cruelty*.[6] He wanted to better understand the people who do horrible things like killing and torture. Hollywood movies portray bad guys as pure evil, intending to hurt others and lacking any conscience. Baumeister in his studies came up with a different picture: perpetrators often don't think what they've done is all that significant. After it's done, they quickly forget about it. In many cases they feel justified in their actions because of all the bad things done to them in their lives. Perpetrators of horrible crimes seldom sit salivating and reminiscing over their exploits, but instead their actions fade from their memories.

Their victims, on the other hand, are frequently traumatised. Far from forgetting, they repeatedly relive, in their minds, the terrible things done to them. The result is a huge asymmetry: the perpetrators don't think it's a big deal and soon forget about what happened, whereas for victims the hurt is huge and lasts a very long time.

---

6 Roy F. Baumeister, *Evil: Inside Human Violence and Cruelty* (New York: Freeman, 1997).

This asymmetry between the perceptions of perpetrators and victims can cause long-lasting feuds. In a family feud, or an armed conflict between nations, the initial victims nourish their resentments and counter-attack when they have the opportunity. Those on the other side then feel they are the real victims. One side calls an assault, a killing or an air strike a reprisal; the other side calls it an unjustified attack.

Not using violence — using only methods of nonviolent action — helps to undermine this process of escalation in which each side forgets or minimises its own actions and responsibility and only pays attention to the terrible things done by the other side. Using the principle of limited harm is a way of avoiding adding to the cycle of harm and resentment.

John's viewpoint about what happened was not favourable to Qafika. He had been smitten with her, loved her and wanted to stay with her. Nevertheless, he felt he had to put up with a lot: her whims, her expensive tastes, her moodiness, her need to be pampered at all times. This was tolerable, but what riled John most of all were Qafika's comments about him. John had a slight stutter, about which he was greatly embarrassed. Yet Qafika was prone to making passing references to it as a way of needling him. Even worse, she would draw attention to it when they were with friends. Eventually this infuriated him.

On top of this, John became convinced that Qafika was cheating on him. He had no formal proof, but the pieces of damning evidence were overwhelming. When Qafika walked out on him, saying he was too controlling, it was the final straw. Putting a photo of her on the web was, for him, a trivial issue. It was far less, indeed nothing at all, compared to the hurt she had caused him.

That Qafika actually was charmed by John's occasional stutter and thought others were too, and that she felt she required some time on her own just to create some distance from John's suffocating demands, need not detain us here. In relationships, differences in perception are commonplace.

The point here is that John may well feel that he was the wronged party, and not feel that putting the photo on the web was anything all that significant. So when Qafika contacted him threatening to sue, he thought "What the hell? She treats me like dirt and now has the gall to make demands." He might do what she wants, but he might be provoked to become more devious in hurting her, for example by surreptitiously giving other photos to friends who post them on a range of websites.

If, on the other hand, Qafika tries to minimise the hurt to John, there is less risk of provoking him. If she apologises for things she did and accepts a share of blame for the break-up, John may be more likely to take down the photo.

The same dynamic applies to John's friends. If he can forward them a high-handed demand, they are more likely to take his side and to help him. If all he can forward is a conciliatory email, they are less likely to assist.

The principle of limited harm needs to be understood in the context that perceptions in a conflict are nearly always different. Assessments of responsibility for injustice sometimes are starkly different. Even though Qafika might feel like she is entirely justified in coming down hard on John for posting the photo, her feelings may not correspond to John's reality. The principle of limited harm, if followed, prevents Qafika from making the situation much worse. In the best-case scenario, it helps John to voluntarily remove the photo and reach an acceptance of the end of their relationship.

Voluntary participation
In most nonviolent actions, it is assumed that participants are there voluntarily. There are some situations in which protesters are induced to participate. Some regimes give incentives for citizens to support it, for example paying them to join pro-government rallies, or giving them a day off work so they can join. The resulting protest actions are far from an authentic expression of sentiment. The ratio of voluntary to paid or coerced participants might be used as a test of how genuine a nonviolent action is.

In struggles over defamation, however, participation is less likely to be voluntary in one particular aspect: the involvement of lawyers, who are paid advocates. When suing someone for defamation, lawyers are often key players, making this unlike a nonviolent action.

Some of the other options for responding to defamation have very limited participation. Complaining to John's boss or to his Internet Service Provider, for example, do not require action by anyone except Qafika. The issue of whether participation is voluntary or not does not even arise.

The main implication here is that relying on legal or other paid advocacy is not characteristic of effective nonviolent action. To have a stronger effect, encouraging involvement of volunteers is more likely to be effective.

Fairness
The principle of fairness in nonviolent action boils down to a simple assessment: do observers think that the actions taken are reasonable, or do they think the actions are too extreme? Of course, different observers will have different views, so seldom is there a simple answer.

If you are defamed, the test of fairness is whether your response seems reasonable to most people. If you have an argument with a friend and, in the heat of the moment, he calls you a twit — and others were around listening to this — what do you do? Most people would say "just forget it" or perhaps "ask for an apology, but after both of you have calmed down." If though, you write a formal letter saying you expect a written apology, many would say you're being unreasonable, maybe telling you, "it wasn't that important, so why are you making such a big deal about it?" If you threatened to sue, that would seem like an extreme over-reaction.

The basic idea here is that the response should seem reasonable in comparison to the harm. This can be difficult to get right, because of differences in perception about the significance of things that are said, and because personal honour is involved.

In many cases, suing, or threatening to sue, is likely to be perceived as an over-reaction. You unwisely sent around an email calling the president of your club a liar. An apology might be in order. A demand for a payment of $10,000 might seem excessive.

Qafika in her reaction to the photo needs to be seen to be fair. The photo is pretty damaging, so many of her options will seem reasonable to observers. However, if she complains to John's boss and he loses his job as a result, that might seem to be a severe penalty — at least to many who know John. Likewise, a legal action demanding damages of one million dollars is likely to be seen as excessive, if not silly. If Qafika posts dozens of demeaning photos of John, that also could be seen as an over-reaction. Indeed, she might be seen as the source of the problem. Observers might think, if those are the sorts of things she does, imagine what she was like when she was with John: he does something that offends her, and she blows it up into a huge issue and pays him back a hundred-fold.

This reasoning might be incorrect, but it is predictable. People often judge a person by the nature of their actions, rather than by the purpose of their actions.[7] This sounds abstract. What it means in practice is that many people will judge Qafika by her actions, not by her goal, which is to get John to remove the photo. Her goal might be legitimate, but people won't think of that when contemplating her actions such as suing for defamation or posting numerous photos of John. John and his supporters are the ones most likely to think along these lines; independent observers might also judge Qafika by her actions rather than the justice of her goal.

---

7 See the discussion of correspondent inference theory on pages 47–49.

There's another factor. What seems reasonable depends on the sequence of actions. If Qafika first politely appeals to John, apologising for any hurt she has caused him, and he brushes her off or posts another photo, many will see it as fair that she escalates her actions. This is analogous to what happens when social movements act for change. They commonly first make rational appeals; when nothing happens, they undertake more forceful agitation.

The implication of the principle of fairness is that Qafika needs to be careful. If she reacts too strongly, she will lose sympathy; some might even think she is the cause of the problem. She can seen to be fair by starting with the most gentle methods — politely asking John to remove the photo, in a message that is sympathetic to him — and gradually escalating to stronger methods. She needs to be careful not to escalate too far, namely to use methods likely to be seen as so heavy-handed that people will sympathise with John.

Prefiguration

The principle of prefiguration is that the means should incorporate the ends. If the goal is peace, then use peaceful methods. If the goal is respectful interactions, then use respectful methods. The idea of prefiguration is that by choosing the appropriate methods, goals can be modelled and fostered. It's not always possible to apply the principle of prefiguration, but when it is, it is worthwhile.

If people are telling lies about you, your goal might be an end to the defamatory comments and an apology. A wider goal might be a culture of respect.

The implication for Qafika is straightforward. She needs to behave towards John the way she'd like him to behave towards her. That rules out legal actions and counter-attack. It suggests she should start with a gentle approach, without passing judgement, and escalate if necessary by talking with others.

Qafika's immediate goal is getting John to remove the photo. However, thinking of means and ends may encourage her to consider longer-range, more fundamental goals, such as fostering an honest and open relationship with John, even if staying together is not feasible. So Qafika might take a step back and think about their time together and how she ended the relationship. She realises now that John was deeply hurt, whereas at the time it was her own hurt that drove her away. If John was deeply hurt by her leaving, or by the way she left, maybe she could imagine a different way, perhaps involving a heart-to-heart talk or gestures of good will.

It's possible, of course, that no matter what Qafika did, John would still be vindictive. Maybe nothing would have made any difference. But at least Qafika would know that she had done all she could to be sensitive towards John's needs along the way.

Non-standard action
What is called nonviolent action is, by definition, something beyond the routine. Literally, "nonviolent" implies not using violence, so just saying hello to someone is an action without physical violence. By convention, though, nonviolent action needs to be something out of the ordinary. In countries with representative government,

voting, lobbying and campaigning are conventional political activities. Nonviolent action includes methods such as boycotts, strikes and sit-ins, that are seldom considered routine. Nonviolent action is non-standard action that doesn't involve physical violence.

When a person is defamed, there are some usual responses. Suing for defamation is legally legitimate, though often an over-reaction. At the other end of the spectrum is doing nothing: not responding at all. This is hardly in the spirit of nonviolent action, though in many cases it may be a good idea. It is useful to remember that carrying out nonviolent action is seldom a goal in itself: it is a means to an end, and in many cases it is better to use conventional methods if they work reasonably well.

Qafika has various options, ranging from doing nothing to suing and counter-attack. It is the ones in between these extremes that are analogous to nonviolent action: the ones that go beyond what is usual but conform to the principles of limited harm, fairness and prefiguration. Some of these were canvassed earlier, such as setting up her own website. It's possible to develop further ideas by examining a wider range of conventional nonviolent actions and seeing how they might apply to a defamation scenario, or suggest original options.

The first category of nonviolent actions, called protest and persuasion, includes petitions, leaflets, picketing, wearing of symbols, vigils, humorous skits, marches and walk-outs. Applied to Qafika's situation, the general idea is to get people expressing their views about John's action, through words or actions. There are quite a number of ways to do this. Today the most obvious candidates involve social media such as Facebook and Twitter.[8] However, there's a problem: involving more people in a protest against what John has done inevitably means giving more visibility to the offending photo. In other words, protesting can potentially cause more harm than benefit to Qafika's reputation.

One way to resolve this tension is to protest more generally against abusive comment on the Internet. Qafika could join with others who have been similarly targeted for spiteful attacks and be involved in various forms of protest, including on blogs, email lists, petitions and the like.

This is analogous to campaigning on some other issues, for example violence against women. Few women want to be named in public as victims of violence — this might trigger further attacks — but women can combine to protest, for example marches on International Women's Day. The idea for Qafika is to work with others who have similar or related problems and come up with ways of protesting that target the problem without naming individuals.

Does this count as non-regular action? Surely, there are so many online campaigns that another protest against some abuse is a routine form of politics. In a general sense, this is true, but the assessment of what is regular and non-regular needs to be more specific. There might be plenty of online protests, but are there organised protests about online defamation, where the targets do not want to

---

[8] These were not available at the time of Qafika's conflict with John.

be named? If not, this suggests that for this issue, a protest action is non-standard. In any case, being non-standard is not a goal in itself. If examination of methods of nonviolent action can lead to ideas that are actually conventional forms of action, but ones that have been neglected, this is worthwhile.

The basic idea here is collective action. This is obvious enough in retrospect, but at the beginning Qafika only thought about ways to address her own individual problem. Furthermore, collective protests are not going to solve Qafika's problem, at least in the short term. Protests are more likely help prevent problems, as well as to put Qafika in touch with others with similar concerns. Possibly the greatest advantage is cross-fertilisation of ideas. If Qafika makes contact with others with similar problems, she will hear about what worked and what didn't work, and possibly get some new ideas about what she can do.

So there are some benefits from protest that may be overlooked: providing moral support, sharing experiences and stimulating ideas for responding. For Qafika, joining or helping organise a protest — even one where her case is not mentioned — can provide support and ideas that may help her.

A second main type of nonviolent action is noncooperation, which includes a wide range of boycotts and strikes. These seem an unlikely option for Qafika. She's not buying anything from John anyway, and not working for him. However, this conclusion is based on a narrow conception of boycotts and strikes, which usually bring to mind consumer boycotts of major companies and strikes by large numbers of workers. Using the concept of noncooperation enables more creative thinking, as well as examining the many types of boycotts and strikes.

One type of noncooperation is called social ostracism. This means refusing to interact with someone. This technique is most commonly used against outcasts in schools and workplaces, and is a common method used against targets of bullying. When used against a more powerful person or group, it fits into the spectrum of nonviolent actions.

Imagine that John is known to a wide circle of friends and work colleagues. If they learn about John posting the photo of Qafika and think his action was repellent, they might complain to John — or they might simply avoid him. The one photo of Qafika is hardly enough to trigger such a response, especially because John didn't attach his name to it. However, if Qafika has created her own website and provided a calm, factual account of her attempts to get John to remove the photo, this could be more influential. Qafika then needs to alert some of John's acquaintances to her site; she can do this because she met quite a few of them during her time with John.

Even so, the one photo and an account of John's refusal to remove it, despite polite, heartfelt appeals, might not be enough to trigger his friends to ostracise him. However, if John has done the same thing to previous girlfriends, and Qafika can find them and get them to join her in a collective effort, more of John's friends might be appalled and decide to stay away. John might not care and be willing to carry on with his few loyal friends. On the other hand, he might think that the effect on his life is becoming too great. At work, his colleagues are less helpful, making his job less pleasant and reducing his career prospects. His social life is crimped because too many women he meets have heard about him posting the photo. With this sort of pressure, he might decide that getting back at Qafika is not worth the cost.

Noncooperation is a form of coercion. Taken to extremes, it can be highly damaging, as anyone who has been ostracised can testify. In using noncooperation in cases of defamation, the basic idea is to apply pressure through people's disapproval of actions taken. The concept is simple but the execution can be difficult, because it involves informing a range of people about defamatory materials and their damaging effect. Doing this is risky because it can worsen the original problem — loss of reputation due to the defamatory materials.

The third major category of nonviolent action is "disruption" via nonviolent intervention. This includes various types of actions, such as fasts, sit-ins, overload of facilities, seizure of assets, land seizures and alternative markets. Few of these look immediately promising for Qafika. She could undertake a fast — but would John care? For this to be effective, she needs to establish communication with him. Unless they share a cultural background in which fasting has significance, it might be useless.

What about a sit-in or some other type of nonviolent intervention? The normal idea in these methods is to put your body between a person and something they desire. Qafika can hardly do this personally; perhaps some friend of hers could do it, but it seems unlikely. So instead of thinking of physical bodies, what might this mean in cyberspace? Is it possible to occupy something of John's online? Perhaps it would be possible to squat in his web domain, but probably only if he forgot to renew it.

There would be possibilities, though, if John has some web presence that allows others to post comments. If, for example, he has a Facebook page, it would be possible for Qafika or her supporters to symbolically occupy the page by regularly posting comments, which might be simple things like "Treat Qafika respectfully" or "Remove unwelcome photos." Comments on John's blog or Facebook page are probably better thought of as forms of protest and persuasion. They might be types of nonviolent intervention if they are so frequent and persistent that John cannot easily avoid them.

Another possibility would be to shadow all of John's contributions on the web. If he posts comments on other people's blogs, it might be possible to keep track of them via a Google Alert. This depends, in part on John's name. If it's a very common name, like John Jones or John Nguyen, and he doesn't post very often, it will require lots of monitoring. If his name is less common, like John Apexz, tracking his comments will be easier. If he likes to comment on particular sites, then shadowing him is easier. He might respond by using a pseudonym. Then there's the question of whether to shadow his different identities.

Sharp identified 198 different methods of nonviolent action, and that was long before the Internet.[9] Rather than

---

9 Gene Sharp, *The Politics of Nonviolent Action* (Boston: Porter Sargent, 1973).

try to apply these methods literally, Qafika and her supporters can use them, and more recent lists, to stimulate ideas about responding to John. Responding to John is different from the usual scenarios envisaged by Sharp in three significant ways. First, what John has done is quite different from the actions normally addressed in nonviolent campaigns, which are major injustices such as repression and war. Second, John's action harms just one individual, Qafika, whereas the harms normally addressed by nonviolent action are collective, affecting many people. Third, John's action is on the Internet; traditional forms of nonviolent action involve people taking physical actions, often in public spaces.

To obtain ideas for responding to defamation, it is worthwhile looking at a wide variety of traditional methods of nonviolent action and figuring out how they might be adapted to a very different set of circumstances. This means that there is no simple formula for responding. Instead, creative thinking is needed.

Skilful use

Methods of nonviolent action do not work automatically. To be effective, they have to be chosen carefully and deployed with great skill. Practice can make a difference. The same thing applies when responding to defamation, whichever method is chosen.

If Qafika decides to sue, or threaten to sue, then picking the right legal advocate is crucial. Some people in this situation think they can do the work themselves, even though they have no legal training. They have little money or perhaps they don't trust lawyers. This is usually a mistake, because the legal system is filled with pitfalls for the unwary.

Finding a suitable lawyer can be difficult. Defamation law is a specialised area. A lawyer might be willing to take on a case but not have the experience to do a good job. If the lawyer for the other side is more skilled, the prospects are not good.

Some lawyers will just go through the motions, satisfying the usual requirements. This often makes the process drag on for months or years, which is good for lawyers to pocket their fees but is not good for getting results. Qafika wants to protect her reputation, but that is not the goal of either the legal system or most lawyers. She might be lucky and find a lawyer who will serve her interests, even one who tells her not to sue.

Then there is the direct approach to John, appealing to his emotional concerns. This requires the most skill of all. Qafika might think she knows enough about John to do this well, but perhaps she only knows one side of John. Even for such a personal matter, it can be useful to prepare and practise, and to seek advice from others. For example, Qafika could draft two or three different email messages to John and show them to a close friend, asking which one seems most likely to be effective. If Qafika decides to ring John, or leave a message on his phone, then preparation and practice can help make this as good as possible. With a friend, she can practise what she plans to say: the friend can respond the way John might. A friend who knows John may have extra insight, but the main point of practice is to help Qafika be able to sound the way she wants. By role-playing the conversation, perhaps over and over in different variations, Qafika can prepare herself for John's possible responses, and avoid the risk that she will trigger one of their standard exchanges — in which Qafika and John started criticising each other — that contributed to her leaving.

Practice will also help Qafika if she decides on the option of talking to others about what happened. She can start by practising what she plans to say on her own, in front of a mirror or with a tape recorder, until she can articulate her concerns in a cogent way. She can then start by talking with a close friend and, if her friend is sympathetic and seems willing to help, ask for assistance in improving and practising her approach to others. Obtaining advice along the way, and continually practising, is an excellent way to develop skills.

In responding to defamation, practice is usually neglected entirely. Yet it is one of the most important ways of becoming more effective. Practice on one's own is useful, and even more useful is having a teacher or guide. Where better to find assistance than from one's friends?

Conclusion

Qafika needed to address a disturbing challenge: what to do about an unwelcome photo of her on the web. She could choose from a range of options, from doing nothing to suing for defamation. In each case, it's valuable to consider the options strategically, in particular to work out how John is likely to respond.

By going through several key characteristics of effective nonviolent action, it's possible to gain greater insight into what is likely to work. Many different points could be noted; three in particular are worth highlighting.

First, in cases of defamation, there is often a dilemma: in putting pressure on John to remove the photo, others may be alerted to its existence. In other words, taking action can easily make the problem worse.

Second, it is worth considering collective responses. In many cases when someone is defamed, their first thought is to make threats, especially legal threats. However, operating through the legal system restricts participation in the issue. Often the only additional people involved are lawyers. Qafika might be able to use legal threats to get the photo removed, but this does nothing about the general problem of defamation on the web. The women's movement gained great strength by women sharing their experiences, providing mutual support and taking collective action. Similarly, a collective response to abuse on the web has much greater promise than lots of separate individual responses.

Third, it is worth trying to re-establish a connection with the person making defamatory comments. Qafika broke up with John and he wanted to get back at her. In such circumstances, trying to understand John's motivations and behaviour can be a path to a more satisfactory solution than legal threats.

However, there are no guarantees. Even though there are regular patterns, cases are different. It can be valuable to use experiences of nonviolent action to give ideas for responding, but this needs to be combined with an understanding of the particular circumstances.

The story of James Lasdun

After completing a draft of this chapter, I read James Lasdun's book *Give Me Everything You Have*.[10] Lasdun is a poet and novelist who sometimes teaches creative writing. In one class he had a promising student, whom he calls Nasreen (not her actual name). A couple of years after the class, Nasreen initiated correspondence about a book she was writing, and other matters, and James was friendly and supportive, referring her to his literary agent. However, their initially cordial relationship degenerated. According to Lasdun, Nasreen became more and more demanding and, when her demands were not met, turned on James, setting out to destroy his reputation.

Initially her verbal abuse was directed only at James. He was bombarded with emails with all sorts of accusations and slurs, for example saying that he had used her ideas in his own work and attacking him for being Jewish. This was distressing enough for James. Gradually Nasreen became more hostile. Her emails were sophisticated in directing her anger: she knew how to upset James through clever references to his writings and common cultural objects.

Nasreen, as well as continuing to send abusive, upsetting emails to James every day, expanded her assault

---

10 James Lasdun, *Give Me Everything You Have: On Being Stalked* (New York: Farrar, Straus and Giroux, 2013).

on his reputation by sending emails to others in his life, making accusations against him, claiming plagiarism, sexual activity with other students and even linking him with rape. She sent emails to James' literary agent and then to staff at the school where he was working.

James' imagination began working overtime. He guessed that Nasreen might write to his publishers, for example magazine editors where his poetry and stories had appeared. But he didn't know for sure, and it would be embarrassing to raise the matter with them. If Nasreen hadn't contacted them, James would be hurting his own reputation by referring to her claims, and even if she had contacted them, how would they respond to his protestations of innocence? He realised that mud would stick.

Nasreen used various aliases to send her missives. Another target was James' online presence. Nasreen sent negative reviews to online services such as *Goodreads*.

Nasreen's assault then took on an even more sinister dimension: she began sending emails to various people that appeared to come from James. She tried to make them sound convincing yet damning.

James was confronted with a major problem, which can be broken down into three aspects. He was being harassed by the continuing abusive emails; he was being stalked, in the digital realm, with every presence of his name or work being subjected to hostile comment; and he was being defamed. Of course these three aspects overlap. Being defamed quite commonly gives rise to a feeling of being harassed.

In terms of the stalking, the advice by one of the most knowledgeable advisers about personal threats is to never give a response.[11] Even responding to one out of 20 emails can provide enough feedback to keep the stalker going strong.

James contacted the FBI and the police, hoping they would take action. Basically, they were not sufficiently interested to do very much, at least not anything effective. When, finally, Nasreen received a warning from the police, she eased off for a while, but then recommenced her email assault, including mocking references to the police threat. For James, seeking assistance from the FBI and police was an exercise in using official channels. As in so many other realms, they came up short.

Furthermore, in some ways he was worse off. The police advised him to read all of Nasreen's emails, in case there was a significant personal threat. However, this caused him continuing mental anguish. James sometimes deleted Nasreen's emails without reading them, thus destroying potential evidence. He obviously felt the choice was between deleting and reading/saving each email. There was a simple alternative: set up a filter for Nasreen's email address, sending all her missives to a special folder. This way James could save all her emails and only have to read, or even know about, ones in which she used a new alias. The police might have felt obliged to tell James to read all the emails but, in practical terms, if she had sent a hundred or a thousand emails and posed no physical threat to James, surely there was no need to read the next hundred or thousand.

---

11 Gavin de Becker, *The Gift of Fear: Survival Signals that Protect Us from Violence* (London: Bloomsbury, 1997).

After Nasreen sent emails to James' workplace, his supervisor came to talk to him about it. James felt his worse fears had come true (though worse was to come). He felt compelled to tell others at the school what was going on, and to his surprise received an outpouring of support. This confirms the value of the strategy of building support. There is power in numbers, if only to provide moral support. Although James feared that dirt would stick and that telling others might make things worse for him, actually it turned out to be one of the best things he did.

Because his online presence was being tarnished by Nasreen's unrelenting campaign to destroy his reputation, James responded by making complaints about posts attacking his books, and often the posts were taken down, usually after a delay. He also undertook a more positive action: setting up his own website. Finally, he decided to embrace the issue that was taking over his life, and write a book about it. Much of *Give Me Everything You Have* is about his interactions with Nasreen, especially her emails and his responses. But the book is more than a chronicle of how a berserk former student harassed him electronically. James devotes much of the book to a deep reflection on his thoughts and experiences, probing his connection with Nasreen through psychological and cultural realms, with commentary on trips he made to New Mexico and to Israel, pilgrimages that provided opportunities for thinking through his circumstances and the meaning of his life. In making his book so broad and deep, James demonstrates his capacity as a writer and his thoughtfulness. Because of the subject matter — the story of being stalked — the book will attract a different readership than his poetry and novels, and may well increase his visibility. It is a nice example of how to turn an attack into a positive.

Appendix: being defamed on the Internet

To learn about how to respond to defamation, a seemingly obvious first stop would be writings about defamation. However, most of the legal writing about defamation gives little or no guidance about what to do if you've been defamed. Instead, this body of writing focuses on laws, judicial interpretations, law reform and prominent cases.

The writings that have especially interested me deal with threats to free speech by the use of defamation law, for example to threaten to sue citizens who protest against property developments or police misconduct.[12] On the practical side, there are some useful guides for journalists on how to avoid being sued for defamation.[13]

A lot of this writing is fascinating, but it's not helpful to someone like Qafika. When she contacted me, I knew of nothing that gave advice for a low-profile defamation case, especially for someone without an ample supply of spare cash to pay lawyers.

Unfortunately there are many other stories like Qafika's, many of them much worse than hers. There is a type of harassment called "revenge porn" in which

---

12 George Pring and Penelope Canan, *SLAPPs: Getting Sued for Speaking Out* (Philadelphia: Temple University Press, 1996).

13 Mark Pearson, *Blogging & Tweeting without Getting Sued: A Global Guide to the Law for Anyone Writing Online* (Sydney: Allen & Unwin, 2012).

individuals — usually former lovers — post or circulate compromising or embarrassing images of others. These images might be posted online or circulated via social media. They can include photos or film clips of the target naked, engaging in intercourse or other activities. Some of these images were taken with agreement but used without permission; others were taken covertly.

Revenge porn is a type of cyber harassment, which means harassment carried out via online means;[14] it can sometimes be combined with other sorts of harassment, such as verbal taunts, pictures posted at work and physical assault. Cyber harassment can be especially difficult to handle, because harassers can operate at a distance and anonymously, and because images can be difficult to remove. If someone calls you a name, bumps into you, knocks over your bag or lets out the air from your car tyres, there is seldom any permanent record. You can be psychologically affected, but outward appearances return to normal. A photo online is like a constant sore, equivalent to a photo near your workplace or home that you cannot remove.

There have been some moves in parts of the US to pass laws to deal with revenge porn, which is an indication that defamation laws are inadequate to the task. However, it is unlikely that laws will be an effective remedy, certainly not for everyone, given the cost, delay and ineffectiveness of legal action in many circumstances.

---

14 Paul Bocij, *Cyberstalking: Harassment in the Internet Age and How to Protect Your Family* (Westport, CT: Praeger, 2004).

Cyber harassment is related to hate speech, which is usually described as speech targeting individuals or groups on the basis of their ethnicity, religion or nationality. An excellent treatment of the problem of hate speech online is the book *Viral Hate* by Abraham Foxman and Christopher Wolf.[15] The authors are involved with the Anti-Defamation League in the US and are especially concerned about anti-Semitism, but also with other forms of hate speech. They describe the problem on online hate speech and examine several remedies. They conclude that the obvious methods — passing laws and enforcing them, or complaining to Internet service providers — have serious limits. They therefore recommend different strategies, especially counter-speech and education, plus liaising with online administering organisations to develop cooperative approaches.

In agreement with my assessment that laws and other official channels are not an effective way of dealing with defamation, Foxman and Wolf state:

> ... this argument about self-governance [using education to strengthen commitments to democracy] reinforces our conviction that laws attempting to prohibit hate speech are probably one of the weakest tools we can use against bigotry. There's no question that hate speech, which includes threats, harassment, incitements to violence, and other criminal actions unprotected by the First Amendment, should be

---

15 Abraham H. Foxman and Christopher Wolf, *Viral Hate: Containing its Spread on the Internet* (New York: Palgrave Macmillan, 2013).

subject to legal sanction. But broader regulation of hate speech may send an "educational message" that actually weakens rather than strengthens our system of democratic values.[16]

Cyber harassment can also be treated as a special type of bullying or mobbing (mobbing is collective bullying). There is plenty of writing about bullying, especially in schools and workplaces.[17] However, only some of it is practical in orientation, and much of it assumes the existence of authorities, such as school principals, bosses or government agencies, that will address the problem. There is much to be learned from studies of bullying, but little that can be applied to Qafika's problem. For example, one recommendation for targets of workplace bullying is to find another job. Another is to develop skills to counter or avoid bullying behaviours. Yet another is to file a formal complaint. These all have parallels in cyber bullying, but have limita-

---

16 Ibid., 171.

17 On workplace bullying see for example Andrea Adams with contributions from Neil Crawford, *Bullying at Work: How to Confront and Overcome It* (London: Virago, 1992); Carol Elbing and Alvar Elbing, *Militant Managers: How to Spot ... How to Work with ... How to Manage ... Your Highly Aggressive Boss* (Burr Ridge, IL: Irwin Professional Publishing, 1994); Susan Marais and Magriet Herman, *Corporate Hyenas at Work: How to Spot and Outwit Them by Being Hyenawise* (Pretoria, South Africa: Kagiso, 1997); Judith Wyatt and Chauncey Hare, *Work Abuse: How to Recognize and Survive It* (Rochester, VT: Schenkman Books, 1997).

tions for cases in which images cannot be easily blocked and the person who posted them is in another part of the world, or even anonymous.

There is a considerable body of writing, both academic and popular, about people with challenging behaviours, including psychopaths, narcissists and other personality types. Some of those who engage in cyber harassment may fit these categories. For me, one of the most insightful treatments is George K. Simon, Jr.'s book *In Sheep's Clothing: Understanding and Dealing with Manipulative People*.[18] Simon's key insight is that traditional psychological frameworks are not relevant for understanding many people today, because genuine neurosis is quite uncommon. The changing structure of society and loosening of constraints mean that the more common source of problems is what Simon calls "character disorders" such as narcissism and aggression. These people aren't inhibited enough: they know what they want and they don't care about hurting others to get it. Simon identifies a new psychological type, in the spectrum of character disorders: covert aggressors. These people use manipulation to get their way. The key is to understand that covert aggressors exist and to deal with their behaviours, not their motivations.

According to Simon, covertly aggressive personalities typically believe everything is a battle and they always have to win; furthermore, they fight unfairly, have a sense

---

18 George K. Simon, Jr., *In Sheep's Clothing: Understanding and Dealing with Manipulative People* (Little Rock, AR: Parkhurst Brothers, 2010).

of entitlement but little empathy or respect, and are willing to exploit the vulnerabilities of others. He recommends dealing with covert aggressors by preventing them from setting the terms of engagement. He advises

- get rid of misconceptions
- become a better judge of character
- understand yourself better, including vulnerabilities such as over-conscientiousness, low self-confidence, over-thinking and emotional dependency
- know the other's tactics
- don't fight losing battles
- change your own behaviour

Simon's approach is compatible with one inspired by nonviolent action. He recommends making direct requests and demanding direct responses, but also avoiding being sarcastic or hostile or making threats. In essence, he advises an informed strategy of assertion.

The most entertaining treatment of online attacks is Jon Ronson's *So You've Been Publicly Shamed*.[19] Ronson interviewed individuals who became targets of massive online abuse, in some cases for minor transgressions. His book highlights the enormous challenge in responding to online shaming. For a readable and insightful personal account by a political scientist who became such a target, see Tom Flanagan's *Persona Non Grata*.[20]

---

19 Jon Ronson, *So You've Been Publicly Shamed* (London: Picador, 2015).

20 Tom Flanagan, *Persona Non Grata: The Death of Free Speech in the Internet Age* (Toronto: McClelland & Stewart, 2014).

7
Euthanasia struggles

Claire had pancreatic cancer, with secondary cancers throughout her body. She had been given three months to live, and each week was less pleasant, with pain and nausea. Claire wanted the option of ending her life when she wanted, before her suffering became too severe. She wanted to go peacefully. She knew she could hang herself, or jump off a tall building, or jump in front of a train. But these options meant she couldn't be with her family when she died, and these methods could traumatise others. However, peaceful options to end her life were limited. It used to be that drug overdoses were a way of committing suicide, but all the drugs that could do this reliably — such as the sleeping pills used by Marilyn Monroe — have been taken off the market.

One drug is widely preferred as a peaceful road to death: pentobarbital, commonly known as Nembutal. It is used by veterinarians, but in most countries it is not available for sale to the public.

Claire would have liked easy access to Nembutal, as a drink, so she could take some and die peacefully in the presence of her closest family and friends. But Claire lived in Australia, where it is illegal for anyone to help someone to die.

Claire's case is a typical one used by advocates of voluntary euthanasia. The word euthanasia literally means "good death." It is now used to describe ending a life to reduce intolerable suffering.

However, there's a danger: someone's life might be ended when actually they wanted to keep living. This would be called involuntary euthanasia. There is no choice involved.

Sometimes people aren't able to express a choice because they are so incapacitated they cannot communicate or comprehend what is going on. Nevertheless, it might be obvious to others that they are suffering extremely and have no hope of recovery, so dying seems to be in their best interests. However, allowing others to decide in such circumstances appears to open the door to involuntary euthanasia that the person would not want.

The word euthanasia acquired strong negative connotations after World War II. In 1939, at the beginning of the war, the Nazis instituted a policy of killing people with mental or intellectual disabilities who resided in institutions. Today often called the T4 programme after the agency in charge, it was termed by the Nazis a programme of "euthanasia" as a way of disguising its actual operation, which involved cold-blooded murder by doctors.[1] After the war, the word "euthanasia" was tainted. The word

---

1 Michael Burleigh, *Death and Deliverance: "Euthanasia" in Germany 1900–1945* (Cambridge: Cambridge University Press, 1994); Henry Friedlander, *The Origins of Nazi Genocide: From Euthanasia to the Final Solution* (Chapel Hill, NC: University of North Carolina Press, 1995); Hugh Gregory Gallagher, *By Trust Betrayed: Patients, Physicians, and the License to Kill in the Third Reich* (Arlington, VA: Vandamere Press, 1995).

continues to have an ambiguity about whether death is voluntary or not, so advocates commonly used the label "voluntary euthanasia." Today, most organisations in favour of voluntary euthanasia have dropped the word altogether in preference for names like "Dying with Dignity."

Proponents of the option of voluntary euthanasia say it is humane — a way to end unnecessary suffering. Many opponents say euthanasia is morally wrong: no one should be allowed to end their life through their own agency. Opponents argue that legalising euthanasia, even with safeguards, will open the door to the risk of involuntary euthanasia. Opponents want to prevent the possibility of abuses by banning euthanasia in any circumstances.[2]

There are many strands to the debate.[3] Opponents say it is unnecessary to allow voluntary euthanasia because good palliative care can reduce most pain and suffering. Advocates counter by saying pain relief does not work for

---

[2] David Jeffrey, *Against Physician Assisted Suicide: A Palliative Care Perspective* (Oxford: Radcliffe, 2009); William J. Smith, *Forced Exit: The Slippery Slope from Assisted Suicide to Legalized Murder* (New York: Times Books, 1997); Margaret Somerville, *Death Talk: The Case against Euthanasia and Physician-Assisted Suicide* (Montreal: McGill-Queen's University Press, 2001).

[3] For analyses of the debate, see Megan-Jane Johnstone, *Alzheimer's Disease, Media Representations and the Politics of Euthanasia: Constructing Risk and Selling Death in an Ageing Society* (Farnham, Surrey: Ashgate, 2013); W. Siu, "Communities of interpretation: euthanasia and assisted suicide debate," *Critical Public Health,* vol. 20, 2010, pp. 169–199.

all conditions and that there are other forms of suffering, for example due to loss of autonomy and dignity, that palliative care cannot fully address.

The push to legalise voluntary euthanasia has been driven, to a considerable extent, by advances in medicine. A century ago, a person with a serious disease usually died at home, with minimal medical intervention. Today, in some countries the majority of people die in hospitals, often in intensive care units. Patients can be kept alive with the aid of remarkable techniques and technologies, including defibrillators, respirators and feeding tubes. The result is that many have their lives extended far more than in previous eras, by months and sometimes years — but in a highly dependent state. For some patients, this is a living death, a state of existence they abhor yet cannot easily escape.

It is not so long ago that suicide was illegal in many countries. People who ended their own lives might be refused church burials, and their families would be humiliated. If they survived a suicide attempt, they could be imprisoned or confined to a mental asylum.

Religious prohibitions against suicide made more sense in times when community solidarity was more important than individual dignity, and when death usually came swiftly, often through diseases such as pneumonia. Cancer was seldom the cause of death.

On the other hand, the breakdown of traditional communities and the rise of individualism have meant increased concern for human rights. In previous eras, newborn children with disabilities were often left to die; today, in many circumstances, parents and doctors make heroic efforts to enable survival and a high quality of life. Euthanasia has a dark history of ties with eugenics, a philosophy and practice of preventing the weak and infirm from having children while encouraging reproduction by those supposedly of the best genetic stock. Eugenics today is largely discredited in most public discourse, yet its underlying ideas still have currency. Legalising euthanasia can bring the spectre of a new application of the idea of culling those who are a burden on society, through their lack of productivity or their poor genes.

One of the arguments against legalising euthanasia is that some people who are ill or infirm will feel they are a burden on society and prefer to die, even though their lives have value to themselves and others. Making it easier to die peacefully could encourage such individuals to claim they are suffering in order to obtain the means to die. Furthermore, some vulnerable people might be encouraged to think this way by greedy relatives.

On the other hand, even without legalisation, euthanasia occurs in practice, usually covertly. Patients who desire death may find an accommodating doctor who can give them drugs to hasten their death. Then there are cases in which doctors make decisions to end a person's life, by withholding treatment, giving more drugs than necessary or even by blunt means such as suffocation with a pillow. In most of such cases, the patient is incapable of giving consent, being unable to communicate or comprehend simple ideas. The doctor judges that the quality of the patient's life is so low that death is a form of deliverance; this is mercy killing in the classic sense. Unfortunately, some of the covert cases can be classified as involuntary euthanasia: the patient is capable of giving or rejecting consent, but the doctor does not seek consent.

For obvious reasons, doctors seldom reveal their involvement in this sort of euthanasia; knowledge that it occurs owes much to a few researchers and outspoken doctors and to surveys in which doctors remain anonymous.[4] Covert euthanasia is fraught with dangers because the doctors may have little experience in assisting death, and secrecy can hide incompetence and abuse. Legalising euthanasia would make many instances of this sort of covert euthanasia unnecessary, as well as ensuring that high standards are maintained in prescribing drugs to end life. Opponents of legalisation almost never refer to covert euthanasia, as it undermines one of their key arguments, the slippery slope, namely that legalisation opens the door to serious abuses. If such abuses are occurring already, and made worse by the secrecy that is necessary to avoid prosecution, then legalisation makes more sense.

Strategies

There are two potential injustices at stake in the euthanasia debate. On the one side is involuntary euthanasia: the killing of a person whose life is worth living and who has not given informed consent. On the other side might be called involuntary life: the refusal to allow a person who

---

4 Roger S. Magnusson, *Angels of Death: Exploring the Euthanasia Underground* (Melbourne: Melbourne University Press, 2002); Clive Seale, "Hastening death in end-of-life care: a survey of doctors," *Social Science & Medicine,* vol. 69, 2009, pp. 1659–1666.

wants to die access to the means to do so in a peaceful way. Some people would consider that not allowing voluntary euthanasia is a form of violence, because it prolongs suffering unnecessarily. Here I'm going to focus primarily on this second injustice. I'll first outline the main strategies of the movement for voluntary euthanasia to achieve law reform, and then consider an alternative, promoting the means for self-deliverance.[5] In each case there are possibilities for using nonviolent action, in its traditional forms, as well as using tactics that follow the spirit of nonviolent action but are adapted for an arena in which the main methods used do not involve physical violence in its usual sense.

Voluntary euthanasia groups have mainly sought to change the law so that it becomes legal to end one's life peacefully. This approach has had success in some parts of the world. In the Netherlands, initial change came through court rulings: in specified circumstances, physicians who

---

5 On the movement for voluntary euthanasia, see especially Richard N. Côté, *In Search of Gentle Death: The Fight for Your Right to Die with Dignity* (Mt. Pleasant, SC: Corinthian Books, 2012). See also Ian Dowbiggin, *A Merciful End: The Euthanasia Movement in Modern America* (New York: Oxford University Press, 2003); Daniel Hillyard and John Dombrink, *Dying Right: The Death with Dignity Movement* (New York: Routledge, 2001); Derek Humphry and Mary Clement, *Freedom to Die: People, Politics, and the Right-to-Die Movement* (New York: St. Martin's Griffin, 2000); Fran McInerney, "'Requested death': a new social movement," *Social Science & Medicine,* vol. 50, 2000, pp. 137–154; Sue Woodman, *Last Rights: The Struggle over the Right to Die* (Cambridge, MA: Perseus, 1998).

helped patients to die were exempt from prosecution. Later the law was changed. Physicians in the Netherlands, by following suitable protocols, can legally give their patients lethal injections, in what is called active euthanasia.

The US state of Oregon introduced a somewhat different approach. Following a referendum, and various appeals, a law was passed allowing physicians to provide drugs to patients who satisfied certain conditions, including being terminally ill and desiring a peaceful death. Physicians can prescribe the drugs, but only the patients can take them, in a process commonly called physician-assisted suicide or physician aid in dying. The words suicide and euthanasia are not part of the Oregon law.

Other places where euthanasia is either legal or where there is no law against it include Belgium, Colombia, Luxembourg, Switzerland and several other US states. In most of these places, only residents can access the legal provisions for peaceful death. In Switzerland, though, it is possible for visitors to legally obtain the means to end their lives peacefully, subject to conditions.

Much writing about euthanasia is about ethical considerations. Another major topic is legal aspects of the issue. Here, my focus is on strategy and tactics. I won't be addressing arguments about whether euthanasia is ethical or should be legalised. All that matters is that significant numbers of people believe in the right to die peacefully, and that on the other side of the debate significant numbers of people oppose anyone being able to have their life ended earlier than what would happen via natural processes.

So to begin. For those supporting access to voluntary euthanasia, who live in countries where this is illegal, how should they proceed? The standard approach by most organisations supporting voluntary euthanasia is to push for legalisation. This is done through lobbying politicians and through publicity and education to change public opinion, with public pressure then used to influence politicians. In some countries it is possible for referendums to be held, and these can be used as vehicles to push for legalisation.

In many countries, public opinion is strongly in favour of access to voluntary euthanasia. Figures of 70% in support are commonly cited.[6] However, on this issue public support rarely translates into political action. Many politicians are reluctant to vote for legalisation because of organised opposition, especially by religious groups.

Traditional forms of nonviolent action are possible. Campaigners can hold rallies and marches. They can hold vigils outside the offices of politicians. In systems of representative government, these are well-established means of political protest. They can be powerful, but they do not push very far beyond the normal political boundaries.

The two main forms of noncooperation are strikes and boycotts. But who is going to go on strike, and what is going to be boycotted? Bringing up the idea of strikes and boycotts points to the difference between the euthanasia issue and struggles against repressive governments or powerful corporations. In a campaign against a powerful and damaging corporation, workers can go on strike and

---

6 See figures cited in Côté, *In Search of Gentle Death*.

consumers can boycott products. Alternatively, the corporation's suppliers or buyers can be targeted via strikes and boycotts. In the case of voluntary euthanasia, the obstacle is supply of a product, namely drugs to enable a peaceful death, or a service, doctors to obtain and prescribe the drugs. Going on strike is not an obvious option, because the goal is the supply of drugs, not interrupting it. The companies that produce Nembutal are not the obstacle: they would be happy to sell the drug; indeed, they sell it to veterinarians. This is not a big industry. Even where euthanasia is legal, the market is small, because any individual needs only one dose of the drugs. Each person dies just once, so repeat prescriptions are not needed, unlike billion-dollar markets for drugs for high blood pressure, arthritis and other chronic conditions. To put it crudely, the business of helping people to end their lives operates in a self-limiting market, whereas extending people's lives offers the possibility of continued sales. This means the market stake in peaceful dying is relatively small. Governments receive negligible revenue from taxes on end-of-life drugs, and few workers are involved.

This means thinking about noncooperation options needs to explore other directions. One possibility is doctors, who have access to means for peaceful death, namely certain drugs. Many doctors assist patients to die, out of compassion, but nearly always this is done covertly, to avoid legal consequences. A doctor can undertake an act of civil disobedience by openly providing a patient with drugs to enable peaceful death. Rodney Syme, a urologist in Melbourne, did just this. In his book *A Good Death,* he tells about his gradual increase in awareness due to encountering patients with terminal diseases and with severe suffering not eased by conventional palliative measures. He began his journey by covertly supplying death-enabling drugs to one patient, and then to another. As his willingness to help became known, more patients came to him for assistance.[7]

Syme sent information to the coroner about his participation in terminal sedation — a common practice with no legal basis — seeking to provoke authorities into making an open declaration about it. If authorities took action against him, this would publicise the issue and probably make Syme a martyr for the cause; if they stated they would not take action, they would set a precedent for others to follow. In this dilemma, the authorities, instead of acting, did nothing, leaving Syme's position in limbo. Syme was not charged with any crime, but neither was there any official statement.

In April 2014, Syme openly admitted supplying Nembutal to a man named Steve Guest, arguing that this was for palliation and was not for the purposes of suicide. Syme aimed to demonstrate that laws addressing medical acts near the end of life were ambiguous and inadequate.[8]

Syme's actions were a form of nonviolent action. However, only a few others could participate in this type of action, namely doctors, and few were prepared to join Syme in openly declaring their involvement. The reason is

---

7 Rodney Syme, *A Good Death: An Argument for Voluntary Euthanasia* (Melbourne: Melbourne University Press, 2008).

8 Julia Medew, "Lifting the lid on a crime of mercy," *The Age* (Melbourne), 28 April 2014, p. 12.

that this was a high-risk form of action, with possible penalties including deregistration and years or decades in prison. Few doctors were willing to risk ending their careers on this issue. If hundreds or thousands of doctors had joined Syme, the consequences would have been dramatic, either the spectre of prosecuting a huge number of doctors or, more probably, the failure to prosecute any of them, resulting in a de facto legitimation of physician-assisted peaceful death.

In September 2014, several doctors in Melbourne spoke to the media, telling about their assistance in helping patients — or in one case the doctor's own mother — to die. Two of them courageously gave their names: Simon Benson and Peter Valentine. The article about their actions mentioned that covert assistance in dying is probably widespread, but has dangers due to being unregulated.[9]

In summary, assisting others to die, and then openly admitting it, is a form of civil disobedience that is potentially potent but has two inherent limits. The first is that only doctors (and perhaps a few others) can participate, and the second that the high risk means only a few of them actually do.

Syme was exceedingly cautious in his actions and his advocacy. Through his experiences with suffering patients, he gradually expanded his view of the circumstances in which he considered it ethical to supply drugs by which patients could end their lives. He approached authorities to clarify the legal status of his actions. Only

---

9 Julia Medew, "Don't-tell doctors supporting secret euthanasia deaths," *The Age* (Melbourne), 7 September 2014.

when this failed to produce a result did he go further by revealing his position to a public audience. In his quiet, compassionate and considered approach, he followed a trajectory that can be likened to Gandhi's approach of first respectfully engaging with authorities to seek a resolution before initiating nonviolent action to create the conditions to enable dialogue.

Kevorkian

The most prominent — or notorious — physician-activist is Jack Kevorkian, who is quite a contrast to Rodney Syme. Based in the US, Kevorkian developed a machine to enable patients seeking death to end their lives. Rather than gradually nudging the authorities, Kevorkian confronted them head-on, pushing the boundaries of ethics and legality.[10]

Kevorkian enabled over a hundred individuals to end their lives. From the beginning, he was a vocal advocate of voluntary euthanasia. With his repeated uses of his technology, he dared authorities to take action; his aim was to challenge laws against voluntary euthanasia. On several occasions, he was arrested and charged with murder, but was found not guilty despite his penchant for flouting legal procedure and frustrating his legal team. Eventually he overreached. He video-recorded his actions ending the life of a patient and challenged authorities to

---

10 Neal Nicol and Harry Wylie, *Between the Dying and the Dead: Dr Jack Kevorkian, the Assisted Suicide Machine and the Battle to Legalise Euthanasia* (London: Vision, 2006).

act. They did. He was convicted of murder and sentenced to prison.

Kevorkian was in such a rush to push the boundaries, and to make a name for himself, that he made mistakes. He did not always seek sufficient information about the condition of his patients, and therefore was not always absolutely sure their diseases were terminal. In the case that led to his imprisonment, he did not take sufficient care to obtain informed consent.

In terms of nonviolent action, Kevorkian's actions in helping people die might be considered direct action or even a form of civil disobedience. Even when his actions were legal, he was confronting current ethical norms, so his "disobedience" was as much to expectations of acceptable behaviour as to laws. However, by pushing the boundaries of acceptable behaviour, Kevorkian took the risk of perpetrating an injustice himself: involuntary euthanasia.

An analogy to nonviolent action might be environmental activists who sabotage equipment to prevent and disrupt forestry operations.[11] Examples are putting sand in the fuel tank of a tractor, pulling up survey stakes and hammering stakes into trees. In this sort of "ecotage," care is taken to avoid harming humans. After putting metal or ceramic stakes into trees, companies are informed of the action to discourage them from logging: the stake can cause sawmill blades to break, a costly process. There is also another risk: a sawmill blade might break and injure a worker. This could happen because the message about

---

11 This was discussed earlier in chapter 2.

staking the trees was not conveyed to the right people, or was incorrect or not taken seriously. Because there is a potential risk of hurting workers, many environmentalists advise against staking. Although the danger is small, a single incident harming a worker could seriously discredit the movement.

Kevorkian can be likened to an environmentalist who takes risks. Although most of the people he helped to die were grateful, it required only a single case of inadequate informed consent for his activities to be judged as murder.

There is much commentary about Kevorkian, including both praise and condemnation. My aim here is not to pass judgement on his actions, but to draw an analogy with nonviolent action. His case shows the risk of going too far — too far in the direction of a different injustice. This is an important point, so it is worth making additional comparisons. In a rally, protesters can harm their case by using even a little violence, such as throwing stones at police. This often legitimises police violence, which is typically much greater. A nonviolent protest in which police use violence is one-sided: the police are causing harm, but no physical harm is being done to them, so witnesses commonly see this as unjust, generating greater sympathy and support for the protesters. As soon as the protesters use violence, no matter how slight, there is a perception of a double injustice: violence against protesters and violence against police. The asymmetry is broken and some of the sympathy for the protesters may be lost.

Kevorkian, by assisting suffering patients to die, was seen by many as serving their interests. Actions taken against him — criminal charges — seemed to many as unfair: he was charged with murder for helping doing what people wanted, namely end their suffering. Of course many opposed Kevorkian because they opposed any intervention to shorten a person's life, no matter what the circumstances. Kevorkian, no matter how careful, was never going to win them over. Similarly, protesters are unlikely to win over members of the public who oppose their cause, or oppose any sort of public protest.

Kevorkian went too far when he was not sufficiently careful in obtaining informed consent. Even if he obtained informed consent in nearly every case, but failed in a single case, the single case would be used against him. This is analogous to protesters who remain resolutely peaceful except for one departure, when a single protester throws a stone. The single departure can be the basis for condemnation. Kevorkian pushed the boundary and paid the penalty. The difference between his action and the protesters is the nature of the boundary. In the case of the protesters, the boundary is between the absence and presence of physical violence. In the case of Kevorkian, the boundary was between voluntary and involuntary euthanasia or, more bluntly, between helping people and harming them.

Kevorkian's story provides a valuable lesson for advocates of voluntary euthanasia. It is exceedingly important to avoid any harm, even though the harm might be small compared to the good. Some might argue that an occasional case in which full consent is not obtained is a minor concern compared to the suffering that is ended in numerous cases. This would be like arguing that a bit of protester violence is not significant compared to the much greater police violence. The trouble is that this moral calculus is not the basis for people's reactions. Just as opponents of the protesters will use a slight bit of violence to condemn the protesters and their cause, so will opponents of euthanasia use any case where consent has not been fully obtained to condemn euthanasia generally.

Self-deliverance

In 1996, voluntary euthanasia became legal in Australia's Northern Territory. Australia is a federation of six states and two territories, one of which, the Northern Territory, covers a huge area with a relatively small population of 200,000. This was the unexpected context for the world's first voluntary euthanasia law, made possible by the commitment of a few individuals, especially the territory's chief minister Marshall Perron.

There was a hitch. Any person seeking to end their lives peacefully had to find three doctors who would vouch that the conditions of the new law were satisfied — including one doctor to certify the person was dying and a psychiatrist to say that the person did not have treatable depression. Because no doctors volunteered, Philip Nitschke decided to become involved. He had had no prior involvement with euthanasia issues, but if no one else would help individuals in need, he would. Nitschke had a prior record as an outspoken doctor, for example speaking out about radiation risks from visiting nuclear warships.[12]

---

12 Philip Nitschke and Fiona Stewart, *Killing Me Softly: Voluntary Euthanasia and the Road to the Peaceful Pill* (Melbourne: Penguin, 2005); Philip Nitschke with Peter Corris,

Taking the initiative, Nitschke found 22 doctors willing to publicly support the new law. Nitschke then designed a computer system to allow the patient to make all the decisions. Nitschke would insert a line into the patient's arm to deliver life-ending drugs. Then, on the computer screen, a series of questions would appear. If the patient provided their consent at this point, giving the go-ahead, the drugs would automatically be administered. Nitschke did not even need to be present.

The first person seeking to take advantage of the law was Max Bell, a taxi driver with stomach cancer. Nitschke needed to find three other doctors — a surgeon, a palliative care specialist and a psychiatrist — willing to say that Max was dying, had had palliative care options explained, and was sane. But no doctors were willing to step forward. Max died the death he had feared, but not in vain: his ordeal travelling to Darwin was filmed, and the resulting national television show was powerful, inducing some doctors to agree to sign the required forms the next time around.[13] Eventually four patients took advantage of the law.

Meanwhile, politicians in Canberra, the national capital, were disturbed by the law. Many of them opposed euthanasia. The Northern Territory, as a territory, was subject to federal control. Soon a bill was drafted to overrule the Northern Territory law, and federal politicians passed it. After only nine months, the Northern

---

Damned If I Do (Melbourne: Melbourne University Press, 2013).

13 Nitschke and Stewart, *Killing Me Softly,* 39–42; Nitschke, *Damned If I Do,* 85–88.

Territory's experiment with voluntary euthanasia was over.

This experience transformed Nitschke. He became committed to helping terminally ill people end their suffering and was convinced that the usual approach of voluntary euthanasia groups, namely to push for law reform, was too weak and too slow. Nitschke turned to a different approach: providing people with the tools to end their own lives peacefully, without requiring the approval of politicians or doctors.

This ideal he called the "peaceful pill." He imagined developing a pill that people could take that would end their lives in a process that would be uncomplicated, dignified, reliable, under the control of the individual, and involve no pain. The peaceful pill is a metaphor for a variety of methods that satisfy the conditions. The drug Nembutal is one option fitting the requirements: drinking just a glass of it reliably causes death, with no pain, in a matter of minutes. The drug tastes incredibly bitter, so it not likely to be taken by mistake.

However, in Australia, Nembutal cannot be obtained legally by members of the public. So Nitschke and his colleague Fiona Stewart investigated ways of obtaining it, for example travelling to Mexico and buying it at veterinary supply shops. This is quite legal, but bringing Nembutal back into Australia is against the law, though penalties are minor for the amount needed by an individual.

Another option is the exit bag. A plastic bag that fits over your head is prepared with a drawstring. A canister of nitrogen or helium is fitted with a valve to set an appropriate flow rate. With the gas continuously filling the bag, you fully exhale, pull the bag down over your head, pull the draw strap and breathe deeply. Now you're breathing only helium or nitrogen — no oxygen. Within seconds you pass out and within minutes you die. This is completely painless.

However, the helium or nitrogen needs to keep flowing to flush carbon dioxide from your exhaled breath out of the bag. If you breathe in carbon-dioxide-rich air, you will desperately gasp for breath, which is not pleasant. The exit bag, if prepared properly, fits all the criteria for a peaceful death: it is painless, reliable, and fully under the control of the individual. Although it is straightforward to obtain the necessary components and prepare an exit bag, it is a bit complicated. It is not something you would do on the spur of the moment, as you might with a gun.

One disadvantage of the exit bag is that, to many people, it seems undignified. Some people don't want a bag over their head. Furthermore, anyone who finds your body will know what you've done. However, if a friend or relative removes the bag and apparatus afterwards, no one else will know you ended your own life. If you used nitrogen, there is no test that can detect how you died. (Removing the apparatus after death could be considered interfering with a corpse, illegal in some jurisdictions.)

One advantage of the exit bag is that it is legal to buy all the components, whereas obtaining Nembutal means breaking the law, at least in a country like Australia. Even so, many people seeking a peaceful death prefer to take the financial and legal risks in obtaining Nembutal, because they prefer this method over an exit bag.

There are various other ways to end your life peacefully. Nitschke and his co-author Fiona Stewart document them in their book *The Peaceful Pill Handbook*.[14] For example, some prescription drugs can be used, but convincing a doctor to prescribe them can be a challenge. If you ask for a drug saying you want to take an overdose and die, the doctor almost certainly will refuse, and then your subsequent request will likely be treated with suspicion. Therefore, you need to be cagey, saying something like, "a friend of mine told me about a green pill that can help my severe arthritic pain." This suggests you don't know much about it. Nitschke and Stewart provide the pros and cons of various options. Nembutal and the exit bag are currently the most reliable methods.

However, circumstances keep changing. For example, whereas it used to be necessary to travel to a place like Mexico to buy Nembutal in liquid form, around 2010 supplies of powdered Nembutal from China became available via mail order. In powered form, Nembutal can be sent in an ordinary letter. However, Australian customs gradually became more alert to this possibility, so some shipments were confiscated. So there's a risk of losing your payment. However, for anyone who is suffering or who wants to be prepared for the end, the loss of a few hundred dollars is unlikely to be a serious deterrent. With the success of online ordering of Nembutal, scammers

---

14 Philip Nitschke and Fiona Stewart, *The Peaceful Pill Handbook* (Bellingham, WA: Exit International US, 2008). For the e-version, see http://www.peacefulpillhandbook.com/.

have entered the scene, collecting money from purchasers but not delivering the product.

Because options keep changing, *The Peaceful Pill Handbook* is available both in print and as an e-book, updated regularly. The book, as well as giving accounts and assessments of various end-of-life options, provides video clips showing how to construct and use an exit bag and photos of bottles of Nembutal for sale in foreign veterinary supply shops, among other information.

The Peaceful Pill Handbook is just one of several manuals of its type.[15] Others are available, usually oriented to circumstances in particular countries, such as Japan or France. These manuals are, in many cases, linked to organisations and activities to inform and campaign. For example, Nitschke set up the organisation Exit International to promote self-deliverance options. He runs workshops in Australia, England, Ireland, US and Canada, covering some of the information in *The Peaceful Pill Handbook* and responding to questions from participants. There are Exit chapters in several parts of Australia, holding meetings and providing support to members. Nitschke has also held seminars over the Internet.

One of the original aims of Exit International was to develop a "peaceful pill" that could be easily synthesised from legal substances. Nembutal is the ideal drug but it is not simple to produce from easily available chemicals, so it does not satisfy Exit's goal. However, despite the

---

15 One of the classics is Derek Humphry, *Final Exit: The Practicalities of Self-deliverance and Assisted Suicide for the Dying,* 3rd edition (New York: Dell, 2002).

participation of some chemists, Exit has not been able to develop its ideal peaceful pill — at least not yet. Whether such a pill would be beneficial for the cause of peaceful death is another question.

One of the prime objections to legalising euthanasia is that this will lead down a slippery slope to abuses. One danger is an increase in involuntary euthanasia, namely killing of people who might prefer to remain alive, especially those most vulnerable, such as people with disabilities. Experiences in places where euthanasia is legal, such as the Netherlands and Oregon, provide little support for this possibility, though the matter is contested.[16] Nevertheless, the possibility of involuntary euthanasia is an important risk that proponents of voluntary euthanasia need to address.

The road of self-deliverance has another danger: if means for peaceful death are readily available, this might lead to more people committing suicide, including people whose mental and physical suffering is only temporary or can be ameliorated. So far, this risk seems small: very few of those attending Nitschke's workshops are young. The initial part of his workshop, where he tells about the issues generally, is open to the public. Attendance at the second

---

16 See for example Margaret P. Battin et al., "Legal physician-assisted dying in Oregon and the Netherlands: evidence concerning the impact on patients in 'vulnerable' groups," *Journal of Medical Ethics,* vol. 33, 2007, pp. 591–597; Penney Lewis, "The empirical slippery slope from voluntary to nonvoluntary euthanasia," *Journal of Law, Medicine & Ethics,* vol. 35, 2007, pp. 197–210.

part requires joining Exit and signing a statement. Participants must be over 50 years of age. In the second part, Nitschke covers material available in *The Peaceful Pill Handbook* and answers questions about it, with the aim of providing accurate information that participants can use to make their own decisions. The workshops neither encourage nor discourage ending one's life.

The precautions are necessary for two reasons. The immediate one is that the Australian government has strict laws against providing information about ending one's life peacefully. Regardless of the law, it might seem inappropriate to be providing this information to young, healthy individuals who are at risk of suicide. Participants in Exit workshops are expected to disclose psychiatric illnesses and, when they do, may be excluded from participation to prevent information being used inappropriately.

However, few young, healthy individuals seem to have any interest in end-of-life options. Even for the first, open part of Exit workshops, very few attendees are under 50 and the average age is probably close to 75.

For people who want to know how to end their lives peacefully, the most common motivation is to prevent unnecessary suffering. Some of those attending are ill, most commonly with cancer, and fear the pain, discomfort and indignity of the final days or weeks. They would like to have the option of going when they are ready. A number of observers suggest that when terminally ill individuals have access to means to end their lives peacefully, they actually live longer, because they know they can end their suffering at any time, if needed.[17] Those without this option may resort to harsher means, such as hanging or drug overdoses, at an earlier time.

Some attendees are healthy but at an age with a limited life expectancy. At age 90, life expectancy is less than 10 years. For those with chronic conditions, such as diabetes or heart arrhythmia, the precariousness of life is apparent daily. They want to be prepared.

Even in places where euthanasia is legal, some individuals may seek their own independent access to means to end their lives. The reason is that the legal requirements to access physician aid in dying may be too onerous for some. A typical requirement is that the requester needs to have a terminal illness with less than six months to live. However, there are some individuals with chronic conditions that cause them extreme suffering but are not life threatening. One case is intractable pain.

Nitschke gradually became sensitised to cases that pushed the boundaries of peaceful death. A key case was Lisette Nigot, a woman in her 70s who was in good health but had decided she had had enough of life. She had done everything she wanted to do and didn't want to live past 80. Nitschke initially refused to help her, thinking this was beyond the bounds of acceptability. Nigot chastised him for his intransigence and inconsistency. If he was seeking to enable people to make decisions to end their suffering, why did he restrict himself to suffering caused by physical conditions and not consider existential suffering?

---

17 Côte, *In Search of Gentle Death*, 210.

Another way to look at this situation to consider the situation of a person who is rationally planning to end their life, not due to depression or a sudden rush of emotion. If a person's desire to die is carefully considered and planned over a lengthy period, there are seldom any obstacles to ending life, assuming some degree of agency. For example, it would be possible to go to the top of a tall building and jump off. Guns and rope provide other means. However, a considerate plan to end one's life takes into account the effect on others, and violent means are usually distressing to others, for example the person who discovers the body. In such circumstances, a request to access means for peaceful dying can seem entirely rational.

If it is considered reasonable, indeed compassionate, to enable Lisette Nigot to end her life peacefully, what is to stop extending the opportunities? Perhaps younger people who are tired of life should have access to assistance in dying. There can be convincing examples, but addressing them involves entering a boundary area where the risks are higher of enabling someone to die who might, on reflection, have preferred not to. This of course is a long-standing rationale for suicide-prevention programmes. Many people who attempt to end their lives are in the midst of depression. With suitable social support, and the passing of time, they may think life is worth living. The point is that these suicide attempts are driven by emotion, usually by extreme psychological distress, rather than a calm, rational consideration of options. Furthermore, these attempts are commonly by people who have — from the perspective of others — prospects for a productive, satisfying life. As such, their circumstances are quite different from those with serious illnesses with little or no prospect of improvement.

This line of thought can lead to several possible conclusions concerning the availability of means for peaceful death. One conclusion is that these means should be illegal or unavailable: by banning these means, fewer people will end their lives prematurely. Another possible conclusion is that extra care is needed to ensure that the means for peaceful death are only available to those who qualify, by some criteria, for this option. This conclusion usually takes the form of arguing for legalisation of assistance in dying, with strict controls, such as having a terminal disease, approval by doctors, and a waiting period. However, this approach, which is standard in places where voluntary euthanasia is not illegal, rules out access by people such as Nigot.

Another conclusion is that anyone should have access to the means for peaceful death, but in a context in which there is considerable social support for people in distress, and where suicide-prevention measures are well supported. In this model, self-deliverance is an option that is only likely to be taken up by those who rationally want to end their lives. It is analogous to the present situation concerning violent suicide. The means for violent suicide are readily available: guns, rope, tall buildings, trains and buses. Making available self-deliverance options would not, according to this line of thinking, do much to encourage suicide among those whose life has potential, because they have plenty of options already.

Another line of thought is that the strictures against peaceful dying are excessive given the ready availability of means for violent death. A society that wanted to be effective in reducing suicide would have the strictest possible gun laws and have barriers to prevent people jumping off cliffs and high buildings. However, there is a limit to this sort of protection. To reduce suicide by drivers purposely crashing their vehicles would require improving public transport and making car ownership more restrictive and expensive. But how could suicide by hanging be reduced? It is hardly feasible to make rope expensive or restricted or to limit the number of things rope could be tied to. The implication is that it is possible to imagine a wide range of protective and preventive measures to reduce the opportunities for people to end their lives violently, but they will never be completely effective. Therefore, the argument that the availability of means for peaceful death will lead to a major increase in suicide by the young does not seem all that plausible. The major problem would arise if it became too easy to end one's life peacefully.

With this background, let me now consider how self-deliverance, as a method of achieving a desired goal, measures up according to the factors involved in effective nonviolent action.

Participation

Nonviolent action is often more effective when many people can be involved. Rallies, boycotts, vigils and many other methods of nonviolent action allow just about anyone to participate, including women, children, the elderly and people with disabilities. In contrast, young fit men are the largest group involved in armed struggle.

People can participate in promoting and enabling self-deliverance in various ways. The most central form of participation is to use this approach to end one's own life. However, this is a very restricted group of people. Even those who advocate and prepare for self-deliverance may not actually use it. Self-deliverance is the antithesis of a participatory direct action. It is more akin to some energetic forms of protest, such as putting banners on tall buildings or sitting atop a tripod to prevent logging. Only a few individuals are capable of or willing to undertake such actions.

Another possibility is to help others prepare for self-deliverance, for example by obtaining Nembutal or constructing an exit bag. However, assisting suicide is a crime in most countries, so this is a highly risky action and unlikely to be the basis for larger participation.

In 2014, an Australian named Laurie Strike recorded a one-minute video in which he requested assistance. He was 84 and was dying of cancer, given only a few weeks to live. In the video, posted online, he asked for means to end his life. An anonymous person supplied him some Nembutal, and Strike used it to die. Strike's appeal served as powerful advocacy for voluntary euthanasia, but did not do much to increase participation in campaigning. Similarly, secret networks in which terminally ill people obtain and share Nembutal can benefit those involved but do little to enable wider participation.

More promising is participating by witnessing someone else's self-deliverance. In Australia in 2002, 69-year-old Nancy Crick ended her life by drinking Nembutal. Having publicised her plight beforehand, at her death she was surrounded by 21 relatives and Exit members who potentially risked being charged with assisting a suicide — though none were. Such support groups have since been called "Nancy's friends."

A group of Nancy's friends can help protect family members or close friends who might be accused of assisting in a death. If anyone is to be criminally charged, then logically all those present should be charged too. Most "Nancy's friends" have themselves been elderly, making them unlikely candidates for criminal proceedings: it would look bad for police and courts to be seen prosecuting elderly members of the community who otherwise have no criminal records or associations. In the US, there was an equivalent support system called Caring Friends.[18]

Being among a group of Nancy's friends at someone's death is a type of civil disobedience. It expands participation beyond the person ending their own life, but so far there have been limits to participation, because suitable events are not that common: only a few people choosing self-deliverance are comfortable having a group of strangers around at the final moment. To increase participation further, some creative thinking is required.

In Australia, one possibility is to challenge censorship of information about self-deliverance. Unlike most other countries, it is illegal to use electronic communication — such as telephone or Internet — to provide any

---

18 Côte, *In Search of Gentle Death*, 201–217.

information about ending one's life. This legislation was targeted at Nitschke and Exit International. In response, Exit hosted its website outside Australia. The Australian government banned *The Peaceful Pill Handbook* — one of the very few books banned in Australia in recent decades. However, because it is possible to obtain the book via mail order and to buy the e-version through the Exit website, banning the book may have been primarily a symbolic action to placate opponents of euthanasia.

The illegality of communicating information about peaceful dying provides an opportunity for civil disobedience actions. For example, hundreds of Exit members — or sympathetic members of the public — might announce together that they have obtained copies of *The Peaceful Pill Handbook,* daring authorities to charge them. If authorities took action, this would provide a platform for publicising the book and the issue; if they declined to act, this would undermine the book ban. The best people to join such an action would be those with the least to lose. If Nitschke joined, he might likely be targeted for reprisals as a means of curtailing his activities, whereas others are unlikely to be.

It is also possible to imagine an expansion of Nancy's friends events by inviting others to participate via online video. If being a member of Nancy's friends is a form of civil disobedience, then the idea is to expand the numbers of those involved. However, this would need careful planning, for example to reveal the location of the event only at the last moment. One person's personal experience of self-deliverance might turn into a spectacle, so only someone who understood exactly what would be involved should even consider this. Furthermore, much prior preparation for participants and observers would be required, so the rationale for self-deliverance — the person's suffering and lack of other options — is fully appreciated. A spectacle is not a problem. The challenge is to make it a spectacle that is educational and motivating.

If actions can be designed to enable large-scale participation in actions in support of self-deliverance, they will achieve several things. First, they will increase the understanding and commitment of those involved. Second, they will provide dramatic endorsement for self-deliverance, much beyond opinion polls. Third, they will make more people willing to consider self-deliverance for themselves, via both publicity and the implied endorsement of mass action.

Direct action in support of the option of self-deliverance can be considered part of the Gandhian constructive programme, which involves acting out the desired goal, and supporting others to do so, rather than trying to put pressure on powerholders to give official permission. In other words, the constructive programme does not rely on convincing or pressuring powerholders. However, ironically, mass action in support of self-deliverance might be the stimulus for governments to legalise voluntary euthanasia — but with the usual tight requirements, such as certification by doctors about a terminal illness, that limit access to it. Self-deliverance, in contrast, does not require the approval of doctors, so for some it will remain an important option even in places where voluntary euthanasia is legal.

Limited harm

Nonviolent action, to be effective, needs to limit any potential or actual harm to the opponent — or to anyone else. In a common form of confrontation, peaceful protesters are met by police, who may use force against the protesters, such as beatings with batons or firing of tear gas. This, to many observers, seems an obvious injustice: it is widely seen as unfair to use violence against peaceful protesters. However, if even a few protesters use violence themselves — for example by hitting police with sticks — this transforms the interaction from violence-versus-nonviolence to violence-versus-violence, and suddenly the police violence seems less objectionable. Even when the protester violence is far less, it can change perceptions about the injustice involved.

In the case of euthanasia, there is no direct harm to the principal opponents of euthanasia, whether religious leaders, politicians or citizen campaigners. Instead, and importantly, there is potential harm to individuals whose lives might be ended prematurely, especially when consent has not been given, as a result of the availability of peaceful means to do so. Furthermore, a person's death, especially if it is seen as premature, can cause psychological pain to some relatives and friends.

Some opponents of euthanasia believe that it is wrong for people to take any steps to end their lives, even when they are in extreme suffering and desperately want their lives to end. For these opponents, euthanasia even under the strictest safeguards is anathema. They see it as causing serious harm, for example as cutting short life without divine authorisation. For these opponents, the goal of limited harm provides no guidance for what to avoid. Drawing an analogy to nonviolent action, this would be parallel to employers who believe any type of workers' strike is a form of violence, or politicians or police who believe that any form of public protest is a threat to public order.

The criterion of limited harm, to make sense, needs to be assessed in relation to a wider, less censorious public. Two prime audiences are those who are sympathetic to the goals of the movement and those who are undecided.

For these groups, concerns may arise if there are cases of *involuntary* euthanasia that are due to or attributed to supporters of *voluntary* euthanasia. For example, in places where euthanasia is legal, if convincing evidence emerged that people were being given lethal injections without consent or being prescribed lethal drugs when they were incapable of understanding their actions, this would discredit the case for voluntary euthanasia. It is telling that opponents of euthanasia make allegations along these lines.

This is precisely where Jack Kevorkian got into trouble. He apparently did not take sufficient care to obtain informed consent. This allowed the police to charge him with murder and discredit him and the case for euthanasia. (Even so, many see him as a hero.)

Self-deliverance involves a somewhat different set of issues connected to harming others. Ending your own life using materials you have personally collected or constructed, such as Nembutal or an exit bag, does not seem likely to physically harm anyone else. In this scenario, the bigger risk is enabling people to end their lives when this is not a carefully considered plan with adequate rationale. For people with terminal illnesses who are experiencing great suffering, the risk is small. However, if young, fit individuals were to use self-deliverance techniques to end their lives, intentionally or inadvertently, this would be a serious problem for the approach, and in many eyes would discredit it. So far, there have been few publicised cases in which this has happened, but it is still useful to consider the possibilities.

Currently, the primary recommended self-deliverance options are Nembutal and the exit bag. These are unlikely to be used accidentally. It would be foolish to leave a bottle of Nembutal sitting in a cupboard where children might decide to drink it, but even if they did, the risk is small because Nembutal is incredibly bitter: most likely they would take a sip and immediately spit it out. However, an adult who knows about how Nembutal can end life and who suffered severe depression might find it an attractive option. Therefore, anyone who obtains Nembutal for their own potential use would be wise to ensure it is as well hidden or securely restricted as other means for suicide such as guns or pesticides.

An exit bag requires special equipment: a canister of helium or nitrogen, a special valve and tubing, and a specially prepared bag. Obtaining this equipment requires forethought: it is not the sort of technique likely to be considered by someone with a sudden suicidal urge, at least compared to options such as shooting or driving a car into a tree at high speed. Nor is the exit bag a likely means for accidental death. Even if the equipment components were foolishly left lying in the open where children could play with them, the technique of using the exit bag is sufficiently complicated that the risk of accidentally dying using it is remote. Only if children repeatedly witnessed practice sessions would this risk become plausible. The implication is to keep children away when practising the steps for using an exit bag.

But what about information on how to use an exit bag? In Nitschke and Stewart's *The Peaceful Pill Handbook*, there is information on constructing an exit bag. The e-version of the book contains a video with an elderly woman, Betty, demonstrating how to use the bag. It might be argued that this information should be kept away from children. Parents who obtain the book might well do so. However, if they were seriously concerned with preventing children from learning how they might end their lives, they would also stop them watching any television or movies showing murder or suicide using guns or other violent methods. The reality is that only a tiny minority of people do not know about violent suicide options. In the movie *The Shawshank Redemption,* rated by audiences as one of the best ever, there is a graphic scene showing preparation for suicide by hanging. Given the glamour or stylishness of many movies involving graphic killing — *Pulp Fiction* is an example — violent suicide is likely to be a far more salient option than the drab scenario of the exit bag as demonstrated by Betty.

One of the goals of Exit International has been to pursue new options for the goal of access to a "peaceful pill," namely a cheap, convenient and reliable means of ending one's life peacefully. In this, Exit has been part of a wider network of self-deliverance advocates called the NuTech group, who started meeting in the 1990s.[19] These pioneers of technological innovation for the purpose of ending life peacefully have investigated various options — but so far have not come up with anything more effective than the exit bag.

Suppose, for the sake of argument, that by purchasing some ordinary chemicals, a Bunsen burner and some test tubes, it was possible to produce an actual pill that, if swallowed, would end life within minutes with no side effects, and with no detectable trace in the body. This would satisfy the ostensible goal of Exit for a peaceful pill, but almost certainly it would create huge new problems. It would become too easy for all sorts of people to use the pill for other purposes.

Because it would be easy to produce, such a pill would have an obvious attraction for anyone who wanted to die, including those in the midst of depression. Many depressed people attempt suicide by swallowing prescription or other drugs; many survive because most available drugs are not lethal, even in large quantities. Many attempted suicides are interpreted as cries for help. If a peaceful pill were available, many more of these attempted suicides would be successful.

Another problem is that such a pill could be used to commit murder. The possibilities would be enormous and horrendous. Hiding a peaceful pill in someone's food would be one possibility. Disguising a peaceful pill as some other pill, for example a vitamin tablet, would be

---

19 Côte, *In Search of Gentle Death*, 109–133.

another. To prevent misuse of such a pill, police might monitor sales of the components or even of Bunsen burners, or might institute a comprehensive surveillance system.

The dangers of such a peaceful pill, leading to government controls and surveillance, then would make it less attractive for the current target group for Exit and other self-deliverance groups: people who rationally want to end their lives because of serious and inescapable suffering.

This line of thought suggests that the NuTech goal of enabling access to a cheap, accessible, simple and reliable means to end one's life peacefully needs to add another criterion: the means should not be too easy to obtain and use inadvertently or surreptitiously.

In places where Nembutal can be purchased legally, for example Mexico, it is not known for being responsible for murders or rash suicides. However, a tasteless or slightly sweet version of Nembutal might be a different story. Similarly, the needed planning and difficulty in constructing an exit bag seem sufficient to deter most spur-of-the-moment suicide attempts.

In summary, self-deliverance can be pursued using direct action, namely development and use of methods for ending one's life in a peaceful way. One of the criteria for this to be an effective approach is that harm be limited. The most likely harm is use of self-deliverance techniques by individuals outside the normal ambit. Therefore, the most appropriate technological options need to make such possibilities difficult.

Voluntary participation

In effective nonviolent action, such as petitions, marches, vigils, boycotts, strikes and sit-ins, participants need to be volunteers. If participants are conscripted or bribed, this undermines their commitment and undermines the credibility of the action. Rallies organised by dictators, in which members of the crowd are paid to attend, are shams and are not the basis for ongoing commitment.

As applied to actions supporting voluntary euthanasia, the implication is that no one should feel any obligation to participate, much less any compulsion. Imagine this scenario: a person arranges to end their life in the presence of a group of Nancy's friends, namely voluntary witnesses. With the preparations complete, 20 Nancy's friends arrive, some travelling a considerable distance. But then the person who is the centre of attention has second thoughts: perhaps it's not time to go just yet. However, all the effort put into making arrangements might seem to impose a sense of obligation to continue. At this point, therefore, it would be opportune to offer a caring, sincere option to cancel or postpone the action. This should always be a possibility; the more high-profile the preparations, the more important it becomes to ensure that proceedings are entirely voluntary.

Some individuals seeking a peaceful death speak out about their situation, becoming temporary stars in the campaign. According to the principle of voluntary participation, the decision to do this should be made entirely by the person concerned, without the slightest pressure. Indeed, it might be worthwhile to have someone play the role of devil's advocate, to articulate the reasons why taking a public role is not a good idea. In this way, a person's commitment to becoming a public figure on the issue needs to be strong enough to overcome careful arguments to the contrary.

A single person who backs out of a planned end-of-life event and claims to have felt coerced would be highly damaging for the cause of voluntary euthanasia. Hence, ensuring consent will continue to be vitally important.

Where euthanasia is legal, protocols for ensuring consent are far more rigorous than the alternative, namely underground euthanasia, in which doctors covertly provide the means for ending life, or sometimes actively end a person's life. This is one of the arguments for legalisation: the necessity for surreptitious activities will be reduced.

Self-deliverance raises a different set of considerations, because it can be carried out whether or not euthanasia is legal. The risk of people being pressured to end their lives against their wishes or best interests exists with legal euthanasia, but is mitigated by the safeguards in the enabling legislation. With self-deliverance, there are no formal safeguards. Therefore, it would probably be useful for proponents of self-deliverance to develop a set of protocols to be recommended to anyone considering this option, to ensure that decisions are completely voluntary. The protocols — which could simply be a series of questions and considerations — might involve questions for friends and relatives as well as the person planning to end their life. For example, if inheritance is involved, the questions might raise concerns if anyone stands to benefit financially from a person's death and has had an influence on the decision.

In one prominent case in Australia, a man, Graeme Wylie, had expressed his desire to die peacefully, because he had developed Alzheimer's disease. A friend, Caren Jennings, visited Mexico to buy Nembutal for herself, and picked up some for Graeme. Caren gave one bottle of Nembutal to another friend, Shirley Justins, who gave it to Graeme. He used it to end his life. Both Caren and Shirley were charged with murder for their assistance in Graeme's death and convicted of manslaughter.[20]

Philip Nitschke has used this example as a warning: "don't do a Graeme Wylie." In other words, don't rely on others to help you die, because in Australia this can be very harmful to them: they could end up with a lengthy prison sentence. Nitschke's message is that you need to make all the preparations yourself. Furthermore, if you suspect you are developing dementia, it might actually be unwise to obtain a diagnosis from a physician because if you do have signs of dementia, courts might deem that you are not competent to make decisions about your health and life.

These sorts of complications indicate that self-deliverance currently operates in a regulatory vacuum. In Australia, this is a direct consequence of the government's attempts to keep information about this option from the

---

20 Nitschke, *Damned If I Do,* 115–122; Australian Broadcasting Corporation, "Additional details about the death of Graeme Wylie," *Australian Story,* 23 March 2009, http://www.abc.net.au/austory/content/2007/s2524595.htm.

public and to make the option as difficult as possible. If, though, self-deliverance becomes more widely known and accepted, it will be all the more important that protocols are developed and applied to prevent abuses. One of the most significant potential abuses is involuntary euthanasia.

Fairness

When actions are seen as unfair, they can generate opposition. One way to assess whether people see a method as fair is the absence of backfire.

Suppose you have to deal with a boss who shouts abuse. If you say nothing, speak in a moderate tone of voice, or just leave, most observers will see your actions as reasonable. If you start shouting, you turn the interaction into a shouting match. However, if you put excrement into the boss's desk drawer, throw red dye on her clothes or let the air out of the tyres of her car, you've gone much further. Some of your co-workers might be sympathetic, if they too have experienced abuse from the boss. However, some observers might think you've gone much too far, and think that you are now the one causing the problem. They might think that the boss is justified in shouting at you, because you're doing much worse things.

If you shoved past the boss and caused her to fall and have a serious injury, you might well be seen as reckless or worse. The boss, whatever her shortcomings, might gain sympathy. Hurting the boss could be seriously counterproductive.

In the case of euthanasia, these considerations might at first seem irrelevant, because only one person is affected: the person who wants to die. But inevitably others are affected too. Indeed, the "fairness" of a method to end one's life is a crucial consideration.

Consider first some violent methods. Suppose you are desperate to die, and you happen to be a commercial pilot. You purposely crash the plane you are flying. You die, but so do many others. This is the height of immorality: you have put your own desires above those of many others.

On a smaller scale, you can end your life by crashing your car, jumping off a building, throwing yourself in front of a train, or hanging yourself. In these and other methods of violent suicide, others can be affected. As well as those closest to you, who will be affected by your sudden death, others may be traumatised, such as train drivers or the person who finds you hanging from a rope.

One of the most important reasons for seeking the option of peaceful death is to reduce the potential trauma to others. So, the push for voluntary euthanasia can be considered to be a quest to enable the use of means to end life that are fair in the sense of reducing one person's suffering — the person wanting to die — while limiting the associated suffering by others affected.

There is one other group to be considered: doctors who are expected or who feel obligated to assist in dying. No doctor is required to help end a person's life, but some who agree to assist nevertheless find the process traumatic, even when they know it is a desired death aimed at reducing suffering.[21] Many doctors feel their primary duty is to save lives, so helping to end lives clashes with the way they conceive their professional mission. For some of them, the goal might be worthy but the means are distasteful. For this group of doctors, self-deliverance should be less disturbing, because doctors do not have to be involved at all, at least not directly.

This discussion of the principle of fairness seems to be somewhat off track: most of the considerations here could just as easily be classified under the principle of limited harm. This is because peaceful dying is, by its nature, non-aggressive. However, there is one group for who it will nearly always be seen as unfair: those who believe human life is sacred and that humans should not take any action to shorten it. For them, euthanasia is inherently unfair. This will remain a fundamental obstacle to full acceptance of this option.

Prefiguration

The idea of incorporating the ends in the means is called prefiguration. A classic example is seeking peace. When using arms to preserve the peace, the means are incompatible with the end: the means or methods are violence and waging war whereas the end or goal is their absence.

---

21 Dr. C, "Narratives from the Netherlands: the euthanasia mountain gets higher and higher," *Cambridge Quarterly of Healthcare Ethics,* vol. 5, no. 1, 1996, pp. 87–92, reprinted in David C. Thomasma et al. (eds.), *Asking to Die: Inside the Dutch Debate about Euthanasia* (Dordrecht: Kluwer, 1998), 313–320; Nitschke, *Damned If I Do,* 96.

Using the principle of prefiguration involves pursuing peace by peaceful means.[22]

Campaigns to legalise voluntary euthanasia are not prefigurative. The goal is people being able to die with dignity. The means are something different: information, education, publicity and lobbying.

Self-deliverance, on the other hand, is an ideal example of prefigurative action. The goal is the option of self-deliverance. The principal method used is to enable more people to plan for self-deliverance themselves, should they so desire, and when the time comes, to end their lives in their desired way.

Non-standard

Nonviolent action, by definition, goes beyond conventional, accepted forms of action. Lots of political actions don't involve physical violence, for example lobbying, election campaigning and voting. However, these are routine activities in systems of representative government. They don't count as nonviolent action, which involves doing something that goes beyond the routine. Strikes, boycotts, sit-ins and vigils are examples. Some methods of nonviolent action are illegal — these sorts of actions are commonly called civil disobedience — but nonviolent actions can be legal too. They just aren't standard.

Nearly all campaigning to legalise voluntary euthanasia has used conventional forms of action, such as leaflets,

---

22 Johan Galtung, *Peace by Peaceful Means: Peace and Conflict, Development and Civilization* (London: Sage, 1996).

newsletters, public talks, films, lobbying and voting. In using conventional methods, the movement remains in the mainstream. It is not seen as extreme, at least not in terms of how it operates. There is nothing wrong with using conventional methods: every major movement for social change has used them. In some places, voluntary euthanasia has been decriminalised or legalised. However, given the overwhelming support for legalisation, the pace of change might seem too slow. If 70% of the population supports legalisation, why doesn't the political system respond?

One of the key roles of nonviolent action is to push for change when conventional methods are unavailable or blocked. Sometimes special-interest groups have a stranglehold on policy-making, so conventional forms of political action do not operate the way they are supposed to in theory. For example, politicians may be elected on the basis of promise to reform the system, but change their minds after being elected.

The movement for self-deliverance can be interpreted as a form of nonviolent action. Self-deliverance sidesteps the push for legalisation, and instead promotes methods for people to end their lives peacefully without legal or medical approval. To the extent that telling people about self-deliverance options and obtaining the means to carry it out is illegal, this option involves a form of civil disobedience, challenging restrictive laws.

Skilful use

Skills and good judgement are needed to use methods of nonviolent action effectively. Organising a rally, for example, can involve much planning and preparation, as well as understanding the issue and circumstances enough to know whether a rally is a suitable method, when and where to hold it, how to publicise it and how to make sure it runs smoothly and achieves its aims.

Similarly, campaigners on euthanasia need skills in advocating their cause. This involves developing and deploying arguments, organising groups, mounting campaigns and warding off attacks.

In the case of self-deliverance, another set of skills is important: knowing how to end one's life, for example by acquiring Nembutal or constructing an exit bag, and using them appropriately. A botched attempt to die can be personally devastating and physically harmful, and also discredit the entire approach.

Conclusion

Some opponents of euthanasia believe life is sacred. Others believe it is risky to legalise euthanasia because it might be used in inappropriate ways, and think improving palliative care is a better option. Most governments have backed the opponents of euthanasia, making it a crime to assist another person to die.

On the other side are those who believe a person who is suffering from a terminal illness should have the option of ending their life in a peaceful manner. They see it as cruel to refuse such a person a means to end their suffering. For supporters of voluntary euthanasia, the key injustice is this refusal. A few governments in the world permit voluntary euthanasia, usually under carefully defined circumstances.

My aim here is to examine this debate using ideas from nonviolent action. This might seem, initially, to be a curious endeavour, in that traditional methods associated with nonviolent action, such as rallies, strikes, boycotts and sit-ins, have seldom played a role in the debate. Furthermore, neither side uses violence in the way commonly encountered by nonviolent campaigners, such as police wielding batons, using torture or shooting protesters.

Overall, the euthanasia debate looks peaceful compared to, for example, struggles against repressive governments. It is possible, though, to draw parallels. Some opponents would say that euthanasia itself, for whatever motivation, is a form of violence, while some supporters would say that preventing access to the means for a peaceful death could be considered a form of torture. However, rather than develop these sorts of analogies, I have proceeded a different way, by extracting key features of successful nonviolent action and seeing their relevance to the euthanasia struggle.

In undertaking this task, I have looked at only one side of the struggle: the campaign for voluntary euthanasia. The main reason is that in most places the power of the state is used against this option. However, it would be quite possible to undertake a parallel examination of the relevance of nonviolence ideas for opposing euthanasia.

Seven features of successful nonviolent action were examined: participation in the campaign; limited harm; voluntary participation; fairness; prefiguration; non-standard action; and skilful use. This examination led to some ideas about action that are not normally contemplated, and also highlight some of the differences between the euthanasia struggle and conventional nonviolent action campaigns.

The movement to legalise voluntary euthanasia has largely proceeded using conventional means of political action, such as education, lobbying and voting. As such, it has seldom moved into the domain of nonviolent action, which involves using non-standard methods. The major exception is the movement for self-deliverance, which involves enabling people to acquire the skills and practical means to end their own lives peacefully, without the need for assistance from doctors or others.

Self-deliverance can be seen as an analogue to nonviolent action. It goes beyond conventional political action; it is, instead, a type of direct action. It has the significant feature of being prefigurative, namely incorporating the goal in the means.

This movement for self-deliverance sidesteps the struggle over legalisation. However, in some places, such as Australia, even to provide information about self-deliverance options is constrained by laws. This opens up a different arena for struggle: opposing or circumventing such laws. In places where providing information about ending one's life peacefully is illegal, there are opportunities to mobilise support by challenging these laws — especially given majority support for voluntary euthanasia.

For the success of nonviolent action, the scale of participation in campaigning is important. For euthanasia, though, creating opportunities for participation in direct action is not so easy. Choosing the self-deliverance option is only suitable for a few individuals. Supporting others, though, is a possibility. If someone is ready to end their life, having witnesses — Nancy's friends — is a form of solidarity and potentially of civil disobedience. Whether to scale this into a larger event is a delicate issue. Participation might be increased, but at the risk of creating a counterproductive spectacle.

In the most common sorts of nonviolent campaigns, remaining nonviolent in the face of violence by opponents, typically governments, can win allies. However, when some campaigners use violence, this can undermine the campaign. In the struggle over euthanasia, there is no potential for harming opponents of euthanasia. However, there is another injustice that can be a potent turning point: euthanasia that is seen to be involuntary. The case against Jack Kevorkian hinged on the claim that he had not obtained informed consent: he had gone beyond a boundary, and this made his actions counterproductive.

Actions by doctors to challenge laws against euthanasia are inherently limited in terms of participation: those who are not doctors cannot join in. As already noted, the option of self-deliverance provides opportunities for greater participation. But it also creates new risks of enabling people to end their lives: the techniques of self-deliverance might be adopted by individuals who do not fit the normal categories for access to peaceful death in places where it is legal. So far, this seems not to have been a problem: there are few publicised cases of young fit individuals choosing suicide by Nembutal or an exit bag. Nevertheless, if self-deliverance techniques became more widely known and accepted, risks might increase. Therefore, developing strict protocols is a wise precaution.

In summary, looking at the euthanasia issue through the lens of nonviolent action offers some intriguing possibilities. So far, the voluntary euthanasia movement has mainly used conventional methods of political action, so there are few analogues to nonviolent action. The one exception is the option of self-deliverance, which can be interpreted as a form of direct action in the tradition of Gandhi's constructive programme. Given that participation is a key to the success of nonviolent action, a key challenge for proponents of self-deliverance is to work out ways of enabling more people to join in actions. The key risk is being seen to support involuntary euthanasia or contribute to suicide in inappropriate groups.

8
A vaccination struggle

Meryl Dorey observed her son's adverse reactions to vaccinations. As a result, in 1994 she set up a group called the Australian Vaccination Network (AVN) whose purpose was to inform parents about the potential adverse consequences of vaccination as well as raising questions about the efficacy of vaccination. Nearly all medical authorities in Australia and internationally endorse and advocate vaccination. The AVN, a voluntary body whose members were ordinary citizens, thus provided a challenge to the dominant pro-vaccination establishment.

Dorey was the primary spokesperson for the AVN, giving talks and media interviews. The AVN published a magazine, had a large website and grew until it had some 2000 paid members. (The magazine had a much broader ambit than vaccination, covering a range of topics in natural health.)

In 2009, another citizens' group was set up calling itself Stop the Australian Vaccination Network (SAVN), with the express aim of shutting down the AVN. SAVN's primary presence was a Facebook page, eventually having thousands of friends. People linked to SAVN used a variety of methods to attack Dorey and the AVN.

My aim here is to examine the AVN-SAVN struggle in light of the features of nonviolent action, adapted to a different domain. There has been no physical violence in the struggle, only some implied threats of violence. The struggle has been waged through words and through the power of government agencies.

I will begin by telling a little about vaccination and the vaccination debate, and then describe the tactics used by SAVN. A key question is, "How should the AVN defend against SAVN's attacks?" A more general, and related question, is how critics of vaccination can use nonviolent action to promote their views. Finally, there is the question of how supporters of vaccination can promote their views.

In telling this story, it is relevant to note that I am not a neutral observer: I've intervened to defend the AVN's free speech and, as a result, come under attack myself. On the other hand, I do not have a strong view about vaccination itself. My main interest is in the struggle, especially the methods used in it, rather than the outcome.

The vaccination debate

Vaccination is a procedure designed to protect people from infectious disease. Polio, a disease that can cause crippling and sometimes death, is caused by a virus, naturally enough called the polio virus. To protect against the disease, scientists developed modified, less virulent forms of the different strains of the polio virus. These modified forms, called "attenuated" strains, are the core of the polio vaccine. When individuals are given the polio vaccine — the attenuated polio virus — by mouth or via injections, the idea is that they react to the vaccine by developing immunity to the virus. The vaccine is intended to be strong enough to stimulate the immune system but not so strong that it gives the disease.

The same principle applies to a large number of other diseases, such as measles, whooping cough and chickenpox. Vaccines can be given at any age. Public health authorities recommend that children have many of their vaccinations at a young age, so they are protected from disease as early as possible. Most vaccines require several doses, separated by months or years, to ensure immunity. In some countries, the flu vaccine is recommended annually for children and adults.

The polio vaccine was developed in the 1950s and was widely administered from the 1960s. Most other vaccines are more recent, with new ones added to the childhood schedule on a regular basis.

Supporters of vaccination say it is one of the most important public health measures in the past century, reducing formerly devastating diseases to relatively minor problems. Authorities remain vigilant, promoting vaccination to prevent a resurgence of disease.

Think of a group of people in an extended family, a workplace or a school. If one person comes down with chickenpox or whooping cough, then others may pick up the virus or bacteria from them: infectious individuals may not show symptoms at first, and so may spread the disease without knowing it; some may have the pathogen but not develop symptoms. If others, who are exposed to chickenpox (for example), have been vaccinated, they are less likely to be infected, because they have immunity, though some may still succumb because their immune response from the vaccine was not strong enough. However, if most people in the group are immune, the virus has a hard time spreading. The result is called "herd immunity" — a sufficient percentage of individuals in the group, or herd, has immunity, so epidemics cannot develop.

The level of vaccination needed to develop herd immunity depends on the disease. It might be 50% or 80% or even 100%, remembering that vaccines are not always effective. In any case, supporters of vaccination say the benefits are both individual and collective. The individual benefit is a lower risk of infectious disease and, if the disease develops nevertheless, a less serious case. The collective benefit is that disease levels drop if most people are vaccinated.

The orthodox position is that vaccination is highly beneficial to a community.[1] Therefore, every effort is made to ensure that vaccination levels are as high as possible and that new vaccines are introduced to deal with additional diseases. This is the position of medical authorities throughout the world. It is backed up by a massive body of research. Nearly all doctors and scientists — including vaccination researchers — support this orthodox position. Within the orthodoxy, there is some level of disagreement, for example whether vaccination should be mandatory, whether vaccines should be stockpiled for diseases like anthrax, and whether a particular

---

1 F. E. Andre, R. Booy, H. L. Bock, et al., "Vaccination greatly reduces disease, disability, death and inequity worldwide," *Journal of the World Health Organization,* vol. 86, no. 2, 2008, pp. 140–146; Paul A. Offit and Louis M. Bell, *Vaccines: What You Should Know,* 3rd edition (Hoboken, NJ: John Wiley, 2003).

new vaccine, such as for hepatitis B, is ready to be introduced. Governments and medical authorities in different countries sometimes differ in their advice concerning the number and timing of childhood vaccinations.

In the face of this overwhelming endorsement of vaccination, there is a small but persistent citizen opposition, supported by a few doctors and scientists. These people are sometimes called "anti-vaccination," but this label is inaccurate: only some are opposed to all vaccines; others are critical of mandatory vaccination, or critical of particular vaccines such as the one for measles, or concerned about health problems caused by vaccination. It is more accurate to refer to them as vaccination critics or sceptics.[2]

There has been criticism of vaccination since its earliest days in the late 1700s. Contemporary criticism has grown since the 1950s, along with the ever increasing number of vaccines in the childhood schedule.[3] The key concern of many critics is the risk posed by vaccines. A few individuals suffer serious adverse reactions, leading to permanent incapacity and occasionally death. Because

---

[2] Pru Hobson-West, "'Trusting blindly can be the biggest risk of all': organised resistance to childhood vaccination in the UK," *Sociology of Health & Illness*, 29(2), 2007, 198–215.

[3] Louise Kuo Habakus and Mary Holland (eds.), *Vaccine Epidemic: How Corporate Greed, Biased Science, and Coercive Government Threaten Our Human Rights, Our Health, and Our Children* (New York: Skyhorse, 2011); Richard Halvorsen, *The Truth about Vaccines: How We Are Used as Guinea Pigs without Knowing It* (London: Gibson Square, 2007).

doctors seldom attribute health problems to vaccines, only a small percentage of adverse reactions are officially reported and acknowledged.

Critics also say that getting diseases such as measles and chickenpox is not so bad. The illness is usually mild, yet confers lifelong immunity, or at least much stronger immunity than vaccination.

Critics point out that death rates from infectious diseases dropped dramatically for decades prior to the widespread introduction of vaccination, a change usually attributed to improvements in sanitation, nutrition and hygiene.[4] They argue that vaccination has not made such a huge difference, given that death rates would have continued to drop even without vaccination. One of the factors is that many diseases are still quite common but are now milder, with a lower death rate.

Critics also suggest that the massive increase in autoimmune disorders such as diabetes and autism may be linked to vaccination. Researchers have not agreed on the cause of the increase in the incidence of autism, allowing critics to claim vaccination might be responsible.

An observer of this clash of viewpoints over vaccination might say, "Let science decide" — in other words, look at research and make a decision based on the findings. However, research seldom is definitive in scientific

---

4 Suzanne Humphries and Roman Bystrianyk, *Dissolving Illusions: Disease, Vaccines, and the Forgotten History* (San Bernardino, CA: The authors, 2013).

controversies.[5] Any findings can be disputed. Vaccination critics point out that most vaccine research is carried out or sponsored by pharmaceutical companies that sell vaccines, and is thus not truly independent. Furthermore, they point to shortcomings of the research on some vaccines, for example insufficient collection of adverse reaction reports, and research on healthy subjects that are not representative of the full population of vaccinated individuals.

The supporters and the critics look at the evidence differently, based on different assumptions about what needs to be proved. Supporters say vaccination is solidly based on science and that critics must provide convincing proof otherwise, whereas critics say that research has not been sufficient to rule out certain types of risks. Each side puts the onus of proof on the other.

Aside from the evidence, there is another source of disagreement. Many of the benefits of vaccination come from herd immunity: they depend on nearly everyone being vaccinated. However, individuals face a very small risk of serious adverse side-effects. This is a classic case of individuals accepting or refusing personal risks with the promise of collective benefit.

I have indicated some of the issues in the vaccination debate, but these are only the basics. As in nearly all scientific controversies, there are untold complications. Campaigners can cite dozens of studies in support of their

---

5 For my comments concerning scientific controversies, see Brian Martin, *The Controversy Manual* (Sparsnäs, Sweden: Irene Publishing, 2014).

position — and point to flaws in studies cited by their opponents. There are claims and counter-claims, and numerous complications, concerning every aspect of the debate.

Only a few well-informed campaigners are familiar with the intricacies of the arguments, on either side of the dispute. The majority of people take their position based on trust in authorities, in accordance with views of family and friends, or their own assessment of the evidence and their personal situation.

Waging the vaccination debate

If decisions about vaccination were based on a calm, careful assessment of the evidence and arguments, in the light of personal values, with respect for those with differing views, there would be little need to examine the debate. However, much of the debate is far from this ideal of open, honest and respectful interaction. Instead, in many cases those on the other side are personally criticised — or worse.

I examine here a particular episode in the global debate over vaccination, involving two Australian groups. My interest in this episode — actually a saga in its own right — is in the way the struggle over vaccination has been carried out. In particular, I want to see how ideas about nonviolent action might be applied.

In Australia, vaccination supporters have mainly relied on authoritative pronouncement and education campaigns, with the main aim being to have nearly all children receive recommended vaccines at the nominated ages. In addition, there have been some additional incentives, for example payments to doctors in years up to 2013 for sufficiently high vaccination levels, and a requirement for parents, if they wish to receive particular welfare benefits, to obtain a waiver if their children are not vaccinated.

Among the various Australian vaccine-critical groups and individuals, my focus here is on the AVN. The group is registered as an incorporated body, which meant it has a constitution and an elected committee to manage its affairs. From membership fees and sales of books, DVDs and other materials, the AVN for a number of years had an income sufficient to pay Dorey a wage and to employ a couple of part-time administrative assistants. Throughout most of the AVN's existence, Dorey has been its prime mover.[6]

Things changed in 2009. Triggered by the death of a child from whooping cough, Stop the Australian Vaccination Network (SAVN) was set up. Its stated aim was to close down the AVN.

SAVN's main presence was a Facebook Page. SAVN had no overt formal organisational structure, apparently not having a constitution, formal leaders or elected officials, or a bank account. SAVN operated as a network of like-minded individuals with a common aim.

Throughout its history, SAVN's Facebook page has been very active, with hundreds of comments each day. Most have been about vaccination, with a special focus on the AVN, naturally enough, but there have also been discussions of other health topics. Some of those active in

---

6 From 2014, she took a lower profile.

SAVN have also been members of the Australian Skeptics, an organisation critical of a variety of topics of research and practice such as psychic phenomena, homeopathy and acupuncture.

SAVN mounted a massive attack on the AVN, using a wide range of methods demonstrating considerable innovation. I became involved in 2010 after I became aware of SAVN's attack. In over 30 years of studying scientific and technological controversies, such as ones over nuclear power, pesticides, fluoridation and nuclear winter, I had never seen such a persistent and wide-ranging attack on a citizens' group whose main activity was providing information. So I became involved to defend free speech by critics of vaccination, in particular the AVN.[7]

On some scientific controversies, I have a strong personal position. For example, for many years I campaigned against nuclear power. However, on vaccination I don't have strong views. I have no children and have never made decisions about anyone else's vaccination. This turned out to be an advantage. I could focus on the dynamics of the struggle without a strong emotional investment in the issues being debated.

The issue of vaccination evokes incredible passions. Some parents, who decide not to have their children vaccinated, find they are condemned or shunned by other

---

7 Brian Martin, "Debating vaccination: understanding the attack on the Australian Vaccination Network," *Living Wisdom*, no. 8, 2011, pp. 14–40. For other publications, see http://www.bmartin.cc/pubs/controversy.html#vaccination

parents. For some supporters, critics of vaccination are a danger to the community and deserve to be censored and pilloried. The critics of vaccination, who are much smaller in number, have a similar level of concern.

Many people have asked me why vaccination is such an emotional issue compared to other controversies such as cancer screening or climate change. It is relevant but simplistic to say that children's health is involved — there are other controversial issues affecting children's health, such as traffic safety and suicide prevention, that do not create the same sorts of passions. The role of infection, and herd immunity from vaccination, may be part of an explanation. It is not necessary to know exactly *why* vaccination is such an emotional issue, but knowing it is this sort of issue helps explain the vehemence of the Australian struggle.

It is important to recognise that both sides in the struggle are well-meaning: they seek the best outcomes for children's health. Their goals are the same; they differ in how to achieve the goal of better children's health, either by vaccinating or not. As will be noted later, vested interests play some role, but almost certainly they cannot be the driving force for most participants.

SAVNers and others have used various methods to censor, discredit, disrupt and harass the AVN, with the intent of destroying the organisation. In the following sections, I describe several of the key methods of attack. After this, I look at methods AVN supporters can use to respond.

Anti-AVN method 1: denigration

When SAVN was set up, its purpose was clearly stated on its Facebook page, along with a colourful description of the AVN's beliefs.

> Name: Stop the Australian Vaccination Network
>
> Category: Organizations - Advocacy Organizations
>
> Description: The Australian Vaccination Network propagates misinformation, telling parents they should not vaccinate their children against such killer diseases as measles, mumps, rubella, whooping cough and polio.
>   They believe that vaccines are part of a global conspiracy to implant mind control chips into every man, woman and child and that the "illuminati" plan a mass cull of humans.
>   They use the line that "vaccines cause injury" as a cover for their conspiracy theory.
>   They lie to their members and the general public and after the death of a 4 week old child from whooping cough their members allegedly sent a barrage of hate mail to the child's grieving parents.
>   The dangerous rhetoric and lies of the AVN must be stopped. They must be held responsible for their campaign of misinformation.

Reading this, it seemed to me extremely unlikely that thousands of members of the AVN could have such preposterous beliefs. If they did, they would constitute a cult of unprecedented size in Australia, and furthermore one that had hidden its existence remarkably well. So I looked further — for evidence.

So far as I could determine, the only evidence SAVNers could produce was that Dorey had made a link to a website by David Icke, who endorsed a conspiracy about lizards ruling the earth. But making a link is not the same as believing anything in the linked page, so I did the obvious: I asked Dorey what she believed. She denied any belief that vaccination had any link to a conspiracy to implant mind control chips. So when I wrote about the attack on the AVN, I said that SAVN's claims were "unsupported."[8]

To my surprise, a couple of SAVNers — Paul Gallagher and Peter Tierney — argued the case. They said that Dorey did indeed believe in the conspiracy, but she had to deny it publicly. They dismissed the issue of whether others in the AVN had the same beliefs as a technicality. To my mind their claims were hollow. So I invited them to test our respective views by sending them to experts on conspiracy theories. They did not take up this offer, indicating to me that they had little confidence that their claims about the AVN would stand up to independent scrutiny.[9]

This reinforced my original assessment: SAVN's claims about the AVN believing in a conspiracy to implant mind control chips via vaccination were intended to

---

8 Martin, "Debating vaccination."

9 Brian Martin, "Caught in the vaccination wars, part 3," http://www.bmartin.cc/pubs/12hpi-comments.html

discredit the AVN. When challenged about these claims, some SAVNers put up a smokescreen of justifications, but were not willing to have their claims independently assessed. Some time after my writings about this appeared, SAVN changed its Facebook description of the AVN, leaving out the mind-control claims.

On the SAVN Facebook page, the amount of derogatory comment about the AVN and Dorey in particular was astounding. She was repeatedly called a baby killer, a liar and other terms of abuse. One of the games played by SAVNers was to produce graphics that criticised Dorey. Some attempted to be amusing. One is titled "The Bangalow nut farm" referring to Bangalow where Dorey lives; her husband is a macadamia nut farmer. The SAVN graphic has a picture of some nuts growing with the caption "Nuts," and a picture of Dorey with the caption "More nuts."

Ken McLeod, a prominent figure in SAVN, produced a lengthy document whose very title encapsulates an attitude of contempt: "Meryl Dorey's trouble with the truth, part 1: how Meryl Dorey lies, obfuscates, prevaricates, exaggerates, confabulates and confuses in promoting her anti-vaccination agenda."[10]

Then there are some especially abusive comments on the SAVN Facebook page.

> **Carol Calderwood**: Meryl now claims that Smallpox has not been eradicated…

---

10 http://www.scribd.com/doc/47704677/Meryl-Doreys-Trouble-With-the-Truth-Part-1

Peter Tierney: Oh crap she's finally gone and broken that medical qualification of hers
Rhianna Miles: I may be drunk — but Meryl is a belligerent fool
Rhianna Miles: And a cunt
Rhianna Miles: "Did I say that? I don't believe I did..."
Amy Ives: Do I see? Yes, I see she's a fucking idiot.
Scott Lewis: One thing that is becoming even more apparent is that the views of Meryl and Greg will never be changed and will never be able to be argued with. The responses have been to make claims (AKA make shit up) that we can't disprove, despite [...].
Simon Vincent: Two for 'Cunt'. I had to promote her from 'Thief'.
Simon Vincent: Pardon the language, apologies etc... but seriously... I'm having trouble finding another word. 'Disgraceful mealymouthed non-sensical science-bastardizing dangerous deceitful behaviour' is too long to type each time. She should hang her head in shame.[11]

---

11 This commentary is no longer available on the SAVN Facebook page. Dorey reproduced it in her blog titled "Poor skeptics — and their right to be cyberbullies," 6 November 2011, http://nocompulsoryvaccination.com/2011/11/06/poor-skeptics-and-their-right-to-be-cyberbullies/. For an analysis of the abuse of Dorey as a form of mobbing — collective bullying — see Brian Martin and Florencia Peña Saint Martin, "El mobbing en la esfera pública: el fenómeno y sus características" [Public mobbing: a

Abusive SAVN comments about the AVN and Dorey were not just on its Facebook page. In letters to government agencies, advertisements and letters to people interacting with the AVN, they were regularly raised. SAVN thus embarked from the beginning on a systematic campaign of vilification.

Anti-AVN method 2: Disruption

The AVN had its own blog, where members could add comments. Dorey regularly made lengthy posts, which were followed by comments. After SAVN was formed, SAVNers sought to post comments on the AVN's blog. Some were polite and constructive; others were nasty and distracting.

When like-minded people post on a blog, there is a sense of mutual support and validation, as well as sharing of information. When hostile individuals join the discussion, this changes the dynamic. There is more disagreement and tension. This disrupts the supportive feel of the blog and diverts the discussion.

Dorey sometimes made comments on blogs run by other vaccine-critical groups. On some occasions, after the formation of SAVN, her comments were soon followed by disruptive comments, for example criticising Dorey or questioning whether children had actually been harmed by

---

phenomenon and its features], in Norma González González (Coordinadora), *Organización social del trabajo en la posmodernidad: salud mental, ambientes laborales y vida cotidiana* (Guadalajara, Jalisco, México: Prometeo Editores, 2014), pp. 91–114.

vaccines. Dorey presumed that SAVNers had put a Google Alert on her name so they were immediately notified when her name appeared on the Internet, and then joined the blog where she had posted, disrupting it.

Anti-AVN method 3: complaints

SAVNers made complaints about the AVN to various government bodies, with the intent of hindering or shutting down the AVN's operations. As one of the administrators of the SAVN Facebook page commented:

> SAVN admins work tirelessly to find new ways to put the AVN out of business and make the world a better place. Every night before we go to bed we trawl through legislation far and wide looking for ways to bring the AVN to account. We trawl through Court judgements old and new. No rubbish bin is safe from us.[12]

Because the AVN was incorporated in the Australian state of New South Wales, and hence subject to state government regulations, many of the complaints were to state agencies.

One early complaint, by Ken McLeod, was to the Health Care Complaints Commission (HCCC), a state government agency set up to handle complaints against health practitioners. On the face of it, the AVN was not an

---

12 Ken McLeod, Stop the Australian (Anti)Vaccination Network, Facebook post, 30 November 2013, https://www.facebook.com/stopavn/posts/10152056015278588

obvious target, given that it was a citizens' organisation raising matters of public debate, rather than a group of health practitioners. McLeod, in his complaint, made the argument that the AVN did fall under the HCCC's ambit, and the HCCC obviously agreed, because it launched an investigation into the AVN.

The AVN was invited to respond to McLeod's complaint, which it did. The HCCC also took into account another complaint, but would not let the AVN see it. On the basis of the complaints and the AVN's response, the HCCC ruled against the AVN.

All the HCCC requested was that the AVN add a disclaimer to its website. This was a pretty mild request and would have had a negligible impact on most people using the website. Many visitors would not even notice that there was a disclaimer, and many others would come to internal pages in the website via searches. The disclaimer requested by the HCCC was more symbolic than effective.

The AVN already had its own disclaimer and unwisely — in my opinion — refused to post the HCCC-mandated disclaimer. Because of its refusal, the HCCC issued a "public warning" stating that the AVN provided inaccurate and misleading information and its failure to post the disclaimer requested by the HCCC was a risk to public health and safety.

The HCCC's public warning did not directly hinder any of the AVN's operations. But in this case its symbolic significance was enormous. The issuing of the public warning was widely reported in the mass media. SAVNers continually cited it in the following months whenever they wrote letters or produced advertisements.

The HCCC was just one of several government agencies to which SAVNers made complaints. Another was the state government's Office of Liquor, Gaming and Racing (OLGR), a curiously named agency handling the charitable status of organisations. The OLGR did not act directly on the basis of complaints, but did respond to the HCCC ruling, making its own ruling that the AVN could not accept donations or new members.

Another state government body, the Department of Fair Trading (DFT), administers incorporated bodies. SAVNers put in various complaints to the DFT. One of them was that the AVN, on its website, had not added "Inc." following "Australian Vaccination Network." Incorporated bodies are supposed to put "Inc." after their names on all occasions, but this legal requirement is frequently ignored. Failing to add "Inc." after an organisation's name is hardly likely to harm anyone. It is an administrative triviality — until it became a means for targeting the AVN. The DFT wrote to the AVN about its breach of regulations. The AVN complied, commenting that few other organisations included "Inc." on their websites as required. The DFT said it only acted on complaints; it did not check adherence to this regulation otherwise.

Later, the DFT became more heavy-handed. It demanded that the AVN change its name. SAVNers started the push for the AVN's name to be changed, with complaints to the DFT. This was eventually taken up by others, such as figures in the Australian Medical Association. This seems to have persuaded the DFT. Behind the forced name change was the threat of closing down the AVN altogether, which the DFT had the power to do.

On the surface, critics of the AVN seemed to have a point about its name. From their point of view, a better name would be the Anti-Vaccination Network, because all its information was critical of vaccination. The name Australian Vaccination Network might seem, at first glance, to be supportive of vaccination.

This is where a double standard test is useful: is the AVN's name especially misleading, or is it being singled out for scrutiny? The reality is that many names of organisations are misleading. Some are so familiar that no one stops to think of their content. The Department of Health perhaps should be renamed the Department of Ill Health, because that is its main orientation. The Liberal Party perhaps should be renamed the Conservative Party, so far has it departed from the principles of liberalism. Then there are front groups, set up by corporations to give the appearance of being local citizens' groups. Their names may be misleading. For example, the Australian Environment Foundation seems to be a front for the timber industry.

Did the DFT target any of these? No. Had the DFT ever before required an organisation to change its name? In a few cases, yes, but apparently not in any similar case involving a non-commercial organisation whose name had been treated as unobjectionable for over a decade. It was apparent that the name-change requirement was part of SAVN's campaign against the AVN. The DFT had become an active participant in the campaign. It put out a media release about requiring the AVN to change its name, though there was no requirement to publicise its action. Furthermore, Anthony Roberts, the Minister of Fair Trading, the politician responsible for the DFT, made statements highly critical of the AVN.

Anti-AVN method 4: censorship

On many occasions when Dorey arranged to give a public talk, SAVNers would try to stop it. They typically would send emails to the organisation sponsoring the talk or the venue hosting it, making adverse comments about Dorey and the AVN, thereby encouraging cancellation of the talk or withdrawal of the venue.

Every year in Woodford, Queensland, there is a major folk festival, accompanied by a wide variety of stalls and talks. Dorey had given a talk about vaccination at several festivals. In 2011, SAVNers mounted a major campaign to stop her scheduled talk, writing letters to the festival organisers, local politicians and the media. Many SAVNers wrote blogs opposing Dorey being allowed to speak, with their main argument being that she was giving false and dangerous information to the public.[13] Ironically, the publicity generated by SAVN led to an extra-large audience for Dorey. However, she was not invited back the next year.

When newspapers and television interviewed Dorey or reported on AVN views, SAVNers would write letters

---

13 Brian Martin, "Censorship and free speech in scientific controversies," *Science and Public Policy*, 2014, doi:10.1093/scipol/scu061.

of complaint. Their goal was to prevent expression of views critical of vaccination in the mass media. As a result of SAVN campaigns, most mass media outlets seem to be less willing to quote Dorey or refer to AVN positions.

Anti-AVN method 5: harassment

A group different from SAVN, Vaccination Awareness and Information Service, had a website on which it hosted a "Hall of Shame." This was a list of alternative health practitioners and businesses that had advertised in the AVN's magazine *Living Wisdom,* complete with names and contact details. Some of these businesses received letters from SAVNers with information critical of the AVN. This was experienced, by some, as harassment. It made them reluctant to advertise in *Living Wisdom.* Starting in 2011, Dorey did not run any new ads in the magazine because she did not want to expose advertisers to harassment.

Someone sent Dorey, and some others in the AVN, pornographic images, by post and by email. Some of these were horrific. SAVN denied responsibility. However, I think it is reasonable to say that SAVN's relentless hostility to Dorey and the AVN provided an atmosphere in which some individuals felt sending pornography was justified.

Dorey received various threats. The most well documented were two phone calls in late 2012, recorded on her answering machine and retained on her computer as audio files. Her answering machine also identified the number of the caller and recorded it. In one of the calls, "Die in a fire" was repeated over and over. Dorey tracked the phone number to the house of a prominent SAVNer.[14]

Interim summary

Meryl Dorey set up the Australian Vaccination Network (AVN) as a means of presenting a critical view about vaccination, to counter or complement the largely uncritical support for vaccination by the medical profession and government health departments. The AVN, as a citizens' group, went about its business disseminating information and perspectives, providing a forum for parents and others with concerns about vaccination or interested in holistic approaches to health. There was nothing remarkable about this. All sorts of groups organise to present their views and provide support to members.

This changed dramatically in 2009 with the establishment of Stop the Australian Vaccination Network (SAVN), also a citizens' group, but with the aim of shutting down the AVN. SAVN added a new dimension to the AVN's agenda: a battle to survive. Previously the AVN's primary struggle was with the medical establishment, namely trying to raise concerns about vaccination in the face of a powerful pro-vaccination orthodoxy. SAVN made the AVN's struggle also one for free speech and organisational survival.

---

14 Meryl Dorey, "Threats to AVN President made from home of Stop the AVN founder," *Australian Vaccination-skeptics Network Inc.*, 3 October 2012,
http://nocompulsoryvaccination.com/2012/10/03/threats-to-avn-president-made-from-home-of-stop-the-avn-founder/.

SAVN used a wide variety of techniques in its attack. SAVN's methods can be usefully divided into three types, according to the forums where they occurred.[15]

> 1. AVN forums. SAVNers tried to post comments on the AVN's blog, thereby diverting and disrupting discussions.
> 2. SAVN forums. SAVNers posted adverse comments about the AVN on SAVN's Facebook page.
> 3. Independent forums. SAVNers tried to enrol various other groups, especially government agencies, to take action against the AVN.

How did the AVN respond to these attacks? What can be learned from the success or failure of different responses? It is relatively easy to describe the AVN's responses, but judging their success is not so straightforward. For this, I use two criteria. The first is promoting the AVN's agenda, namely alerting people to possible problems with vaccination and with their right to choose whether they, or their children, will be vaccinated. The second is organisational survival, namely whether the AVN continues to function.

AVN responses 1: dealing with denigration

On SAVN's Facebook page, and on various blogs, SAVNers posted abusive comments about the AVN and especially about Dorey. This served to discredit the AVN, for those who read these pages and took them seriously. They also served to discourage AVN members from posting comments on the AVN's own blog. One technique

---

15 I thank Danny Yee for suggesting this classification.

used by SAVNers was to take a screen shot of comments on the AVN's blog and post it on the SAVN Facebook page, along with a hostile commentary, making fun of the supposed ignorance or danger attributed to the person and the comment. These sorts of postings discouraged some AVN members from making any comments, at least under their own names.

One possible response was simply to ignore the SAVN Facebook page and other anti-AVN online commentary. This would allow the AVN to get on with its business. However, SAVN's online campaign had an impact: some of its pages rose up within search engine results. Someone doing a search for the Australian Vaccination Network or Meryl Dorey would obtain first-page links to SAVN commentary. For some individuals targeted by SAVN, for example those with practices as naturopaths or homeopaths, the online impact could be significant. The result was that individuals were discouraged from posting under their own names. Ignoring SAVN's efforts allowed this impact to continue.

Another option was to complain to Facebook that SAVN's page violated the terms of agreement. The AVN did indeed complain, but with limited results. Although Facebook does not allow pages that attack others, its interest in enforcing its policy was limited. From the point of view of Facebook, getting involved in disputes between groups with Facebook pages did not seem to be a high priority. Many of the disputes were complicated and not easy for an outsider to understand and assess. Initially, Facebook administrators did not react to the AVN's complaints.

In 2010, apparently in response to AVN complaints to Facebook, SAVN closed its Facebook page to outsiders: only friends could access the page. At the same time, SAVN set up a new Facebook page — an open page — that carried on the same sort of criticism of the AVN. Then, some months later, SAVN reopened its original page for general viewing.

The AVN's complaints thus led to no lasting change. SAVN was initially inconvenienced by having to close its Facebook page, but this caused no serious interruption to its campaign. This reflects a general feature of the Internet: it is very hard to censor information, no matter how unwelcome. Once information is posted, others can copy it and post it elsewhere. Therefore, complaints and legal actions have a limited power to eliminate the information. This is most obvious with WikiLeaks. The US government has used its considerable powers to squash WikiLeaks, a very small operation, but has never been able to prevent distribution of information after it has been posted.

In the face of SAVN's relentless hostile commentary about the AVN, a different AVN strategy was to post a dossier on SAVN abuse.[16] The dossier collected instances of derogatory language, ridicule, veiled threats and other hostile comment and listed them under the names of the perpetrators, some of whom were the most active opponents of the AVN on several fronts. The basic idea here is to expose SAVN's activities to a wider audience.

---

16 Australian Vaccination-skeptics Network, "Dossier of attacks on the AVN," http://avn.org.au/dossier-of-attacks-on-the-avn/.

Most of the abuse on SAVN's Facebook page was unknown to anyone who didn't visit the page; many AVN members would not have been aware of it.

When the attacks were in SAVN's forums — its Facebook page and blogs of SAVNers — there was not much that the AVN could do in the same forums. It lacked large numbers of energetic supporters willing to engage directly on SAVN's forums, and in any case such supporters probably would have been blocked if they had become effective. The second main type of response was to enrol third parties to intervene. This included contacting Facebook and complaining about violation of its terms of use. The third arena for response was the forum controlled by the AVN, namely its own website, with the dossier. This was the most effective response: it could not easily be censored by SAVNers. Note that the effectiveness of this response depended on the AVN having a well-developed website with a significant audience. Setting up a new website to post the dossier would not have been as effective.

Let's apply this framework — the three options of engaging in the opponent's forums, enrolling third parties, and using one's own forums — to protests against governments at official events, such as meetings of the World Trade Organisation or leaders of major governments. In these events, the protesters aim to disrupt the activities of their targets, namely governments. The forum is one chosen and controlled by governments who, if prepared, can pick a venue convenient for privacy and security and can draw on police for containing protest. In such situations, governments have overwhelming superiority in force.

A second option for protesters would be to call upon some third party to intervene, for example to go to court to say what the governments are planning is illegal. In the case of government meetings, such an intervention is implausible, because governments control the rules. Even in the face of an adverse ruling, if one were forthcoming, governments could probably ignore the courts without much consequence.

A third option for protesters is to hold their own counter-events, such as public meetings or discussion forums questioning the agendas and views of the governments. This has occurred in some cases — for example, a soup kitchen outside the venue of an extravagant official dinner — often as a parallel activity to attempts to intervene.

This example of protests against governments at meetings illustrates that the likelihood of success depends greatly on the relative resources of the different groups involved, both the principal players (protesters and governments) and third parties that might be enrolled in the struggle (such as courts or media).

Another example is action against nuclear weapons. Some protesters attempt to directly intervene in the domain of the weapons states, for example by entering facilities and using hammers to damage the nosecones of nuclear missiles — and then turning themselves in to authorities.[17] This is the first option: entering the venue of the opponent.

The second option is to draw on the authority of third parties. Opponents of nuclear weapons have gone to court seeking rulings against them. In 1996, the International Court of Justice unanimously ruled that governments have a duty to negotiate and achieve nuclear disarmament. (Other rulings by the court in the same judgement were more ambiguous.) However, nuclear weapons powers seem to have ignored the ruling.

The third option is to organise events in the protesters' own forums, for example in public meetings that they organise. This is a regular occurrence.

These examples show the value of examining actions according to the domain in which they occur: the opponent's domain, one's own domain, or a domain run by some third party. The other key factor is the relative power of the groups involved. In the case of nuclear weapons, the governments with significant numbers of weapons have considerably more power than their citizen opponents. There is no third party with the authority or capacity to take action to disarm arsenals. Civil disobedience against weapons — a form of intervention into the domain of the weapons states — usually leads to arrest and often to imprisonment.

---

17 Sharon Erickson Nepstad, *Religion and War Resistance in the Plowshares Movement* (Cambridge: Cambridge University Press, 2008).

In the case of the attack on the AVN, the situation is reversed. The AVN is relatively weak and has no powerful backers, whereas SAVN's position on vaccination is the same as government health authorities and pharmaceutical companies. So few third parties with power and influence are likely to take up the cause of the AVN. Indeed, the situation is exactly the opposite: third parties can potentially be used by SAVN for purposes of attack.

AVN responses 2: dealing with disruption

First consider AVN forums, starting with its blog. SAVNers tried to post on the AVN blog, sometimes diverting and disrupting the discussion and thereby discouraging others from posting.

One possible response would be to allow SAVN posts, using them as a learning tool, as engaging with the issues of concern. This seemed to work when the number of SAVN posts was small, and they were polite. However, some posts were confrontational and abusive. This changed the tone of the discussions. Rather than being supportive exchanges of people with a shared concern about the problems with vaccination, they became debates about whether vaccination should be supported. When SAVN debaters were not respectful to AVN members, this made the blog less attractive to them.

The option chosen by AVN blog moderators was to block posts by SAVNers, at least when they were abusive or disruptive. This meant deleting their posts and blocking the individual SAVNers from making any posts. This was an ongoing effort, because some SAVNers who had been blocked would set up new accounts under different identities and try to join the AVN's blog.

Meanwhile, SAVNers repeatedly complained about the AVN's alleged censorship, namely that SAVNers were being blocked from the AVN's blog. Such a complaint is curious, given that the stated purpose of SAVN was to shut down the AVN, and SAVNers repeatedly tried to censor AVN talks. However, they saw things differently. They saw the AVN's speech as false and dangerous and therefore not warranting any protection, whereas their own efforts were merely an attempt to protect the public. SAVNers made these complaints on SAVN's Facebook page, in letters to others and seemingly on any possible occasion.

SAVNers, in making claims about AVN censorship, have displayed a double standard. They say anyone is allowed to comment on the SAVN Facebook page, but some critics of SAVN who post on the SAVN page receive an extremely hostile response, with numerous SAVNers making derogatory and accusatory comments. For example Mina Hunt made a post on the AVN's page; SAVNer Peter Tierney took a screen shot of Hunt's post and put it on SAVN's page, accompanied by hostile commentary, with SAVNers calling her repugnant, vicious and contemptible, among other epithets. Hunt claims she was blocked from responding.[18]

The claims by SAVNers about AVN censorship thus might be considered to be hypocritical in two senses. First, SAVN was set up to shut down the AVN, a drastic form of

---

18 Martin and Peña, "Public mobbing."

censorship. Second, some SAVNers have censored comment on their own blogs and on the SAVN Facebook page. Despite this, SAVN claims about AVN censorship were important. These claims were repeated on numerous occasions and in diverse venues, for example in letters to venues and government bodies. To those unfamiliar with the SAVN-AVN struggle and with SAVN's own censorship record, these claims seemed to have substance. Just as importantly, SAVNers convinced themselves that the AVN was practising unconscionable censorship, which thereby seemed to justify SAVN's own behaviour.

In response to SAVNers complaining about AVN censorship, the AVN set up a separate forum called "Vaccination: respectful debate."[19] Those who made comments considered disruptive or abusive were referred to this separate blog, where the rules about the style and content of comments were explicit and could be used to exclude violators. In this way, the main AVN blog was freed from disruption, while making the claim about censorship less credible.

Another option the AVN could have taken was to make its blog private, namely not visible to non-members. In this way, it would be possible to legitimately exclude non-members. It would still be possible for SAVNers to disrupt the blog, but they would have to join the AVN first. However, the AVN did not adopt this option because it would have meant limiting the visibility of its discus-

---

19 "Vaccination — respectful debate," Google Groups, https://groups.google.com/forum/#!forum/vaccination-respectful-debate

sions: open discussions were important for making ideas available to wider audiences.

There is an analogy here to meetings of activist groups, such as environmentalists. In many cases, these groups are open to any interested person, which is useful for attracting new members. On the other hand, this also makes the group susceptible to infiltration by opponents and paid informers and, more commonly, to individuals who are just looking for a place to interact and to air their own personal concerns and grievances. Keeping the group closed seems exclusive but can provide greater security and stability.

At some rallies, there is a system called the "open mike": the main microphone is made available to anyone who would like to speak to the audience. This seems democratic — no one is excluded — but in practice it is risky unless everyone in the audience is respectful and in tune with the crowd. The risk is that some who choose to speak have their own agenda, for example wanting to talk about a different topic. If there are only a dozen people attending the rally, the damage is not very great, but if there are a thousand, the level of disruption can be considerable. This is the primary reason why the open mike is seldom used. Instead, most rallies are carefully planned by the organisers, who choose speakers and other performers.

If there are known disrupters who would take any opportunity to hog the open mike and disrupt the rally, then organisers would be foolish indeed to allow this; instead, they would screen speakers. Likewise, if an activist group knows that infiltration and disruption are likely, then careful assessment of potential members makes sense.

Open meetings and open mikes are feasible when prospects for disruption are limited. When opponents have greater numbers and consciously seek to disrupt meetings, then some sort of screening of participants or speakers is necessary to prevent hostile takeover.

This is the situation in which the AVN found itself. SAVN had much greater numbers and energy and embarked on a consistent campaign of disruption. If the AVN had allowed all comers on its blog, it would have been taken over by SAVNers.

The AVN's defence — blocking disrupters and referring polite critics to "Vaccination: respectful debate" — was relatively successful by both criteria: it enabled the AVN to continue its efforts and to survive as an organisation. The price paid was continually being criticised for alleged censorship — even though the critics were, arguably, the primary censors.

AVN responses 3: dealing with complaints

Complaints have been a crucial part of SAVN's strategy to shut down the AVN. When agencies ignored or dismissed complaints, they had no direct effect on the AVN. However, agencies took some complaints seriously enough to conduct an investigation and require the AVN to respond. In these cases, there was an impact on the AVN: time and effort were required to prepare a response. In some cases, the time and effort were considerable, because the claims were many and varied and the stakes were high if a ruling was made against the AVN. So as well as time and effort, there was a psychological cost: the AVN's future was imperilled, and this put stress on the AVN members involved.

Thus, SAVN's strategy of repeated complaints could be successful even if the AVN defended successfully against all of them. When agencies launched investigations requiring an AVN response, the complaints served as a form of harassment, requiring time and effort to prepare a response, causing stress in the process. When an agency made a ruling against the AVN, that was a tremendous bonus for SAVN. Instead of the AVN being criticised only by a partisan group with no formal standing, the AVN would be condemned by a government agency with the credibility attached to its role.

The success of SAVN's strategy thus depended on the response of the agencies involved. What is important is that some complaints were treated seriously enough to warrant asking the AVN for a response. Because vaccination is backed by government health authorities and the medical profession, it is far more likely that complaints against critics of vaccination will be taken seriously. Imagine the contrary scenario: complaints to the Health Care Complaints Commission from the AVN, saying that campaigners for vaccination have misrepresented the evidence and that children are being harmed by vaccines. This would have a negligible chance of becoming the basis for an investigation. The HCCC would hardly want to take on the medical establishment.

The AVN, when subject to a complaint and an investigation, has had several options for responding. The most important initial instance involved the HCCC, which received a lengthy submission from Ken McLeod, a key figure in the attack on the AVN, and launched an investigation requiring the AVN to respond. The HCCC also received a complaint from the parents of a child who died from whooping cough — the death that triggered the formation of SAVN. I do not propose here to look at the content of the complaints, but instead at options for the AVN in response.

1. The AVN could simply ignore the complaints, and carry on with its usual business. However, the likely result would be that the complaints would be upheld, with the consequence that the AVN's activities would be hampered or even the organisation shut down. This is not a viable option unless the agency has little power or credibility.

2. The AVN could conscientiously respond to the complaints. This reduces the risk of adverse findings. However, it soaks up time and effort that might otherwise be devoted to the AVN's usual business.

3. The AVN could challenge the validity or jurisdiction of the agency, for example by filing a formal appeal to a review body or challenging the agency in court. If successful, this option discredits the agency and prevents further action by the agency. However, it is a high risk strategy, because it requires a large effort and cost to mount the appeal, with no guarantee of success, distracting the AVN from its usual business.

4. The AVN could use the agency investigations to call for greater support from its members and from the general public. In this option, the complaints are treated as a mode of attack — as I've presented them here — with

the defence being mobilisation of support. This option has the advantage of building commitment from members and forging alliances with allies. Its disadvantage is taking the AVN away from its usual activities concerning vaccination and reorienting efforts towards organisational autonomy and free speech. On the other hand, by taking the issues to wider audiences, there is a potential for some of them to become aware of and sympathetic to the AVN's central concerns.

5. The AVN could transform itself so that its operations are less susceptible to complaint-based attacks. As an incorporated body in the state of New South Wales, the AVN was subject to regulatory control by a number of bodies, such as the Department of Fair Trading. If, for example, the AVN dissolved and reconstituted itself as a network, it would no longer be subject to DFT rules.

To assess these options is not easy. Imagine that it is possible to create parallel universes, each one developing separately from a common origin. In the first universe, the AVN used option 1, in the second universe option 2 and so forth. With such an experiment, different outcomes for different options could be observed and assessed. However, even with such a hypothetical process, assessing outcomes would not be easy. Perhaps what happened depended sensitively on a few quirks of the circumstances, such as an agency official's attitude towards vaccination when a complaint arrived. Despite the difficulties, it is possible to make some observations based on what actually happened, recognising that if circumstances had been somewhat different, the outcomes may not have been the same.

Option 1 was to ignore the complaints. This is sometimes a sensible strategy when the complaint is like a threat. Sometimes people threaten to sue for defamation, which scares the target of the threat, but few of such threats ever result in legal actions. The threats that are not followed up can be called bluffs. However, it is not always easy to know when someone is bluffing.

When agencies asked the AVN to respond to complaints, they might have been bluffing. But it would have been a big risk for the AVN to assume this. One key reason was the watchful eyes of SAVNers. When a SAVNer had made a complaint that led to an investigation, the complainant was informed, and other SAVNers then knew about it. Their active discussion of what was being demanded of the AVN made it difficult for agencies to quietly drop an investigation.

When in 2012 the Department of Fair Trading (DFT) demanded that the AVN change its name, if the AVN had done nothing, the likely result was that the DFT would have shut it down.

In 2011, the HCCC, after an investigation, made a ruling that the AVN must put a specified disclaimer on its website. It seemed like this ruling could be ignored, because the HCCC, unlike the DFT, had no power to shut down the AVN. The AVN, for its own reasons, decided not to put up the HCCC's disclaimer, being advised by its lawyers that nothing much could happen. The HCCC's subsequent public warning was one of the most damaging outcomes imaginable, but this depended on the context, namely the existence of a hostile group doing everything possible to undermine the AVN.

If the HCCC had made a public warning about some obscure company, with no attendant media coverage or citizen action, the warning might have largely passed unnoticed. Even when prominent companies are found guilty of fraud and fined hundreds of millions of dollars — as has happened in the US — there is relatively little publicity and the companies continue with their activities.[20] The companies are wealthy, profitable and influential, and there are no major citizen organisations analogous to SAVN campaigning to challenge and expose the companies. So the impact of a public warning from an official body like the HCCC depends, to a great extent, on the efforts made by opponents like SAVN, as well as the reputation and efforts of the official body itself. The HCCC publicised its warning, and even put a link to its report, hosted on SAVN's website.

Option 2 is to conscientiously respond to demands made by agencies as a result of complaints. This was the AVN's regular choice. When the HCCC launched an investigation in response to Ken McLeod's complaint, Dorey, on behalf of the AVN, prepared a detailed response. When the Office of Liquor, Gaming and Racing examined the

---

20 Peter C. Gøtzsche, *Deadly Medicines and Organised Crime: How Big Pharma Has Corrupted Healthcare* (London: Radcliffe, 2013).

AVN's charitable status, the AVN supplied all information required.

Judging by the results, responding conscientiously worked well for the AVN in many cases, staving off adverse findings. Furthermore, when the AVN's response was informative and well argued, it could provide the basis for agencies to dismiss subsequent complaints that covered the same ground. Preparing careful responses to complaints has some similarities with building a defensive fortification: the effort that goes into the defence can ward off repeated attacks — but only if they come from the same direction.

The down side of option 2 was a serious diversion of the AVN's efforts into defence against complaints. Time, energy and money normally used for collecting and preparing information about vaccination, editing the AVN's magazine *Living Wisdom,* giving talks, answering queries and raising money were instead channelled into the complaint-responding process. This sort of diversion was a key result of SAVN's harassment via complaints. SAVNers then criticised the AVN for its resulting shortcomings as an organisation, repeatedly citing the failure to publish *Living Wisdom* at the normal rate. In other words, SAVN did what it could to cripple the AVN and then claimed that the AVN's reduced capacity to function showed it was deficient. This is roughly equivalent to tripping someone and then saying to others, "Look, they can't even walk properly!"

Option 3 is to challenge the validity or jurisdiction of the agencies making an adverse finding against the AVN. This is expensive and time-consuming. It is also risky, because there is no guarantee of a favourable outcome.

The HCCC's warning was open to challenge because the HCCC was set up to deal with complaints about health care practitioners, such as doctors and nurses, not to adjudicate about disputed social issues. If criticising vaccination falls under the HCCC's mandate, then why not criticism of pesticides, nuclear power or climate change? These all have major health consequences, and one side or the other in these controversial issues could claim their opponents were dangerous to public health.

The AVN decided to go to court to challenge the HCCC's jurisdiction. This was a major enterprise, requiring considerable expense and much time and effort. It could not have been achieved without pro bono legal support, illustrating the imbalance in resources between a government agency and a citizens' group like the AVN. Despite these obstacles, the AVN won its case. The HCCC immediately withdrew its warning. Furthermore, the Office of Liquor, Gaming and Racing (OLGR) reinstated the AVN's ability to receive donations and accept new members; the OLGR's restrictions had been imposed on the basis of the HCCC warning.

However, the AVN's victory in court over the HCCC was not the end of the story. SAVNer complaints against the AVN continued, indeed seemed to increase in frequency, including new complaints to the HCCC seeking to get around the technicalities of the court ruling in favour of the AVN. Furthermore, a push developed to change the law specifying the powers of the HCCC, to give it the ability to do exactly what the court had ruled it couldn't, namely investigate and take action against groups like the AVN without there needing to be any complaint and without evidence of harm to any individual.

The legislative change in the HCCC's powers is an example of a recurring feature in struggles to challenge abuses of power. When the abuses are by a powerful group against a much weaker one, playing by the rules may provide a temporary respite for the weaker party, but determined opponents will, if frustrated, seek to change the rules that restrain their actions. The HCCC, with its new powers, proceeded to launch a new investigation into the AVN: the AVN's court victory turned out not to protect it from the HCCC, because the rules were changed.

After the Department of Fair Trading (DFT) demanded that the AVN change its name, the AVN delayed as long as possible and then appealed the decision to the Administrative Decisions Tribunal. This appeal was unsuccessful. There followed a game of cat and mouse, with the AVN seeking to register names with various agencies, and to reserve Internet domain names, and SAVNers — somehow having discovered what the AVN was doing, possibly through DFT leaks — seeking to register them first. The upshot was that the AVN changed its name to Australian Vaccination-skeptics Network, thereby retaining its acronym AVN. This was much to the annoyance of SAVN and the Australian Skeptics, who seemed to believe they were the only ones who could legitimately use the word "skeptic."[21]

---

21 In Australia, the usual spelling is "sceptic." SAVN reserved various names with this spelling but was outflanked when the

Option 4 is to respond to complaints in ways that mobilise support from AVN members and the wider public. This is not easy. The very nature of formal complaints processes is to take a public issue, in this case the debate about vaccination, and turn it into a procedural issue, requiring input from specialists such as lawyers.

One approach is to publicise the complaints as a means of generating awareness and, from some, sympathy. The AVN did this on a regular basis, notifying members about complaints and sometimes posting both the complaints and its responses on its website. For the AVN, posting complaints and responses served to increase awareness but it did not provide a ready avenue for participation, except financial support for some of the AVN's legal actions.

One way to escape the regulatory morass is to acquiesce to some of the demands made by agencies, using the process of acquiescence as an opportunity for publicity. When the HCCC ruled that the AVN should post a disclaimer on its website, the AVN could have acquiesced and posted it. But as well, the AVN could have posted a response to the disclaimer immediately after it (or via a link), exposing the political agendas involved. Here is a possibility.

AVN used the US spelling "skeptic" which, ironically, was the spelling used by the Australian Skeptics.

> "1. The Australian Vaccination Network's purpose is to provide information against vaccination in order to balance what it believes is the substantial amount of pro-vaccination information available elsewhere.
> 2. The information provided should not be read as medical advice; and
> 3. The decision about whether or not to vaccinate should be made in consultation with a health care provider."

This is the statement that the Health Care Complaints Commission recommended be put on the AVN's website (and here it is!), after making an investigation into two complaints against the AVN. If the AVN did not put up this statement, the HCCC proposed to issue a public warning on the basis that "the AVN provides information that is inaccurate and misleading" that affects decisions about whether to vaccinate and "therefore poses a risk to public health and safety."

The AVN has serious reservations about the HCCC's recommendation.

1. The HCCC does not have the authority to require the AVN to put this or any other statement on its website. The AVN is not a health service provider in the usual sense: it does not provide clinical management or care for individual clients. Instead, the AVN is a non-government organisation providing a point of view on a matter of public debate.

2. The HCCC misunderstands the role of public debate on controversial issues affecting public health. In the vaccination controversy, different participants operate on the basis of different assumptions and values, for example about the importance of individual choice. The HCCC has adopted pro-vaccination assumptions and values. In other words, it has adopted a partisan position. That is not its role.

By accepting complaints against the AVN, the HCCC has overstepped its mandate. By the logic of its investigation, it might also accept complaints against organisations presenting information and viewpoints about pesticides, climate change, nuclear power, stem cells, genetic engineering, nanotechnology and nuclear weapons, because in each of these areas of debate, incorrect statements might pose a risk to public health and safety.

It is widely accepted that campaigners on these and other controversial issues have a right to present strong viewpoints without being subject to HCCC-style "public warnings" because they have allegedly provided information that is "inaccurate and misleading."

Public debate is vitally needed on issues that affect the public. The HCCC is intervening in the vaccination debate in a one-sided fashion. This is completely inappropriate.

3. The complaints to the HCCC against the AVN are part of a systematic campaign to shut down the AVN and deny its ability to provide information about the

disadvantages of vaccination. Those who have attacked the AVN have ridiculed and slandered AVN members, made false claims about their beliefs, made numerous complaints to a variety of official bodies, and made personal threats to individuals.

The AVN understands that others believe in vaccination and respects their right to present their viewpoints. The AVN invites them to provide information and viewpoints — in other words, to participate in free and open debate — rather than attempting to shut down debate by attacking the AVN.

The AVN chose not to use this approach, so it is only possible to speculate about possible responses. SAVN might have publicised the disclaimer itself, without mentioning the AVN's response. Would the HCCC have objected to a response immediately following the disclaimer? Possibly, but if so the AVN could have found other ways of highlighting its response, for example through links elsewhere on its website. Whatever the response to this approach, it could hardly have been as damaging as the HCCC's subsequent public warning.

In relation to the Department of Fair Trading's demand that the AVN change its name, one response would have been to choose a new name that enhanced the AVN's profile while foiling SAVN. One possibility would have been the name Vaccination Choice, highlighting a key argument presented by the AVN, that parents should have a choice whether their children are vaccinated. SAVN would have been in a quandary. If it changed its name to Stop Vaccination Choice, it would be perceived as unacceptable, because nearly all supporters of vaccination say they accept that parents should have a choice. As a name, Vaccination Choice combines a description with widely accepted stance. The name Australian Vaccination Network, on the other hand, serves as the name of the organisation but does not incorporate a stance. SAVN's name, Stop the Australian Vaccination Network, expresses opposition to an organisation. Stop Vaccination Choice would uncomfortably mix opposition to an organisation with opposition to a widely accepted stance.[22]

Option 5 is for the AVN to transform itself so that it becomes less vulnerable to harassment and control via regulatory agencies. One possibility would be to wind up the AVN as an incorporated body and to relaunch the AVN, perhaps under a different name, in a different form. Another possibility is to set up the AVN as a business in another country. Its operations in Australia would not be subject to the same controls as a business registered in Australia.

The N in the abbreviation AVN stands for Network. Actually, though, it has operated as an organisation, with a constitution, elected office bearers and other aspects

---

[22] One complication involved the AVN's website. If the AVN changed its name to Vaccination Choice, SAVN would have challenged the AVN's domain name of http://avn.org.au/ and, if possible, taken it over. A possible counter option for the AVN would have been to set up a spin-off organisation to host the web domain. This is a small indication of the machinations involved in the SAVN-versus-AVN struggle.

required by legislation covering incorporated bodies. In contrast, SAVN is an actual network, without the formal features associated with an organisation.

Option 5 has high transition costs. It might involve getting rid of assets, ensuring continuity of website operations, and enabling the membership list to become a contact list in a network. The DFT has rules covering closing down of an incorporated body, and these could be applied in an onerous fashion. (Many incorporated bodies fizzle out through lack of activity, but given the scrutiny of the AVN, this would have been an unlikely scenario.)

Imagine that the AVN closed down and reconstituted itself as a network called Vaccination Concerns (VC). The next step is to imagine the reaction of SAVNers. They might close down their Facebook page — mission accomplished — but more likely would turn their attention to VC and any other activity critical of vaccination. Prime targets would be those in VC who remained or became active in questioning vaccination.

SAVNers might attempt to go after individuals, making complaints to the HCCC and other bodies. If some agencies took action against individuals — for example, those with practices in alternative health or involved in businesses — their ability or willingness to comment about vaccination might be inhibited. In such a scenario, one option would be for VC to choose individuals with the fewest vulnerabilities to be spokespeople. This sounds good in principle, but in practice it can take years of effort and a special commitment to become a knowledgeable and effective proponent of a cause.

If SAVNers attempted to attack individuals, another option would be to operate from outside Australia. A VC campaigner might live in another country, thereby avoiding Australian regulatory agencies, and send messages to those living in Australia. Alternatively, an Australian resident might covertly send messages to others in VC, using encryption, anonymous remailers and an intermediary in another country.

This sounds like a resistance movement in a repressive state, and there are important similarities. When expressing an opinion on a controversial topic predictably leads to reprisals, it is necessary to consider options for resistance that reduce vulnerability, allow participation and win greater support. If intolerance of vaccination dissent in Australia became extreme, then support might come from other countries, in the same way that human rights organisations such as Amnesty International take up the cause of targets of state repression in other parts of the world. This suggests there might be a natural limit to the ability of Australian pro-vaccinationists to limit the speech of critics: if their attempts at censorship become too effective, support from other parts of the world will emerge. Censorship, when it becomes too great, can backfire, at least if opponents of censorship use appropriate tactics.[23]

---

23 Sue Curry Jansen and Brian Martin, "Making censorship backfire," *Counterpoise,* vol. 7, no. 3, July 2003, pp. 5–15; "The Streisand effect and censorship backfire," *International Journal of Communication,* vol. 9, 2015, pp. 656–671.

AVN responses 4: dealing with censorship

The AVN has responded in various ways to SAVN's attempts to censor talks. One effective technique is, when booking a venue for a talk, to warn the host about the likelihood of receiving complaints. When hosts are forewarned in this way, they can decline in a timely fashion or prepare for the complaints. The AVN can also get its members and allies to send messages of support to beleaguered hosts. Another effective technique is to reveal SAVN's efforts, appeal to others to oppose this sort of censorship, and increase the AVN's visibility.

Another technique is to not announce talks publicly, but instead organise them privately through personal networks and send out the location of the talk via text messages the day beforehand. In this way, opponents do not have sufficient time or information to organise a censorship campaign. This method has been used by some critics of vaccination. It shows similarities to the sort of organising required under a repressive government.

AVN responses 5: dealing with harassment

When Dorey received threatening phone calls, she would sometimes go to the police. This was a frustrating process. Even in the case of the calls recorded on her phone, one of them saying "Die in a fire," along with the phone number of the caller, the police were reluctant to act and then accepted the word of the SAVN member at the house that he had not made the calls. In other cases, with less evidence, police did nothing.

Dorey applied in 2012 for apprehended violence orders (AVOs) against three SAVNers based on their continued abusive and threatening messages. Applying for AVOs is a legal process, most commonly used by women whose former partners assault them or their children. One SAVNer did not contest the AVO application, but the others did, and Dorey's applications were unsuccessful, and furthermore she had to pay for their court costs. More importantly, the failure of these AVO application seemed to provide a stamp of legitimacy to what the SAVNers had been doing. Dorey's AVO applications backfired on her.

More effective was her compilation of a dossier of attacks on the AVN. This revealed abuse and harassment to a wider audience. After receiving the "Die in a fire" message, Dorey prepared a blog about it and put a recording of the message on the web.[24]

Interim summary 2

The Australian Vaccination Network was going about its business of providing a critical perspective on vaccination until 2009, when it came under sustained attack by a network of pro-vaccinationists, mainly under the banner of Stop the Australian Vaccination Network (SAVN). The methods used by SAVN and other opponents of the AVN included abusive comment on its Facebook page and in the individual blogs by SAVNers, attempts to disrupt

---

24 "Threats to AVN president made from home of Stop the AVN founder," *No Compulsory Vaccination,* 3 October 2012, http://nocompulsoryvaccination.com/2012/10/03/threats-to-avn-president-made-from-home-of-stop-the-avn-founder/.

discussions on the AVN blog and elsewhere, harassment of some AVN members, attempts to block public talks organised by the AVN, and numerous complaints to government agencies. SAVN's stated goal from the beginning was to shut down the AVN, and it has been remarkably innovative and persistent in its attempts to achieve this goal.

In the face of this onslaught, the AVN defended in various ways. Its attempts to deal with abusive SAVN commentary have had only limited success: few AVN members or supporters have the energy or willingness to confront SAVNers on their own territory. To defend against disruption on the AVN's blog, the main strategy has been to block SAVNers from commenting. When Meryl Dorey, the key figure in the AVN, received pornography and threatening phone calls, she complained to the police, to little effect. She also publicised this harassment, building greater support.

One of the most potent forms of attack used by SAVNers was to make complaints to government agencies. Few of these complaints led to official action, but in some cases the AVN was asked to respond, soaking up time and energy even when the agency took no further action. In the few cases in which agencies made adverse findings about the AVN, requiring it to comply with directions, the consequences for the AVN have been severe, including negative media coverage, loss of credibility and in some cases hampering of the AVN's regular activities. In the face of agency demands, the AVN has had quite a few options. The AVN's experience in these circumstances provides a rich body of evidence for assessing ways of defending against attack via complaints to government agencies.

Next I will analyse the AVN's ways of responding to attacks using the seven criteria for effective nonviolent action laid out in chapter 4. This is one way of assessing the AVN's strategies, and also a way of seeing whether concepts from nonviolent action are relevant to a different domain — the public controversy over vaccination — where no physical violence is directly involved.[25]

Some of this analysis is based on the AVN's actual actions; some of it is more speculative, being based on what the AVN might have done.

Nonviolent analogies

In chapter 4, I identified features of nonviolent action that distinguish it from other forms of action and that make it effective. These were widespread participation, limited harm, voluntary participation, fairness, prefiguration, nonstandard methods and skilful use. The AVN's responses to attack can be assessed according to these features.

First, though, it should be noted that SAVN tactics, while not involving physical violence, violate several of these features. SAVN's goal is to cause harm to the AVN as an organisation. Their methods of personal abuse, disruption and making complaints cause harm. Many

---

25 Each side would claim that damage to health — due to vaccines or to insufficient vaccination — results from the other side's position. However, the supporters and critics of vaccination have not used direct physical violence against each other.

people would see abuse and disruption as unfair. As a way of prefiguring or modelling their desirable society, SAVN's tactics are not appropriate. Increasing the amount of abuse or the level of censorship of vaccine critics is not the goal of pro-vaccinationists, which presumably is a society with universal vaccination in which everyone favours vaccination based on a rational consideration of benefits and costs. SAVN's tactics are based on shutting down debate; they do not model the rational approach to decision-making to which they aspire. Finally, some opponents of the AVN have resorted to sending pornography and making threats, tactics obviously not compatible with the goal of rational acceptance of universal vaccination.

In a later section, I will propose some ideas for how to promote vaccination in a way more compatible with principles of fairness and prefiguration. For now, I will focus on strategies for the AVN in defending against attack and in promoting its own agenda.

Participation

Participation is a key element in many methods of nonviolent action. When more people can participate, a campaign or movement has a greater capacity to mobilise supporters and stimulate action. On the other hand, if a method of action allows only a few individuals to join in, then it is less likely to do much to help.

Few of the AVN's responses to SAVN created opportunities for greater participation. Dorey, as the key figure in the AVN, has done much of the work, including responding to SAVN, until 2013, when Greg Beattie took over as president. She has been the primary speaker and the person contacted most often for media interviews. She wrote most of the responses to government agencies, and managed the AVN's website. She carried out an extensive correspondence, including responding to numerous enquiries. Dorey's effort and contribution were enormous — but at the expense of wider participation.

Possibilities for greater participation by AVN members and supporters include:

- being a supporting speaker
- monitoring SAVN's Facebook page and blogs by SAVNers
- contributing to a dossier of abuse by SAVNers
- running a portion of the AVN's website
- learning about specific vaccination issues and responding to queries about them.

In practice, a few other AVN members have helped with such activities, and so have a few individuals and groups aligned with but separate from the AVN. The Australian network of vaccination critics contains a spectrum of activists. SAVN focused on the AVN because it was the largest and most active group, due especially to Dorey's effort. To increase overall participation, the challenge would have been to encourage greater involvement by more of the AVN's membership.

As long as Dorey tried to do so much, the opportunities for wider participation were limited. This is a common issue in activist groups. Those who are most experienced and knowledgeable often prefer to do things themselves, knowing they will be accomplished reliably and competently. It takes time to mentor others, at a cost to short-term efficiency. Nevertheless, if the goal is greater participation, activities need to be designed to encourage others to take on more tasks and roles. Dorey would have had to reduce her campaigning in order to spend more time as a teacher and guide. Changing in this way is difficult at the best of times and exceedingly difficult when a group is under attack.

One way of increasing participation would be to organise a "statement of defiance" in support of free speech. This would take the form of a petition opposing censorship of vaccination criticism, written in a way that permitted signers to hold diverse views about vaccination itself. Such a petition could be set up so it only became public after a target number of signatures was obtained — maybe 100 or even 500 — so there would be safety in numbers. The aim in such a petition is to encourage participation in the struggle by reducing the risk.

Limited harm

Harm is central to the vaccination debate, which is centrally about the benefits and harms of vaccinating or not vaccinating. In contrast, "limited harm" here refers to harm to opponents in the debate over vaccination.

The struggle between the AVN and SAVN has not involved physical violence between protagonists, but there are other sorts of harm involved. The sending of pornography and making of threats to AVN members are certainly types of harm. The goal of SAVN, to shut down the AVN, could be said to harm an organisation. The wider goal of SAVN, to shut down public criticisms of vaccination, might be considered harm to free speech.

In terms of nonviolent responses to SAVN's attacks, the question is whether the AVN has caused any equivalent harm. To my knowledge, critics of vaccination have not seen it as their goal to terminate promotion of vaccination; this is so far away from the current reality as to be only hypothetical.

One possible harm to SAVN would be shutting it down. The AVN made complaints to Facebook about SAVN's violation of rules for groups, and at one point SAVN closed down its public operations. The question of harm to SAVN raises interesting questions about censorship: is it censorship to curtail the activities of a censor? For example, is opposing government censorship causing harm to the jobs of government-employed censors? Studies of nonviolent action seldom address this point. For example, commentary on the US civil rights movement do not talk about the harm the movement caused to politicians, police and businesses that supported segregation. There are two key issues here. The first is that segregation is, today, seen as wrong, so any harm to its promoters is not of major concern. The second is that supporters of segregation were not physically harmed; only their jobs and businesses might have been affected. By the same token, the AVN did not try to stop SAVNers from advocating for vaccination, only to stop abuse and disruption from SAVN campaigns.

Voluntary participation

A key feature of nonviolent action is that it is voluntary. All members of the AVN joined the organisation voluntarily, and likewise their participation in AVN activities was voluntary.

It is possible to imagine non-voluntary participation in debates like the one over vaccination. For example, some corporations employ staff to make comments on social media and to make changes on Wikipedia, to make the corporations look good. Some of these staff would not undertake such activity without being paid, and in this sense they are not volunteers.

Fairness

Most people think defending against attack is more justified than launching an attack, though the boundaries between these are often blurred. When the AVN sticks to defence, for example blocking abusive comment from its website or exposing threats, it is more likely to be seen as justified. When it appears to attack, for example making complaints to Facebook, it is less likely to be seen as justified.

Another perspective is to see whether the AVN uses some of the same techniques as SAVN. One of the signature SAVN methods is making complaints to authorities. The AVN has tried this on a few occasions, with limited or no success. However, the most significant disadvantage of the AVN making formal complaints is that it seems to provide a justification for SAVN's tactics.

This is analogous to protester tactics at a rally, in the face of police violence. If protesters use even the slightest amount of violence, this is likely to be used as a justification for the much greater police violence. There is a double standard in the way tactics by the two sides are evaluated. The point here is the pragmatic one of public perceptions. That protester violence is so regularly exaggerated by authorities, and sometimes provoked, signals that it is likely to be counterproductive. This is a key reason for insisting on avoiding violence. When protesters are resolutely nonviolent, the violence of police is more likely to generate greater support, with sympathisers becoming more committed and active, many witnesses having greater sympathy, and even some opponents shifting their viewpoints.[26]

In the case of complaint-based attacks against a relatively weak group, counter-complaining thus has serious weaknesses. It is very unlikely to be effective and it provides a justification for the attackers to continue or escalate their efforts. The implication is that the AVN was unwise to try to shut down SAVN, for example by complaining to Facebook. Far more effective, according to this line of thinking, is to expose SAVN's tactics.

To generalise from this experience, when a powerful attacker group uses methods that can be perceived as unfair, targets should consider avoiding using the same methods in response. This is the parallel to the recommendation, by advocates of nonviolent action, for protesters to

---

26 See the chapter "Political jiu-jitsu" in Gene Sharp, *The Politics of Nonviolent Action* (Boston: Porter Sargent, 1973), 657–703.

"maintain nonviolent discipline," namely to avoid using violence when violence is used against them.

Prefiguration

The principle here is for a group's methods to be compatible with its goals. An example is anti-war activism. The goal is a world without war, so the methods should not involve war. A "war to bring about peace" violates the principle of prefiguration.

The goal of the AVN is a society in which people have an informed choice about whether they and their children are vaccinated. The key idea here is choice. If the AVN tried to block access to vaccination, have some vaccines withdrawn, or otherwise advocated government restrictions on vaccinations or information about vaccination, this would be incompatible with a commitment to informed choice. The AVN has never pursued any such goals, and in any case is far too weak to achieve them.

The AVN's setting up of a "respectful debate" about vaccination provides a model for how it would like the discussion on vaccination to proceed. Dorey's offer to debate vaccination is another model. These are methods of engaging in the vaccination controversy that are compatible with the goal of a respectful exchange of ideas.

How prefiguration applies to defending against SAVN is not immediately obvious. Abusing SAVNers certainly does not, nor does trying to shut SAVN down.

Non-standard methods

Methods of nonviolent action go beyond the usual, officially sanctioned methods of political action. Voting is a standard method of political engagement, whereas refusing to pay taxes is not. For the AVN, parallels to nonviolent action need to involve doing something different from or stronger than the usual accepted methods.

First consider the issue of promoting the AVN's agenda, including informing members of the public about the risks of vaccination and arguing for parental choice. The routine, accepted ways of doing this include lobbying politicians, making submissions to government bodies, writing articles, giving talks, holding meetings and all the other sorts of methods associated with freedom of speech and assembly. The AVN has organised a number of protest marches, including some with hundreds of people attending, but did not continue with this form of action because of the effort required and the lack of any media coverage. In Australia, rallies and marches are commonplace and might be considered a form of conventional action, though not as institutionalised as voting.

Going beyond this are various methods of noncooperation and intervention, such as vigils at health department offices, boycotts of pharmaceutical companies, and refusals by nurses and doctors to administer vaccinations to newborns. Nurses and doctors who are critical of vaccination policy probably would seek positions where they are not directly involved in vaccinations; in Australia, there are no well-known examples of conscientious objection by medical professionals to vaccination policy.

If AVN supporters launched a boycott of a pharmaceutical company, it probably would have no significant effect, due to low numbers. Calling for a boycott would mainly be a symbolic gesture. Holding a vigil outside health department offices would be possible, because a vigil can be carried out with only a few participants, or even just one. However, there are no well-known examples of such actions in Australia.

In summary, the AVN proceeded without adopting any of the assertive methods characteristic of nonviolent action. However, circumstances changed in 2009 with the emergence of SAVN. The attacks by SAVN were intended to shut down the AVN and to hinder the AVN from getting its message out. In short, SAVN's agenda can be said to be to censor AVN criticism of vaccination.

Whether an action counts as conventional political action or nonviolent action depends on the context. In a country such as Australia, handing out a leaflet is normally a conventional political action: it happens all the time, and no one thinks much about it. However, in a dictatorship, handing out a leaflet critical of the government may be considered a subversive act, sometimes leading to arrest and imprisonment. In such circumstances, handing out a leaflet certainly counts as a method of nonviolent action: it is not standard and not sanctioned by authorities.

When SAVNers began attempting to censor speech by the AVN, the circumstances changed dramatically. From carrying out its business in a generally tolerant, if largely unsympathetic, context, the AVN entered a new context of sustained hostility. Suddenly, what had been normal and unproblematic, for example making blog posts and giving public talks, became occasions for opponents to attack.

For political activists, circumstances can change dramatically through election of a new government or through a military coup, so that routine activities like holding a rally become illegal or highly regulated, and group activities are monitored. What counted previously as normal political activities — like handing out a leaflet — can become methods of nonviolent action, because they are unauthorised.

For an organisation, a change in the environment can have parallel impacts, and that is what happened to the AVN after the formation of SAVN. Some of the AVN's activities, such as giving talks, became analogous to nonviolent action.

Which particular AVN activities fitted this category of non-regular, assertive action? They included, most obviously, blog comments and giving public talks. These became methods of protest and persuasion.[27] SAVN created a context in which the mere expression of views critical of vaccination became acts of courage and resistance.

SAVN's aim was to shut down the AVN. Initially, this was an aspiration rather than a serious proposition; it came closer to reality as various individuals and agencies joined SAVN's campaign. In this context, for the AVN to

---

27 Gene Sharp, in part 2 of *The Politics of Nonviolent Action*, gives "protest and persuasion" as the first of three main categories of nonviolent action.

attempt to survive became a form of resistance. As long as it used conventional methods — such as writing replies to formal complaints and going to court against adverse judgements — this resistance might be considered "normal politics." In contrast, some creative ways of reconstituting the AVN, or vaccine criticism more generally, might be classified as analogous to nonviolent action. However, this is hard to fit into a traditional picture of the methods of nonviolent action, which focuses on actions and puts matters of organisation into the background. This is a point by which nonviolent activists can learn from organisational struggles. For vaccine critics, organisational form and the ability to speak out become closely connected when the climate becomes hostile. So it is useful to think of transforming modes of organisation as an aspect of resistance, and in some way analogous to nonviolent action.

Skilful use of methods

Nonviolent actions do not work automatically. To be effective, they need to be chosen carefully and executed skilfully. The same applies to struggles in the vaccination debate. The AVN, in responding to attacks, needs to choose its methods carefully and use them well. For example, taking the HCCC to court is unwise unless backed by capable lawyers, and setting up a dossier of SAVN abuse is unwise unless it is well documented and accurately expressed.

One of the key requirements for effective nonviolent action is avoiding the use of violence. If some activists are violent, this can undermine the entire group. For the AVN, an analogous requirement is not being abusive in the face of abuse. If AVN members openly express contempt for SAVNers, this gives greater legitimacy to SAVN's tactics of verbal abuse.

The importance of avoiding abuse is shown by repeated SAVNer claims that they are, in fact, subject to abuse from vaccination critics. AVN spokespeople have disowned abusive threatening language from supporters. SAVN spokespeople have done the same in regard to theirs.[28]

Summary

When the AVN came under sustained attack from SAVN, it entered a different, harsher political environment. In this new context, ideas from nonviolent action became more relevant. SAVN was able to use or stimulate government agencies into becoming antagonists of the AVN, which meant that the normal sorts of fairness principles became less commonly applied. Furthermore, for members of the AVN to exercise free speech became far more difficult.

---

28 It is hard to get to the bottom of many of the claims about being abused, because so many participants operate online using false names. Some of these "sock puppets" may be loose cannons, unwelcome by those they claim to support, or they could even be the equivalent of *agents provocateurs,* falsely presenting themselves as being on the opposite side and behaving badly as a means of discrediting it. How to deal with these sorts of anonymous behaviours has been little studied.

In this new context, finding an effective way of responding was difficult. Using SAVN's own techniques, such as making derogatory comments or making formal complaints, was a losing proposition, being either futile or counterproductive. Mimicking SAVN in any way meant relinquishing the high ground of behaving politely and respecting free speech, and allowed SAVNers to treat their own methods as legitimate. On the other hand, simply acquiescing to the demands of SAVN and the agencies that adopted its agenda meant giving up.

The alternative is what can be called assertive action: going beyond conventional forms of action, yet not adopting SAVN's aggressive techniques. Some of the most effective of these were continuing to exercise free speech — for example, by holding talks and making posts — and calling attention to SAVN's attempted censorship, for example through posts to members, press releases and compiling a dossier of attacks.

More generally, the AVN could have responded by adopting tactics that reduced risks from direct confrontation. For example, instead of ignoring the HCCC request that it post a disclaimer, it could have posted the disclaimer with a rebuttal. Similarly, the AVN could have transformed its operations to become less of a target. Rather than continue as an incorporated body, it could have closed down and reconstituted its operations in network form, or dispersed them into different entities. This is analogous to moving from conventional warfare to guerrilla warfare, except that this is a conflict without violence.

A comparison with the criteria for effective nonviolent resistance suggests that the AVN's actions were more likely to be effective when they protected the AVN but did not attempt to shut down SAVN, and when they exposed SAVN's attacks as a means of promoting awareness and building support. The most important facet not developed by the AVN was to choose actions that increased participation in the struggle.

There are some lessons here for the study and practice of nonviolent action in more conventional contexts, namely as a method against an opponent willing to use violence. The key in asymmetrical struggles, in this case nonviolence versus violence, is to avoid using the opponents' most aggressive methods, especially when those methods are widely seen as harmful and unfair. This suggests that the arguments about what counts as nonviolent action may sometimes miss the point: what is appropriate depends, in part, on the opponents' tactics, especially the ones that can be documented and exposed to wider audiences. For example, if police are not overtly using force, then protesters might be wise to avoid even the appearance of confrontation: yelling abusive slogans might be counterproductive. On the other hand, if police are beating and killing protesters, then more aggressive protester actions may not hurt their cause as much.

The more important lesson concerns the transition from direct confrontation to dispersed resistance. The AVN was an attractive target for pro-vaccination attackers because it was a formal organisation subject to all sorts of government regulations. In the face of relentless attack, the AVN could have adopted the strategy of dispersal, by disbanding and reconstituting its activities through separate email lists, websites, newsletters and support networks.

For nonviolent action in the face of violent attacks, the implication is that the way a movement is organised is a vital part of any resistance strategy. This is well known to activists on the ground, who learn from experience which organisational forms are vulnerable and which are more resilient. However, discussions of organisational form are not so common in nonviolence theory, which focuses on methods of action and on strategy.[29]

Anders Boserup and Andrew Mack wrote *War Without Weapons,* a classic treatment of nonviolent resistance as an alternative to military defence.[30] If a country or community gets rid of its military forces and relies instead on nonviolent methods, this is called nonviolent defence, social defence, civilian-based defence or defence by civil resistance. It is basically an application of ideas from nonviolent action to the special case of defending against military threats.

---

[29] Among discussions of the value of decentralised structures for unarmed resistance movements facing repression are Robert J. Burrowes, *The Strategy of Nonviolent Defense: A Gandhian Approach* (Albany, NY: State University of New York Press, 1996), 184–199, and Kurt Schock, *Unarmed Insurrections: People Power Movements in Nondemocracies* (Minneapolis, MN: University of Minnesota Press, 2005), 143–144.

[30] Anders Boserup and Andrew Mack, *War Without Weapons: Non-Violence in National Defence* (London: Frances Pinter, 1974).

Boserup and Mack said nonviolent defence is analogous to guerrilla warfare. In conventional warfare, two armies directly clash, and usually the army with the greatest numbers and firepower is victorious. It is futile for an "army" of 100 men, armed only with rifles, to try to take on a force of 10,000 armed with machine guns and aeroplanes. In such a situation of unequal forces, the weaker side may adopt a different strategy: avoiding direct confrontation and instead operating in the shadows, occasionally making raids and then fading away, either into a hinterland or into the civilian population. Guerrilla warfare is essentially a form of political struggle. The central aim is to win over the people through honest behaviour, progressive political action such as supporting the poor against exploiters, and symbolically challenging a repressive opponent through armed exploits.

Nonviolent action is like a guerrilla operation, except with no violence. The resisters do not take on the armed forces in a direct way but rather seek to win support through principled behaviour and showing their commitment to a different system of governance. Nonviolent action against violence is a form of asymmetric struggle, indeed even more asymmetric than guerrilla warfare: the asymmetry is in the tools of engagement (nonviolent methods versus violence) rather than just the modes of engagement (hit-and-run tactics versus frontal attack).

For the AVN, direct engagement with its opponents was a losing proposition: SAVN had vastly superior numbers and energy as well as the backing of the medical profession and government. Therefore, it makes sense for the AVN to adopt asymmetric struggle techniques. One implication is to dissolve its organisational equivalent of a "standing army" — its status as an incorporated body — and to operate through a less formal set of arrangements.

Applied to traditional nonviolent action scenarios, such as challenges to a repressive government, the implication is that organisational form is of crucial importance. As well as choosing appropriate methods of resistance, whether vigils, strikes or symbolic actions such as quiet marches or banging of pots and pans, resisters need to choose a way of organising their activities that reduces vulnerability to attack.

Promoting vaccination

So far, I have focused on strategy for critics of vaccination in the face of a relentless attack. It is also worth looking at strategy to promote vaccination.

Participants in SAVN and other promoters of vaccination have the best of intentions: to increase the rate of vaccination in order to reduce disease and death, especially of children. They see the activities of the AVN in questioning vaccination as a serious danger to public health, by discouraging parents from having their children vaccinated. SAVN was set up to counter this danger. In attacking and destroying the AVN, their aim was to discredit and silence what they considered to be uninformed criticism of vaccination, thereby allowing more parents to better recognise the truth about the benefits of vaccination, increasing vaccination rates and thereby improving the health of the population. SAVNers have noted that their campaigns have led the mass media to become more sceptical of the AVN, giving it less credibility in stories. They see this as a signal success.

SAVN's strategy sounds plausible enough. It has certainly provided sufficient rationale for years of effort involving thousands of hours in commenting on Facebook and blogs, preparing complaints and much else. Yet it is reasonable to ask whether there is any evidence to support SAVN's strategy.

SAVNers often raise the banner of evidence-based medicine. The idea is that medical interventions should be backed up by evidence of their effectiveness. For example, a new vaccine should be introduced only after evidence has been provided that it reduces disease or increases the body's immune response, an indicator of improved resistance to disease. The most impressive evidence in support of an intervention is a double-blind controlled trial. In a drug trial, for example, subjects are randomly assigned to two groups. Subjects in one group, the control group, are given pills with no active components; subjects in the other group, the experimental group, are given pills containing the drug. Neither the subjects nor the researchers know who is getting which pills: that's the double-blind part. In a trial like this, the differences between the groups are not due to either the subjects' expectations (a placebo effect) or the researchers' expectations.

SAVNers, in choosing their strategy to promote vaccination, have not provided any evidence in its support except their belief that it is effective. They haven't compared shutting down the AVN with, for example, better information for parents or training for doctors to deal with parents. Furthermore, there are obvious negative effects of SAVN's campaign, including being seen as heavy-handed censors, causing some vaccine critics to become more committed, and generating a huge struggle that brings vaccination disputes to the public eye, making some people pay more attention to vaccine criticisms.

There is even the possibility that SAVN's campaign is entirely misguided. The campaign is premised on the assumption that the AVN and other vaccine-critical groups have a significant influence on public opinion about vaccination, and in particular discourage some parents from vaccinating. However, there is little evidence to support this view. Social scientist Stuart Blume, having studied the vaccination debate, suggests that vaccine-critical groups may be largely the consequence, rather than the cause, of resistance to vaccination by members of the public.[31] His view is that individuals develop critical views on their own, for example as a result of a child's apparent adverse reaction to a vaccine or due to a doctor who haughtily dismisses their expressions of concern about some vaccines. On the basis of their experiences, they then search to find relevant information and make contact with others with similar experiences, or even set up groups themselves. Furthermore, according to Blume, strident attacks on vaccine-critical groups can distract attention from behaviours of health professionals that stimulate critical views about vaccination.

---

31 Stuart Blume, "Anti-vaccination movements and their interpretations," *Social Science & Medicine,* vol. 62, 2006, pp. 628–642.

Blume's assessment accords with the results of a survey of AVN members carried out in 2012.[32] Few respondents said they had formed their views about vaccination solely as a result of the AVN's information. More commonly, they developed concerns about vaccination before joining the AVN. The implication is that if the AVN had not existed, they might have joined a different organisation or, what is much the same thing, subscribed to a different magazine or email list. Even if all the vaccine-critical groups in Australia were shut down, people could still obtain information from other countries, as indeed many do.

If Blume's assessment is correct and the survey of AVN members is accurate, then SAVN's campaign might be judged to have had little impact on public views and behaviours concerning vaccination. In this perspective, the key driver of public concern is personal experience, not AVN activity. SAVN, in this picture, has attacked the symptom, not the cause, of public concerns about vaccination.

Some pro-vaccination social researchers have taken a different approach, investigating the response of parents to doctors when obtaining advice about vaccination.[33] They

---

32 Trevor Wilson, *A Profile of the Australian Vaccination Network 2012* (Bangalow, NSW: Australian Vaccination Network, 2013).

33 Julie Leask et al., "Communicating with parents about vaccination: a framework for health professionals," *BMC Pediatrics,* vol. 12, no. 154, 2012, http://www.biomedcentral.com/1471-2431/12/154.

are concerned that when doctors too quickly dismiss parents' concerns about the actual or potential hazards of vaccination, this may alienate parents from vaccinating their children and more generally from the health system. The researchers advise that doctors adopt an approach sensitive to the attitudes and concerns of their patients. For example, when encountering a parent who is critical of vaccination, the researchers advise against trying to directly argue against the parent's views, but rather enquire about the parent's concern for their children's health. This approach involves a tacit acknowledgement of the counterproductive effects of being arrogant and assuming that parents who question vaccination are ignorant or misguided.

The same sort of approach could be adopted by citizen campaigners for vaccination. Rather than assuming that critics are ignorant, misguided and dangerous, and like SAVN trying to shut them down, more savvy campaigners could promote vaccination through door-to-door personal contact.[34] Rather than approaching people as bearers of "the truth," campaigners could instead seek to learn about the concerns expressed by members of the community, remembering that even those without children or who have followed vaccination recommendations to the letter can be influential with family, friends and co-workers. Through personally talking with a wide variety

---

34 A group in northern New South Wales has done something like this, to the acclaim of SAVNers: Heidi Robertson, "Love, peace and no vaccinations," *The Skeptic* (Australia), June 2014, pp. 8–9.

of people, campaigners would learn about the most commonly expressed concerns, whether about the necessity or hazards of particular vaccines, about the likely consequences of diseases targeted by vaccines or about condescending or dismissive doctors. They would learn about the reasons why some parents delay or decline particular vaccines.

The advantage of a grassroots campaign based on the principles of community organising is that it respects people's good judgement. The road of condemnation and censorship, on the other hand, assumes that people are gullible and cannot be trusted to make decisions based on the evidence available, but must be protected from allegedly dangerous information. Grassroots organising builds the capacity of community members to make autonomous decisions and to be able to judge new claims by critics. Organising opens the prospect of fostering community leaders, namely individuals who decide, based on sensitive and respectful approaches and provision of balanced information, to become more knowledgeable and join the campaign. Local opinion leaders, attracted by such a campaign, are likely to be especially influential.

A broader approach would be to orient the campaign around children's health more generally, addressing the roles of disease, accidents, nutrition, exercise and education, with vaccination being just one component in a wider picture. Children's health organisers would be open to learning about all the factors that affect parents and their children. They would be seen as more balanced than single-minded vaccination proponents. Their credibility would be increased even among those parents who have reservations about vaccination.

From the point of view of vaccination advocates, a broader approach has the advantage of embedding vaccination in a suite of measures that are likely to be favourably received, whether it is neighbourhood safety, fostering of exercise and sport, addressing nutritional deficiencies and tackling the challenges of poverty and child abuse. By adopting a broad approach like this, it is possible that campaigners might find common cause with some vaccination critics. In this way, some of the negativity and damaging conflict in the vaccination debate might be converted to a more productive engagement with promotion of child health.

This sort of community-based campaign is entirely in keeping with the principles of nonviolent action. It fits within what Gandhi called the "constructive programme," namely building a fair society that meets the needs of all, including those who are most deprived.

9
Conclusion

Nonviolent action is commonly thought of as a collection of methods, such as rallies, strikes, boycotts and sit-ins. It is better thought of as a philosophy or an approach to conflict and social change.

Nonviolent action is widely used in struggles against injustice, including repressive governments, exploitation of workers, discrimination, environmental problems and much else. Activists and scholars have learned from these struggles, and there is now a fairly well developed understanding of the sorts of things needed for success using nonviolent action, as well as an understanding of the strengths and weaknesses of nonviolent action compared to alternatives, especially violence and conventional political action.

Nonviolent action is commonly used against opponents who have the capacity to use force against activists, and who often use that capacity. A classic example is a rally by protesters, in which police use force to beat and arrest protesters. In these and similar scenarios, nonviolent action is most effective when protesters avoid using violence themselves, as indeed the term "nonviolent action" would suggest.

The question I have addressed in this book is how to apply ideas from nonviolent action to arenas where there is little or no physical violence. To this end, I've examined four areas involving struggles between individuals or groups: verbal interaction, defamation, euthanasia and vaccination.

This may seem a disparate and peculiar group of topics. It largely reflects areas that I've studied for other purposes. I decided that knowledge of the issue, including contact with campaigners, was more important than starting with some arbitrary group of issues chosen for theoretical reasons.

All four case studies have one important similarity: they involve speech that is unwelcome to someone. Verbal defence has the elements of communication and personal relationships, whereas being defamed has the elements of damage to reputation and potential legal remedies. The euthanasia issue is largely a social controversy, with some technical details in dispute; vaccination is a scientific and social controversy.

In all four case studies, there is normally no physical violence involved in the struggle. Euthanasia itself might be considered, by some, to be a violent act, but the *debate* over euthanasia has mainly involved words. Verbal interactions sometimes lead to fighting, but the verbal interactions themselves do not involve physical force. Because these struggles seldom involve physical violence, it might be asked, what is there to learn from the experiences with nonviolent action undertaken against opponents who can and do use force against challengers?

A first step in answering this question is to identify key features of effective nonviolent action. The ones I selected for this purpose are participation, limited harm, voluntary participation, fairness, nonstandard methods, prefiguration and skilful use. Applying these to the arenas of verbal interaction, defamation, euthanasia and vaccination requires some adaptation and modification of the features, perhaps amounting to distortion. This process is not necessarily straightforward, and others might choose different ways of going about it.

This process of applying insights from one field, namely nonviolent action, to others, is stimulating because it can open up new ways of thinking about an issue. Campaigners on vaccination and targets of defamation know an incredible amount about their particular issues and circumstances, but may benefit from seeing things from a different perspective. There is another potential benefit from this process of cross-pollination. By applying ideas from nonviolent action to other domains, new insights may arise that can be returned to the traditional arenas of nonviolent action.

Verbal defence

Several writers, including Suzette Haden Elgin, Sam Horn and George Thompson, have developed methods for individuals to respond to verbal attacks. The common feature of their approaches is finding a path between weakness and counter-attack. One weak option is to accept the assumptions of the attacker. Elgin says many attacks include a bait and a presupposition, for example when someone says to you, "If you really loved me, you would buy this car." Responding to the bait is to fall into the attacker's trap. If you start explaining why buying the car is a bad idea, you're in a weak, defensive position. Instead, Elgin recommends responding to the presupposition, and undermining it, for example by asking "When did you start thinking I don't love you?" Verbal counter-attack — for example, "You're such a spendthrift" — is often disastrous because it escalates the confrontation and sometimes makes the original attacker seem like the calm, reasonable one, as Elgin shows in many examples.

Experts in verbal defence recommend an assertive strategy that operates between weakness and aggression, and thus is analogous to the strategy of nonviolent action. Many effective methods of verbal defence involve a jiu-jitsu effect: the attacker's energy and momentum are turned against them. The verbal barb shoots right past you and the attacker ends up with something unwelcome or unexpected. Horn titled her book *Tongue Fu!* and Thompson his book *Verbal Judo,* each of them invoking the imagery of martial arts.

The many tools of verbal self-defence presented by Elgin, Horn, Thompson and others are insightful, but can be overwhelming at first. There are many methods of verbal attack. Figuring out how to respond to an initial comment can be challenging enough. Then there's the need for well-formulated follow-up responses, as the attacker renews the assault or shifts to another technique. The verbal domain can be complex, and some attackers have honed their skills over many years. Furthermore, many on the receiving end fall into habits of response that are hard to change.

The parallel in the realm of nonviolent action is that it can take time and effort to develop skills in strategy and action. Choosing the most appropriate form of action can be a challenge, and then the opponent may do something unexpected, requiring a creative response. In the template of protesters versus police, protesters may fall into a pattern of always using the same method — rallies, marches, pickets or whatever — for challenging a wide range of injustices. This would be like always responding to verbal attack using the same sorts of comments. The diversity of verbal defence techniques suggests that activists should aim to develop skills in a wider range of methods and strategies. The implication is that developing skills in strategic thinking and tactical innovation should be a priority. This is exactly the conclusion made by some researchers and activists involved with nonviolent action.

In interpersonal relations, being assertive is often positioned as being intermediate between being passive and being aggressive. The idea is to respond, but not so strongly that it escalates a confrontation or becomes a form of abuse. Although one end of the spectrum is called "passive," this can be misleading, because sometimes an apparently passive response is highly effective, especially when it is unexpected. This is highlighted by William Irvine's approach to insults based on the philosophy of the Stoics from ancient Greece. Irvine suggests that the Stoics would have responded to insults by saying nothing or perhaps by saying "Thanks." Although this response might be thought of as passive, it can be effective because it causes the energy of the insult, and the insulter, to be expended without effect. It is like dodging a punch rather than taking a hit without resistance.

The sort of weak response that doesn't work well is the most predictable one, which may be defensive, for example responding to the bait in one of the scenarios presented by Elgin. In the face of verbal attack, either a defensive or an aggressive response plays into the hands of the attackers. The intermediate positions, which can be called assertive, are often unexpected, and a non-response can fit into the category of assertiveness. The Stoic strategy is based on quiet self-confidence that is not shaken by insults. A Stoic-inspired ignoring of an insult or saying "Thanks" is premised on a refusal to play the verbal and emotional games of abuse and countering of abuse. Perhaps, in a nonviolent campaign against a repressive government, there are occasions when doing nothing in response to provocations may be a powerful mode of behaviour.

Defamation

The issue of defamation involves competing injustices. On the one side is free speech, which sometimes damages another person's reputation; on the other side is protection of reputation, which sometimes involves curtailing someone's freedom of speech. I've looked at this from the point of view of being defamed and examined options for dealing with the problem. Ideally, a resolution might involve dialogue between the parties involved. However, there are many cases in which dialogue seems impossible or futile.

Among the options for responding to defamatory comments and images are doing nothing and, on the other end of the spectrum, suing. These can be thought of as passive and aggressive responses. In between are various assertive and avoidance options, some of which are analogous to nonviolent action.

Looking at the features of successful nonviolent action offers some tips for responding to being defamed. One of them is participation, which means getting more people involved in applying pressure on the defamer. However, there is a cost in doing this: the defamatory material becomes more widely known. Many people are uncomfortable about recruiting support if it means making them aware of damaging text or images.

This then leads to avoidance and defensive options. Qafika, with her distinctive name, was dogged on the Internet by links to the degrading image posted by her ex-boyfriend. She could take the drastic step of changing her name. Alternatively, she could post positive information about herself, thus making the damaging image less prominent in web searches.

The options for defending against defamation can be fed back into scenarios involving conventional forms of nonviolent action. Calling a rally can be effective, but in some circumstances it only makes people vulnerable to attack. So sometimes avoidance is a better option, ensuring survival until circumstances are better. The point is to do what is required to survive and to continue activities in a different way.

Euthanasia

In a few countries, voluntary euthanasia is legal; in many other countries, legalisation is supported by a majority of the population, often 70 to 80%. Yet most politicians are resistant, refusing to support proposed laws. Those who oppose voluntary euthanasia — who themselves often feel like an embattled minority — can draw on support from some church leaders and medical associations.

The euthanasia debate involves competing concerns about justice. Proponents of voluntary euthanasia are concerned about the suffering of individuals, typically with terminal diseases or intractable conditions, for which they seek release through dying on their own terms, typically among family and friends in their own homes. Opponents of euthanasia are concerned about the potential for abuse, with euthanasia imposed without consent, including on people who are depressed, disabled or whose suffering can be controlled with palliative care.

I have chosen to examine the application of ideas from nonviolent action to one side in this debate, the campaign for voluntary euthanasia, because in most countries these campaigners are opposed by the power of the state, including the threat of arrest and imprisonment for assisting someone to die. The euthanasia debate has been largely carried out through the means of conventional politics, including distributing information to win public support and trying to influence politicians. This sort of engagement with the political process is a conventional approach to change; in most countries it has proved to be ineffectual in legalising voluntary euthanasia. This is an example of the shortcomings of "official channels."

Many of the typical methods of nonviolent action, for example strikes, boycotts and occupations, would be difficult to use to promote voluntary euthanasia because economic factors do not play a major role, and there are no obvious physical locations to mount a challenge. Furthermore, the immediate constituency for voluntary euthanasia includes many who are frail and ill, and thus less able to be participants. Traditional methods of nonviolent action should be considered as options, as there are no fundamental obstacles to using them, but thus far they have played relatively minor roles in euthanasia struggles.

The major direct challenge to government laws against euthanasia has been the do-it-yourself movement, in which people learn ways to end their lives peacefully without relying on others. In most countries, it is legal to commit suicide, but most of the familiar means available for doing so — hanging, guns, jumping out of buildings or in front of trains — are not peaceful, and can be traumatic for others. Many people would prefer to take a pill or a drink, but ending one's life this way has become more difficult with controls over medicines.

Exit International is one of the groups providing information for people who want to end their lives peacefully, most commonly by obtaining the drug Nembutal or constructing an exit bag. The approach has parallels with Gandhi's constructive programme, in that it involves directly creating a desirable society rather than asking or pressuring government leaders to bring about changes.

One of the important lessons from the euthanasia debate is the role of competing injustices. Advocates of having the option of voluntary euthanasia focus on the injustice of people having to suffer when they would prefer a peaceful death. On the other hand, opponents of euthanasia focus on the injustice of lives being ended prematurely should euthanasia become legal and extended to vulnerable groups such as people with dementia.

When there are competing injustices, the principle of fairness becomes especially important when planning actions. Although different people have different assessments of what constitutes injustice, often there is a boundary beyond which actions can become counterproductive because many people are offended. For proponents of voluntary euthanasia, it is disastrous when individuals have their lives ended without clearly giving consent. This was a key factor in Jack Kevorkian's conviction for murder.

The same principle of fairness applies to opponents of euthanasia. When an individual is suffering greatly from a terminal disease, palliative care is insufficient to ease the suffering, and the individual asks to die, but is refused this option, the case against voluntary euthanasia is damaged. From these examples, it is apparent that cases that seem unfair to significant audiences provide powerful messages that can be used by one side or the other.

The idea of competing injustices, and the need to avoid situations of apparent unfairness, can be applied to familiar scenarios involving nonviolent action, for example protesters versus police. The protesters might be opposing militarism: they draw on popular concerns about the damage due to war and military spending. Opponents of the protesters can draw on concerns about the need for defence against aggression. Opponents can also draw on concerns about the behaviour of the protesters, if they are aggressive towards the police, for example pushing or shouting abuse — this can be seen as unfair towards the police, who are thought to be just doing their duty.

The message from these examples is that it is worthwhile thinking of the situation from the other side of a debate or confrontation, and figuring out what might be considered unfair by those on the other side, or by third parties. The two sides in the euthanasia debate can readily do this, and so can protesters and authorities. Sometimes there is nothing that can be done in the short term to change perceptions of unfairness: if some people think public protest is a disturbance of public order and therefore inappropriate, this would rule out protest or perhaps even disagreement. But in other cases, small things, such as expressing sympathy or avoiding derogatory comments, can make a big difference in perceptions.

Vaccination

The examination of the campaign to shut down a vaccine-critical group, the Australian Vaccination Network, reveals that some of the group's defensive measures were far more effective than others. In particular, the AVN's attempts to use the law and other formal processes turned out to be futile. In one case the AVN was successful: it challenged the Health Care Complaints Commission in court, and won the case. But this was a pyrrhic victory, because the state government then changed the law to give the HCCC greater powers.

The AVN spent enormous efforts trying to defend its organisational entity, an incorporated body in the state of New South Wales. However, in the face of a tremendous onslaught, another strategy was worth considering: dissolving the organisation and reconstituting as a true network. As a network of individuals, there would be far fewer targets for opponents.

There is an important lesson here for nonviolent activists. Often the main focus of attention is on methods of action, for example whether to initiate a boycott and how to run it. Less attention is given to how the group and movement are organised. Possibilities include a traditional organisation with formal leaders, a network of local groups, and a loose collection of ad hoc operations. There is no right or wrong form of organisation, because much depends on the issue, the goals and the opposition. The point is that the way the movement is organised can be very important for its success or failure. Furthermore, the way people interact with each other in actions has a major influence on their satisfaction, commitment and energy.

Many activists are highly attuned to group dynamics and spend a lot of time maintaining relationships and supporting individuals. The same attention needs to be given to organisational forms. The key point here is that in developing a campaign, often the main focus is on action. Activists need to reflect on the way they are organised. Getting the organisational form right may make the difference between survival and collapse in the face of a ruthless opponent, or make the difference between temporary success and long-term transformation in an ongoing struggle.

To learn from the vaccination struggle in Australia, it is not necessary to take a stand on vaccination. It is possible to support vaccination and yet learn from the challenges faced by the AVN. This points to the value of seeing all sorts of conflicts as strategic encounters and of learning from the experiences of others.

Future directions

Nonviolent action has proved to be a powerful approach to popular social action. It is more forceful than conventional political action such as lobbying and voting while avoiding the damaging and counterproductive consequences of physical violence. Because of the success of nonviolent action in dramatic challenges to repressive regimes and its widespread use by campaigners in social movements such as the labour, feminist, environmental, anti-racist and peace movements, there seems to be potential to apply the basic approach of successful nonviolent action to other arenas — arenas seemingly outside the template of nonviolence versus violence.

To do this, I first needed to identify key features of successful nonviolent action. This is not so easy, because some of these features are implicit in the normal way practitioners think about nonviolent action. Furthermore, different people might well come up with different "key features." What I've done here is just one way of doing it.

I chose case studies in which I could rely on work by experienced practitioners (verbal abuse) or about which I had some familiarity (being defamed, euthanasia, vaccination). Others might choose different case studies. Possibilities include lying, file sharing (including music downloads), surveillance, the abortion debate, the climate change debate, and bullying. Sometimes the most unlikely arena can offer unexpected insights.

My approach to each of these case studies has been to examine the typical techniques and strategies used by participants and analyse them in light of the features of successful nonviolent action. This sounds straightforward but actually requires a fair bit of creative thinking. Nonviolent action is a huge realm within its traditional domains, such as protesters versus police, so it is not surprising there is no simple application of nonviolent action to other domains.

An important lesson from this exercise is that applying ideas from nonviolent action to different arenas can lead to new approaches to action. Nonviolent action can generally be thought of as an assertive option, different from conventional action and from aggression. What this means in practice depends quite a lot on the arena. The other benefit is that this process of applying nonviolent action can lead to insights that can be fed back into traditional arenas for nonviolent struggle.

The study of nonviolent action has been neglected. History books and media stories are filled with attention to conventional politics, especially politicians and elections, and violence, such as wars and terrorism. In comparison, nonviolent action is invisible, and often misunderstood as well. This means there remains an enormous amount to be learned about nonviolent action. Applying ideas about successful nonviolent action to unusual arenas is one way to go about this. There is plenty more to do.

Index

9/11, 48, 195–198

A Good Death, 217
armed struggle, 2, 54–55, 75–78. *See also* guerrilla warfare
A Slap in the Face, 131
asymmetric struggle, 55, 327
Australia, 14, 30, 208, 224–229, 231, 236–238, 248, 256. *See also* AVN; SAVN; Whistleblowers Australia
AVN (Australian Vaccination Network), 259–260, 267–285, 288–332, 345, 347

backfire, 55–72, 75, 88, 93, 97, 123, 159, 249, 307, 309
Baumeister, Roy, 180
behind-the-scenes work, 32–33
Bell, Max, 225
Blume, Stuart, 330–331
Boserup, Anders, 326–327
boycotts, 6, 18–20, 31, 45–46, 91, 102, 105, 122, 190–191, 216–217, 319–320. *See also* noncooperation; nonviolent action
Britain, 58–59, 72–73. *See also* Indian independence struggle
bullying, 141, 146, 191, 205, 273
Burma, 38–39, 83

censorship, 70, 152, 237, 279–280, 289–290, 292, 307–308, 312, 314–315, 320–321, 324, 333
Chenoweth, Erica, 2, 81–86

Chile, 41
China, 2, 17, 38, 72, 77–78, 228
civil resistance, 24–25. *See also* nonviolent action; *Why Civil Resistance Works*
civil rights movement, 18, 36–37, 39, 62–63, 315
competing injustices. *See* injustice, competing
complaints, 66–67, 166–168, 175, 201, 205, 275–280, 283–284, 292–308, 310–311, 315–317, 322, 324, 329. *See also* HCCC
conspiracy, 270–272
constructive programme, 120–121, 239, 258, 334, 343
conversations. *See* verbal defence
correspondent inference theory, 47–49
cover-up, 64, 66. *See also* backfire
Crick, Nancy, 237
Cuba, 40
cyber harassment, 202–206. *See also* harassment
Czechoslovakia, 51–54

defamation, 4, 148–207, 340–341
denigration, 270–274, 282–288. *See also* defamation
Department of Fair Trading. *See* DFT
devaluation, 64–66. *See also* backfire; defamation
DFT, 277–279, 295–296, 300, 304, 306

Dharasana, 57, 61–64. *See also* salt satyagraha
disruption, 274–275, 288–292
doctors, 209, 211–213, 217–219, 224–226, 228, 234, 239, 247, 250–251, 256–257, 262–264, 267, 319, 329–333. *See also* Nitschke, Philip; Syme, Rodney
Dorey, Meryl, 259, 267, 271–275, 279–283, 297, 308–310, 312–314, 318

Earth First!, 10
East Germany, 34–36
East Timor, 28–30, 63
Elgin, Suzette Haden, 106–123, 126, 128, 136–137, 146, 337–340
Ellison, Sharon, 142
El Salvador, 41
empirical evidence, 81–87
ends. *See* prefiguration
eugenics, 212
euthanasia, 4–5, 208–258, 341–345; covert, 212–213; involuntary, 209–210, 212–213, 221, 223, 230, 241, 249, 257–258
Evil, 180
examples, 34–44
exit bag, 226–229, 241–245, 254, 258, 343
Exit International, 229–231, 237–238, 243–245, 343

Facebook, 171, 189, 193, 259, 267, 270, 272–275, 282–285, 289–290, 306, 309, 313, 315–317, 329. *See also* SAVN; social media

fairness, 63, 67, 97–98, 102, 117–119, 184–186, 249–251, 316–318, 323, 344–345. *See also* injustice
Fighting with Gandhi, 145–146
Flanagan, Tom, 207
Foxman, Abraham, 204–205
fraternisation, 50–55, 85. *See also* loyalty

Gallagher, Paul, 271
Gandhi (film), 62
Gandhi, 17–18, 24, 26, 56–57, 64, 71–72, 86, 100, 120, 144–146, 220, 239, 258, 334, 343. *See also* constructive programme; nonviolence, principled; salt satyagraha
Gandhian approaches, 144–146. *See also* constructive programme; Gandhi
Give Me Everything You Have, 198–202
goals, 47–50. *See also* prefiguration
good cause, 18–20
Gordon, Thomas, 144
Gorsevski, Ellen, 140
Gregg, Richard, 56–57, 59
guerrilla warfare, 40, 55, 74–76, 96, 324, 327. *See also* armed struggle

harassment, 148, 166, 173–174, 202–206, 280–281, 293, 298, 305, 308–310. *See also* complaints; cyber harassment; defamation
harm. *See* limited harm
HCCC, 275–277, 293–294, 296–297, 299–304, 306, 322, 324, 345
Health Care Complaints Commission. *See* HCCC
herd immunity, 262

Horn, Sam, 123–126, 138, 337–338
Hunt, Mina, 289

In Sheep's Clothing, 206–207
Indian independence movement, 37, 57–62, 64–65, 78. *See also* Gandhi
Indonesia, 29–30
injustice, 4–5, 12–13, 22, 56–57, 63–71, 134, 182, 213–214, 221–222, 240, 255, 257, 335, 340, 342–344; competing, 5, 213–214, 222, 340, 342–344. *See also* fairness; limited harm; official channels
International Court of Justice, 287
Internet, defamation on, 202–207
intifada, 31, 38, 83. *See also* Israel; Palestine
intimidation, 65, 68–71, 149. *See also* backfire
involuntary euthanasia. *See* euthanasia, involuntary
Iran, 42–43, 78, 83
Irvine, William, 131–137, 339–340
Israel, 31, 38, 42–43, 48, 63, 201

jiu-jitsu, 56, 58. *See also* backfire; moral jiu-jitsu; political jiu-jitsu
Juergensmeyer, Mark, 145–146
justice. *See* injustice

Kenya, 73
Kevorkian, Jack, 220–223, 241, 257, 344
Keyes, Gene, 74

language, 16–18, 23–26. *See also* verbal abuse
Lasdun, James, 198–202

lawyers, 67–68, 150, 152, 154, 156, 158, 173–175, 183, 194–195, 197, 202, 296, 301, 322. *See also* defamation; official channels
Leader Effectiveness Training, 144
legal system. *See* defamation; lawyers; official channels
libel. *See* defamation
limited harm, 91–94, 102, 116, 176–183, 240–245, 251, 314–315
Living Wisdom, 280, 298
loyalty, 49–50, 54, 59–60, 76, 84–85, 87–88. *See also* fraternisation

Mack, Andrew, 326–327
Mao, 86
McLeod, Ken, 272, 275–276, 294, 297
means. *See* prefiguration
methods, 47–50. *See also* prefiguration
military, 3, 10, 25, 29, 35, 39–41, 49–56, 75–77, 88, 135, 326, 344. *See also* armed struggle; fraternisation; guerrilla warfare; police
Miller, Webb, 58, 64, 70. *See also* salt satyagraha
mobbing. *See* bullying
Moore, Jr., Barrington, 56
moral jiu-jitsu, 56, 58–59. *See also* Gregg, Richard; political jiu-jitsu

Nancy's friends, 237–239, 246, 257
Nazis, 3, 9–10, 18–19, 209
Nembutal, 208, 217–218, 226–229, 236–237, 241–242, 245, 248, 254, 258, 343. *See also* peaceful pill
Netherlands, 214–215, 230
networks, 236, 244, 267, 295, 305–306, 324, 346. *See also* AVN; SAVN

Nigot, Lisette, 232–234
Nitschke, Philip, 224–232, 238, 243, 248, 251
noncooperation, 6, 14, 20, 33, 79, 135, 140–141, 146, 190–192, 216–217, 319. *See also* boycotts; nonviolent action; strikes
non-standard, 90–91, 102, 121–122, 187–194, 252–253, 256, 319–322
nonviolence, 24; pragmatic, 99–100, 146–147; principled, 99–100, 146–147. *See also* nonviolent action
nonviolent action, 1–4; boundary with language, 16–18; boundary with physical violence, 7–11; boundary with usual politics, 12–16; and communication, 140–141; effectiveness of, 27–88; expressions for, 23–26; features of, 3–4; participation in, 20–21, 44–46; training, 143; transportable features of, 89–103; violence, compared with, 81–86; what is, 6–26. *See also* nonviolence; protest
Nonviolent Communication, 142–143
nonviolent defence, 326–327
Northern Territory, 224–225
nuclear weapons, 286–287
NuTech, 244–245

Occupy movement, 15
Office of Liquor, Gaming and Racing. *See* OLGR
official channels, 64, 67–68, 166–168, 200, 204–205, 342. *See also* backfire
OLGR, 277, 297–298
open mike, 291–292
Oregon, 215, 230

ostracism, 105, 126, 135, 148, 191–192

pacifism, 79, 133
Palestine, 31, 38, 48, 63, 83
palliative care, 210–211
participation, 21, 44–46, 77–78, 80–81, 84–88, 92–96, 102, 115–117, 138, 174–176, 183–184, 197, 218–219, 235–239, 246–249, 257–258, 301, 312–314, 316, 325, 341. *See also* voluntary participation
passive resistance, 25–26. *See* nonviolent action
Peaceful Persuasion, 140
peaceful pill, 226, 243–245. *See also* exit bag; Nembutal
Peaceful Pill Handbook, 228, 238, 243
people power, 24. *See* nonviolent action
Philippines, 37, 39, 83
police, 7, 15, 34, 48–51, 56–59, 61–67, 92–93, 118, 123, 126–128, 130–131, 138–139, 153–155, 162–163, 176, 200, 222–224, 240–241, 308, 310, 317, 325, 335, 344–345. *See also* fraternisation; military; Thompson, George
polio vaccine, 260–261
political jiu-jitsu, 59–65, 69–70, 123, 138, 317. *See also* backfire; Sharp, Gene
politics, 12–16. *See also* political jiu-jitsu
prefiguration, 98–100, 102, 119–121, 186–187, 251–252, 256, 312, 318
protest, 1, 7–11, 13, 15–20, 25, 27–30, 32–35, 37–39, 42, 45, 48–52, 55–75, 88, 92–93, 97, 102, 118, 123,

130–131, 138–139, 143, 146, 176, 183, 188–190, 193, 216, 222–224, 236, 240–241, 285–287, 317–319, 321, 325, 335, 339, 344–345, 348. *See also* nonviolent action; police

refusal to obey orders, 135. *See also* fraternisation
reinterpretation, 64–67. *See also* backfire
revenge porn, 202–203
Ronson, Jon, 207
Rosenberg, Marshall, 142–143

sabotage, 9–11, 221–222
salt satyagraha, 57–65, 70–71, 73. *See also* Dharasana; satyagraha
Satir modes, 107
satyagraha, 17–18, 26, 145. *See also* Gandhi; nonviolent action; salt satyagraha
SAVN, 259–260, 267–285, 288–332
self-deliverance, 214, 224–258. *See also* euthanasia; Exit International
self-immolation, 7–8
Serbia, 37, 49–50
Sharp, Gene, 6, 8, 11, 13, 17–19, 59, 61, 70, 100, 123, 138, 146–147, 193–194, 317, 321. *See also* political jiu-jitsu
Simon, George, 206–207
skills, 28, 45, 86, 100–102, 110, 122–123, 125, 130, 138–139, 147, 194–196, 205, 254, 256, 322–323, 338–339
slander. *See* defamation
social media, 189, 203, 316. *See also* cyber harassment; Facebook
South Africa, 37, 62–63, 78

statement of defiance, 314
Stephan, Maria, 2, 81–86
Stewart, Fiona, 226, 228, 243
Stoics, 133–136, 339–340
stone throwing, 8
Stop the Australian Vaccination Network. *See* SAVN
Strike, Laurie, 236
suicide. *See* euthanasia
Syme, Rodney, 217–220

Thompson, George, 126–131, 138–139, 337–338
Tiananmen Square, 38
Tierney, Peter, 271, 289
Tongue Fu!, 123–126, 138, 338
transportable features, 89–103

unarmed resistance, 25. *See* nonviolent action
US, 40–41, 48. *See also* civil rights movement

vaccination, 4–5, 259–334, 345–347; debate, 260–266; promoting, 328–334
Varney, Wendy, 140–141
verbal defence, 4, 17, 104–147, 336–340
Verbal Judo, 127–130, 138–139, 338
Vietnam, 2, 7–8, 75, 77–78
violence: against objects, 9–11; boundary with nonviolent action, 7–11. *See also* limited harm
Viral Hate, 204–205
voluntary compliance, 128–129
voluntary euthanasia. *See* euthanasia

voluntary participation, 77, 96–97,
 102, 116–117, 183–184, 246–249,
 316

War Without Weapons, 326
Weber, Thomas, 144–145
Whistleblowers Australia, 32, 148. *See also* whistleblowing
whistleblowing, 148–152
Why Civil Resistance Works, 81–86
WikiLeaks, 284
Wolf, Christopher, 204–205
Woodford, 279
Wylie, Graeme, 248

www.ingramcontent.com/pod-product-compliance
Lightning Source LLC
Chambersburg PA
CBHW051803230426
43672CB00012B/2620